LONGRUN DYNAMICS

A companion volume by the same author

ECONOMICS WITHOUT TIME

Longrun Dynamics

A General Economic and Political Theory

Graeme Donald Snooks
Coghlan Professor in Economics
Institute of Advanced Studies
Australian National University

First published in Great Britain 1998 by
MACMILLAN PRESS LTD
Houndmills, Basingstoke, Hampshire RG21 6XS and London
Companies and representatives throughout the world

A catalogue record for this book is available from the British Library.

ISBN 0–333–72726–6

First published in the United States of America 1998 by
ST. MARTIN'S PRESS, INC.,
Scholarly and Reference Division,
175 Fifth Avenue, New York, N.Y. 10010

ISBN 0–312–21422–7

Library of Congress Cataloging-in-Publication Data
Snooks, G. D. (Graeme Donald)
Longrun dynamics : a general economic and political theory /
Graeme Donald Snooks.
p. cm.
Includes bibliographical references and index.
ISBN 0–312–21422–7 (cloth)
1. Economic forecasting. 2. Economics. 3. Statics and dynamics
(Social sciences) 4. Economic policy. I. Title.
HB3730.S53 1998
330—dc21 97–52348
CIP

This book is printed on paper suitable for recycling and made from fully managed and sustained forest sources.

10   9   8   7   6   5   4   3   2   1
07   06   05   04   03   02   01   00   99   98

Printed in Great Britain by
The Ipswich Book Company Ltd
Ipswich, Suffolk

To the memory of my father
William Donald Snooks
1920–1966

'...it is in the essence of his behaviour that he should be eccentric, unconventional and rash in the eyes of public opinion. If he is successful, that will only confirm the general belief in his rashness; and if in the short run he is unsuccessful, which is very likely, he will not receive much mercy. Worldly wisdom teaches that it is better for reputation to fail conventionally than to succeed unconventionally.'

J. M. Keynes
The General Theory (1936)

Contents

List of Figures

List of Tables

Preface

This book has been many years in the making. Its origins can be traced back to the dissatisfaction I felt as an undergraduate in the mid-1960s with the avalanche of abstract and unrealistic articles on neoclassical growth theory. These models had little to tell young economic students eager to learn the secrets of economic progress. As the only way to understand economic dynamics seemed to be by examining the way real economies grew, I turned in earnest to the study of historical economics. Would it be possible, I wondered, to develop a general dynamic theory from the systematic study of the economic transformation of real societies through historical time? There seemed no other way.

That was 30 years ago. While a number of interesting theoretical developments have occurred since then, our profession is still no closer to a general understanding of real dynamic processes. It was hardly surprising to see the early neoclassical growth theory (based on the Solow–Swan model) wither on the vine. Once the theoretical possibilities had been exhausted, not long after I was first introduced to it, interest in this totally unrealistic growth model rapidly declined. It could tell us next to nothing about the real world. Only with the passage of a further decade or so and the attempt to introduce technological change as an endogenous variable into the neoclassical growth model did this field once more appear to offer further research possibilities. Yet, a decade on, the so-called 'new' growth theory has still to come to grips with real dynamic processes, or to offer insights that have not been known to development economists and historical economists for generations. This lack of success has led a growing number of theoretical economists to look for inspiration beyond the boundaries of economics. Yet this borrowing of evolutionary concepts from biology has, in my opinion, failed to fill the void.

During these decades, my own exploration of dynamic issues, which has taken place over widening stretches of space and time, has only gradually come to fruition. The road has been long and hard. While some of the ideas in this book can be traced back to my *Depression and Recovery* (1974), they did not appear sufficiently substantial to warrant any challenge to economic orthodoxy until my *Economics without Time* (1993), which is a manifesto of sorts. Underlying this challenge was the research for a series of dynamic studies that have recently appeared as *The Dynamic Society* (1996), *The Ephemeral Civilization* (1997a), and *The Laws of History* (1998). The current book is an outcome of these, and is an attempt to distil dynamic theory from the systematic study of real societies in historical time. It is an attempt to fulfil not only my recent (1993) manifesto but also the much earlier (1965) desire for a general theory that could explain the changing fortunes of real societies. It places time within economics.

This book has a practical as well as an intellectual purpose. It is my conviction that economic policies currently being advocated by orthodox economists and adopted by the governments of developed societies are actually undermining the longrun viability of these nations. This is an outcome of the pursuit of balance and stability at the expense of economic growth and full employment. Not only is this an unnecessary waste of scarce resources, it also endangers the survival of the societies concerned. This book attempts to provide the theoretical basis necessary to reverse this tragically flawed policy thrust and to promote the longrun viability of the advanced democracies. An outcome of this work is a new dynamic theory of inflation and the discovery of the longrun and shortrun growth–inflation curves. A forthcoming book will examine the performance and prospects of lesser developed societies.

This work has benefited from the most important encouragement and support an author can receive – that of his publisher. Tim Farmiloe at Macmillan saw something of value not only in this volume but also in the preceding *Economics without Time*. For this I thank him. Also, as in the case of my last two books, I am delighted to thank Gary Magee for reading the penultimate draft, asking many penetrating questions, and discussing at length some of the key concepts (particularly those in Chapters 11, 14, and 17). The final version is much improved because of his contribution. It is a rare privilege to have such an intellectually stimulating and supportive colleague. Finally, the speed and expertise with which this book was produced owes much to the professionalism of Jeannie Haxell and Barbara Trewin for the word-processing and formatting, Min Mee Teh for the research assistance, Wayne Naughton for drawing the graphs, and Barry Howarth for the copy-editing and for compiling the index. Once again I am in their debt. And, as always, I am grateful for the unfailing encouragement and wise advice from my wife, Loma Graham.

Sevenoaks   G.D. SNOOKS
Canberra
July 1997

Part I
Introduction

1 Social Statics and Social Dynamics

This book seeks to explore the complex issue of social dynamics. And it does so in an entirely new way. The method, focus, conclusions, and policy implications of this study stand in marked contrast to those of orthodox growth or evolutionary models. It is hoped that those readers dissatisfied with existing dynamic theory may find something of interest and value here.

The basic method is inductive rather than deductive. Of course this is a relative matter because both induction and deduction are intertwined in scientific work. What I mean is that the main source of the ideas in this book come from a systematic exploration of historical reality. My objective is to explain the complexity of dynamic reality, as far as that is possible, by deriving theory inductively rather than by employing existing neoclassical production theory developed for an entirely different purpose, or by borrowing deductive theory from entirely different disciplines such as evolutionary biology and sociobiology.

An attempt has been made to develop a formal, but non-mathematical, dynamic model. This is the outcome of both comparative advantage and a desire to maximize the flexibility and generality of the resulting theory. Like John Maynard Keynes, I maintain that the flux of reality is too complex to be represented by a set of simultaneous equations. The model-building has been undertaken as concisely as possible in order to focus on the main dynamic forces in reality. All extraneous supporting argument and evidence can be found in three books that I have recently published: *The Dynamic Society* (1996), *The Ephemeral Civilization* (1997a), and *The Laws of History* (1998). In developing this new theory, which I call dynamic-strategy theory, I am attempting to identify the main dynamic forces, rather than all the forces, irrespective of their significance, that might be involved. My focus is on the role of **strategic demand** (or dynamic demand) in a dynamic world experiencing changing markets and institutions. This contrasts with the Keynesian focus on effective demand (or aggregate demand) in a static world characterized by imperfect markets and institutions, and with the neoclassical focus on aggregate supply in a static world with perfect markets and institutions.

SOCIAL STATICS AND SOCIAL DYNAMICS

John Stuart Mill (1843), under the influence of Auguste Comte (1896), divided the wider field of economics into two main sections that he called 'social statics' and 'social dynamics'. He argued that, while political economy had made considerable progress in the field of social statics, social dynamics was virtually non-existent. Mill's great unfulfilled objective was to develop the new field of social dynamics so that it could stand beside, but a little higher, than social statics. He also asserted that these two branches of economics must be based on two very different methods. While social statics had successfully employed deduction, social dynamics, owing to its greater complexity, would need to be based on induction, the 'historical method'.

Mill discovered, however, that he had no comparative advantage in the historical method. For this reason, his serious attempt to discover the 'laws of dynamics' – through a study he called 'Ethology' – failed completely. Because of this failure he returned to social statics, and placed his faith in the Ricardian 'growth' model that focused on convergence to the stationary state. He even came to believe that the stationary state would be a kind of 'Mecca' in which humankind would pursue moral improvement rather than material advantage. This was a major retreat for Mill because the Ricardian convergence model was constructed from static classical theory.

Since Mill's day, no mainstream economist has attempted to develop the field of social dynamics using the historical method.[1] Instead, economic growth models have continued to be teased from the corpus of static theory. As we shall see, the objective of neoclassical growth theorists is not to observe the real-world growth process in order to construct the most effective model to explain it, but rather to use the existing body of static production theory to construct a model that generates *outcomes* (rather than *processes*) that might meet a formal abstract definition of economic growth, such as convergence to the steady state. These abstract growth outcomes have no reality other than a theoretical reality. In other words, economic growth theory is based not on the dynamics of reality but on the statics of neoclassical microeconomics. This certainly does not meet Mill's original objective for social dynamics.

In developing his macroeconomic model, John Maynard Keynes (1936) distanced himself from the existing body of supply-side theory. He was able to develop a macroeconomic model that was not – indeed could not be – derived directly from neoclassical microeconomics.[2] It was for this very reason that Keynes made an important demand-side breakthrough. As *The General Theory* is not dynamic, although there are some dynamic elements in it, he did not need to adopt the historical method. Instead he employed an impressive intuition together with an acute observation of the world around him. Had he attempted to go further and develop a dynamic model, Keynes would have needed to replace casual observation with systematic historical study. But, owing to his theory of knowledge (Fitzgibbons 1988), this is something he would never have attempted.

Some, the new evolutionary economists, have abandoned orthodox economic theory completely in their search for a dynamic theory, and have replaced it with deductive theory from biology. This provides a dramatic demonstration of the growing lack of confidence in the dynamic qualities of neoclassical economics. Yet this step into the dark is regrettable because it has imposed a totally inappropriate biological model on the changing fortunes of human society. When he said that 'the Mecca of the economist lies in economic biology', Alfred Marshall (1920: xii) was well wide of the mark.

The argument in this book is that a realist dynamic model of human society can only be constructed from within the discipline of economics. And this can only be achieved if we distance ourselves from static neoclassical microeconomics as Keynes did, and if we employ the historical method as Mill advocated. Yet this should not be interpreted as an attack on neoclassical economics as such. What orthodox theory was designed to do – the study of shortrun static issues of production and distribution – it does well. For some purposes it provides a powerful instrument of analysis. But it is just not possible to create dynamic theory from static ingredients. And it is not possible, as we shall see in Chapter 17, to use static theory to formulate successful policy for a dynamic society.

By adopting the inductive method a whole new world is opened up. For the first time in the history of economics we are able to see the existence and operation of the forces of dynamic demand. This knowledge transforms our perception of economics, both in terms of the real forces driving human society and the dynamic mechanisms by which this is achieved. And, in the process, a penetrating light is cast upon a number of key supply-side concepts that have been employed arbitrarily in orthodox economics to compensate for the inability of the deductive approach to model dynamic demand successfully. These concepts include the 'stationary state' or the equilibrium to which any society is tending; the natural or equilibrium rate of unemployment to which an economy is continually gravitating; the 'steady state' or equilibrium (even optimum) growth path on which we should be travelling; the shape of the aggregate supply curve (reflecting the degree of price flexibility) which is the main determinant of total output; rational expectations which has been employed to undermine demand-side analysis; and Pareto optimality which is the only objective test of economic performance. In the following chapters I argue that, had it been possible in the past to model dynamic demand, none of these artificial supply-side concepts would have been required.

What do I mean by 'social dynamics'? The approach to this issue has changed quite dramatically over the course of the twentieth century. When Alfred Marshall contrasted 'economic evolution' with 'economic dynamics', he thought of evolution in biological terms, and dynamics in physical or mechanical terms. Since then 'dynamics' has taken on the more general meaning of growth or change and is not limited to the physical concept of mechanics. It is in this more general sense that I use the term 'social dynamics'.

The study of social dynamics, or economic change, is influenced by the metaphor that is adopted. Neoclassical theory employs the metaphors of physics while evolutionary theory employs the metaphors of biology. As we shall see, the new evolutionary economists, like Marshall a century earlier, call for the replacement of the metaphors of physics with those of biology, as if that will provide a better theory of economic dynamics. No one has suggested that social dynamics should create its own metaphors. I will argue that the metaphors of social dynamics should arise from our systematic analysis of the economic transformation of real societies through historical time. One such metaphor is the riders in the chariot of change that emerged from the systematic study in *The Dynamic Society* (1996) of the dynamics of human society throughout recorded time. Another, employed below, is the skilled athlete who is able to convert a sequence of unstable lunges into an elegant running motion (or dynamic process). Such metaphors will invariably be human-centred.

THE SIGNIFICANCE OF DYNAMIC THEORY

The significance of dynamic theory can hardly be in doubt. We inhabit a world that is never static, that is always in flux. The only reason orthodox economics has focused on static theory to the exclusion of realist dynamic theory is that the latter has proved so intractable. In order to understand and resolve the larger issues facing humankind we must be able to model real-world dynamic processes. Our continued neglect of this essential task will compound the distorted picture we have of reality. This is particularly important when, as in Chapters 16 and 17, we come to examine economic policy of both the shortrun and longrun variety. As we will find, orthodox policy in the developed world is undermining our longrun viability and must, with some urgency, be redressed.

The distorted picture we have of the real world can be briefly illustrated. The flaw in the glass is the outcome of employing static models to explore dynamic issues. Owing to the absence of a suitable dynamic theory, applied economists have been tempted to use static partial and general equilibrium models to explain elements of longrun economic change. Counterfactual questions that have been examined include: What would the level of real GDP per capita have been in the USA in the late nineteenth century had railroads not existed? and What would the level of real wages be in the USA in the late twentieth century if immigration had been curtailed after the Second World War? The estimated size of these impacts is invariably and substantially incorrect because the static models employed implicitly assume that the dynamic strategy pursued by the society remains unchanged. Needless to say, this is a totally invalid assumption.

Over a period of more than five years, a major counterfactual change would result in the adoption of a new dynamic substrategy. When the change in dynamic substrategy is taken into account our interpretation of these events changes dramatically. Hence, the dynamic-strategy model presented in this book has major implications for past work in applied economics that is based on testing longrun counterfactual propositions using static partial or general equilibrium models. While the computed results of these models are precise, they are, as demonstrated in *The Ephemeral Civilization*, meaningless.

HOW GENERAL IS DYNAMIC-STRATEGY THEORY?

Dynamic-strategy theory can be regarded as general in the following three senses. First, it has universal applicability to different societies throughout the modern and pre-modern worlds. This is important because the implication is that it will also be relevant to the future. Orthodox models are, at best, limited in scope to developed societies in the modern world. Secondly, the dynamic-strategy theory can explain both economic and political change in the longrun. This unusual attribute also has important implications for its predictive power. Finally, this model has been able to encompass and integrate three disparate fields of orthodox economics. The three fields are economic growth theory, the theory of economic fluctuations, and the interaction between economic and political agents. This integration is possible because dynamic-strategy theory is able to model dynamic demand as well as the supply response. **Strategic demand** is the key. Through it we are able to link analytically these three fields of orthodox economic interest.

SOME DEFINITIONS

While the meaning of the central concepts employed in my dynamic-strategy theory will become clear as the book progresses, some concepts need to be defined at the outset to avoid unnecessary confusion. These include my definitions of the shortrun and longrun, rent-seeking and profit-seeking, and the term 'dynamic strategy'.

What is meant by 'dynamic strategy'?

It is important to realize that the dynamic-strategy concept was not derived from either game theory or business-management studies. Both of these fields employ the word 'strategy' when they mean 'tactic'. In this book I have returned to the common usage of these terms. Hence, a 'strategy' is a plan designed to achieve broad objectives, whereas a 'tactic' is a skilful device or procedure employed to achieve a certain limited objective within the broader strategy. A dynamic strategy, therefore, is a broad economic programme, such as conquest, commerce, or technological change, designed to achieve the general objective of survival and prosperity. These dynamic strategies are composed of a number of substrategies. And a dynamic tactic is a procedure required to implement aspects of these strategies and substrategies. This usage arose from my systematic study of the dynamics of real societies in the past, rather than from the imitation of methods employed in the deductive disciplines. The point of this definition is not to be pedantic but to avoid any confusion that could easily arise from readers believing that my dynamic strategies have anything to do with game theory or business management.

The nature of time

While the basic distinction involving time is between the shortrun and longrun, we also need to consider the very shortrun and the very longrun. These distinctions in this book are based on the concept of the dynamic strategy. 'Longrun' is employed as a single word because it refers to an important and integrated concept.

The shortrun is the period in which a dynamic strategy cannot be changed. During this period, of up to five years, decision-makers are forced to operate within the boundaries of an old dynamic substrategy even if it has been exhausted. The theoretical and practical implications of this are important, because over the duration of this period it is valid to employ the static general equilibrium model, which implicitly assumes that the dynamic strategy remains constant. Yet there may be other grounds for not employing the Walrasian–Arrow–Debreu model.

The longrun is the period in which a dynamic substrategy is not only able to change, but also has time to work itself out. As we shall see, the longrun ranges from *about* 5 to 50 years. Over this period of time it is not valid to use the general (or partial) equilibrium model to explore counterfactual propositions, because the dynamic strategy cannot be assumed to remain constant. Static models, therefore, will give entirely misleading estimates of variables under longrun analysis. A dynamic model that allows for a change in strategy must be used.

The very longrun is defined as the period in which a full dynamic strategy (say commerce, conquest, or technological change) can be replaced by a new one. It is during the very longrun, of up to 300 years, that we can observe the life history of a complete dynamic strategy composed of a series of substrategies. Finally, the very shortrun is the period in which even small investment projects cannot be changed. This is equivalent to the Marshallian definition of the shortrun.

Strategic objectives

While it is well known that decision-makers can opt for either profit-seeking or rent-seeking, the distinction between these objectives is not always clear. Indeed, there are a variety of definitions of these terms, including those of neoclassical economics and new political economy. The neoclassical definition of economic rent is the extranormal return received by the owners of resources that are in fixed supply either in the longrun or the shortrun (quasi-rents). It is assumed that quasi-rents will be eliminated in the longrun through competition.

The new political economy, on the other hand, draws an important distinction between rent-seeking and profit-seeking based on perceived social outcomes. James Buchanan (1980: 8–9) argues that the pursuit of extraordinary returns is an important part of a society's entrepreneurial activity which, provided there are no artificial barriers to entry, will lead to a 'socially desirable outcome' in the form of economic progress. This is profit-seeking rather than rent-seeking. It is an outcome consistent, he claims, with minimal governmental action 'restricted largely, if not entirely, to protecting individual rights, personal and property, and enforcing voluntary negotiated private contracts'. But, if governmental action 'moves significantly beyond the limits defined by the minimal or protective state', artificial barriers to entry will be erected, thereby preventing the natural and healthy erosion of economic rents. This will lead to a waste of resources as individuals attempt to capture these artificially contrived rents. Governments, therefore, can transform socially desirable profit-seeking into wasteful rent-seeking.

While I agree with Buchanan and other new political economists that the pursuit of extraordinary returns is a central part of the dynamic process and should be regarded as profit-seeking, I cannot accept the criterion used to draw a distinction between profit-seeking and rent-seeking. They employ the 'social consequences' criterion, whereas I employ the 'dynamic-strategy' criterion. The dynamic-strategy criterion states that a profit-seeker is one who pursues a dynamic strategy, whereas a rent-seeker is one who attempts to reap the rewards of frustrating the strategic pursuit. The profit-seeker is the dynamic **strategist** and the rent-seeker is the **antistrategist**. It is a distinction essential to the discussion of political change in Chapter 15.

This is not just a semantic distinction because it envisages entirely different roles for both the individual decision-maker and the government. In the first place, the dynamic-strategy criterion suggests a more proactive role for individuals in attempting to create rent-generating circumstances. The most extreme of these is where a group of antistrategists takes over government and hijacks the dynamic strategy, as in the USSR in 1917. Also this criterion assumes a different role for government. In the dynamic-strategy model there is important, indeed essential, scope for the government to provide

strategic leadership. This role exceeds the Buchanan minimum. Strategic leadership may even involve the erection of artificial barriers to provide extraordinary profits for those who are required to pioneer a new dynamic strategy. Examples of this type of strategic leadership include trade protection provided for European industrialists against British goods in the mid-nineteenth century, and protection for American industrialists against European goods in the late nineteenth and early twentieth centuries. While resources were directed to the achievement and maintenance of this governmental protection – resources that Buchanan would regard as 'wasted' – this action led to the emergence of new dynamic substrategies that, in turn, generated sustained economic growth in these economies. What I am arguing is that the real test for governmental involvement is not static efficiency but whether it leads to the effective development of a dominant dynamic strategy. Strategic progress, as will be discussed in Chapter 15, can be measured in terms of longrun growth rates.

THE BOOK'S STRATEGY

The strategy underlying the book's structure is the desire to contrast the approach of dynamic-strategy theory with that of orthodox theory. I begin in Part I by sketching the bare outlines of my dynamic model to provide a hint of what is to come. Then, in Part II, I contrast the three main approaches to economic dynamics – growth theory, evolutionary theory, and strategic theory. The intention is to suggest how the nature of these competing models is determined by the basic methods employed.

Part III focuses on the various approaches to what I call dynamic order. Before developing a new dynamic model we need to address the issue of how human societies are able to successfully achieve orderly material and socioeconomic progress without consciously planning it. This issue has been central to the discipline of economics since the time of Adam Smith. In this section I contrast the orthodox concepts of 'the invisible hand' and 'spontaneous order' with the strategic principle of 'dynamic order'. The central conditions for dynamic order are **strategic demand** and **strategic confidence** that emerge from an unfolding dynamic strategy.

Parts IV and V are concerned with the central elements of the dynamic-strategy model, namely the driving force and the dynamic mechanism. In Part IV, I focus on the dynamic nature of what I call 'materialist man', which is contrasted with the passive concept of *homo economicus*. Part V examines strategic demand, which is the core of the dynamic-strategy model. It elicits a **strategic response** through a process of rising prices that I call **strategic inflation**. The empirical testing of this mechanism has led to the discovery of the longrun and shortrun growth–inflation curves. Part VI focuses on dynamic outcomes, contrasting orthodox and strategic explanations of economic fluctuations. In the process, economic fluctuations are integrated into my theory of economic growth.

Finally, Part VII deals with politics and policy. It attempts to integrate political change and the process of policy formulation into the strategic model of economic change. This is contrasted with the lack of connection between orthodox growth theory and the new political economy. In the final chapter I also outline the general principles of strategic policy, and contrast these with the policy implications of neoclassical and new political economy theory. It is argued that the dynamic-strategy model calls for a new policy approach in order to reverse the current trend in developed nations that is undermining their longrun viability.

2 A Realist Dynamic Theory

While the dynamic-strategy model will be discussed in detail in the chapters that follow, a brief overview at the outset will provide the necessary perspective. The model, which is self-starting and self-sustaining, is built around a dynamic mechanism that generates both strategic confidence and strategic demand for new units of capital, labour, materials, ideas, and institutions. It is a model capable of generating fluctuations of a shortrun (3 to 10 years), longrun (20–60 years) and very longrun (300 years) nature. It can explain why some societies have been successful and others have stagnated and collapsed. It can show how political systems are transformed to accommodate changes in this fundamental dynamic mechanism. It can make sensible predictions about the future in both the short and long term. And it can generate far-reaching policy measures.

A LONGRUN DYNAMIC MODEL

The driving force within the dynamic-strategy model is an outcome of human nature operating within a typically competitive environment. This dynamic principle was derived from the detailed historical study undertaken in *The Dynamic Society* (1996) not only of human behaviour during the past two million years but of life itself during the past four billion years. I have called the motivating force 'materialist man' to differentiate it from the more familiar 'economic man' which is little more than a convenient and abstract collection of preferences and rational choices in neoclassical production theory. Materialist man, on the other hand, is a real-world decision-maker whose biological evolution has, in a typically competitive context, given him an overwhelming determination to survive and, having survived, to maximize individual material advantage *over his lifetime*. This objective, which provides human society with its fundamentally dynamic nature, is achieved through investment in one of four possible dynamic strategies (family multiplication, conquest, commerce, and technological change) and through a number of substrategies (such as steam power, iron and mechanical engineering; or nuclear power, space-age materials and microelectronics, both in the wider technological strategy). Materialist man, therefore, is a realistic inhabitant of a dynamic world, and the longrun consistency of his actions provide our first dynamic law – the law of human motivation – which is to survive and prosper (Snooks 1998).

As orthodox economic theory is concerned primarily with shortrun static, rather than longrun dynamic, analysis, 'economic man' does not aggressively adopt the dynamic strategies of materialist man. He merely expresses preferences for goods and services or coolly and effortlessly maximizes his profits, consumption, or utility. And he does this secure in the perfection of his knowledge of the world and its future, and in the bewildering speed and unerringness of his rational calculations. *Homo economicus* is clearly not a dynamic force, nor is he called upon to be so by orthodox economists. The motive force in most orthodox growth models is supplied by exogenous shocks.

The pursuit of strategies and substrategies in the dynamic-strategy model requires neither perfect knowledge about benefits and costs of investment in a wide range of alternative projects, nor sophisticated abilities to calculate rapidly their various rates of return. The reason is simple. In reality human decision-making does not conform to the neoclassical model, particularly in its rational expectations form. In reality the bulk of investment decisions are made through the imitation of successful individuals and projects. The initiators are the **strategic pioneers** and the imitators are the **strategic followers** who are powerfully attracted by extraordinary profits. I have called this the law of **strategic imitation**. This decision-making process, which is discussed in detail in *The Ephemeral Civilization* (1997a: ch. 2), places only minimal demand on the scarcest of all resources in nature – the human intellect. It is also responsible for the nature of societal rules or institutions (and, ultimately, artificial intelligence), which have been devised to economize on intelligence, not on benefit–cost information as institutionalists believe. While many others, especially Joseph Schumpeter (1949), have called attention to the imitation phenomenon, this is the first time it has been integrated into a general dynamic model as a complete explanation of human decision-making.

The second distinctive feature of the model is its central dynamic mechanism. This mechanism can be characterized in the first instance as the unfolding of a society's dominant dynamic strategy and its sequence of related substrategies. The strategic unfolding describes a development pathway that can be traced through time by the familiar macroeconomic measures of real GDP, population, and real GDP per capita. This **strategic pathway**, which defines the **dynamic form** of our model, is an outcome of competitive materialist man interacting with his physical and social environments. The physical environment can be characterized as an endowment of factors – of natural resources, labour, and capital – which is perceived through a set of relative factor prices. And the social environment consists of a large number of competing individuals together with a set of institutions required to conserve intelligence and facilitate the unfolding of the dominant dynamic strategy. The social cement that holds this all together is **strategic confidence** which is generated by a successful dynamic strategy and which in turn provides the trust and co-operation required for individuals to achieve their maximizing objectives. When strategic confidence evaporates, so too does trust and co-operation.

Individuals and (through the strategic imitation process) societies adopt the dynamic strategy that achieves their materialistic objectives most efficiently. This is the law of strategy optimization (Snooks 1998: ch. 8). In the abstract, efficiency can be thought of in benefit–cost terms as between alternative dynamic strategies and substrategies. It is, of course, a relative rather than an abstract concept. A strategy or substrategy is chosen because, at a point in time, it is more efficient than the alternatives, not because it is, in some timeless sense, absolutely the most efficient strategy. In the real world this is the outcome of a process of trial and error, with the strategic pioneers exploring the profitability of various alternatives and the great mass of followers imitating those who are conspicuously successful.

In any competitive environment, the potential of a dynamic strategy or substrategy is explored by materialist man, who responds to relative factor prices and to his peers. It is this interaction that leads to the unfolding of a dynamic strategy. Of course there is nothing inevitable or preordained about this unfolding process. There is no internal principle of strategic growth as, for example, in the germination of a seed. The nature and speed of an unfolding strategy depends upon conditions of competition and the nature of the physical and societal environment. In the early stages of this strategic unfolding, increasing strategic returns are experienced that encourage the growth of strategic infrastructure. But, at some point, decreasing strategic returns set in, thereby leading to a slowdown in economic growth and, once the dynamic strategy has been exhausted, the onset of stagnation.

These laws of increasing and decreasing *strategic* returns arise not from the production process but from the wider dynamic strategies and substrategies that are responsible for the dynamics of human society. As explained in Chapter 10, this strategic law encompasses the classical law of diminishing returns that is based on the misleading assumption of a fixed supply of natural resources (or 'land'). Also it resolves the difficulty inherent in the neoclassical version of diminishing returns which transfers the law from a situation in which natural resources are fixed in the longrun to a situation where all factors of production are fixed in the shortrun. Owing to technological change, dynamic strategies, but not natural resources, are capable of exhaustion.

Strategic demand is the central active principle in our model. It, together with strategic confidence, is generated by the unfolding dynamic strategy driven by materialist man. Owing to its dynamic origins, strategic demand is always changing, but in a logical rather than a chaotic way. As we have seen, a dominant dynamic strategy unfolds as a result of investors exploring its economic potential in a particular place over a particular period of time. It is because the unfolding dynamic strategy gives a predictable shape – the dynamic form – to a particular economic environment that the everchanging strategic demand traces out a logical and broadly predictable pattern. In this way demand is generated for a range of inputs required to facilitate the development of the dynamic strategy. These inputs include labour, fixed investment, working capital, material inputs, ideas, institutions, and organizations ranging from small firms to mega-states. It is the interaction between strategic demand and the strategic response of these supply-side variables that gives rise to the strategic pathway.

Strategic demand brings together a number of real, institutional, and cultural variables that are not usually associated in a causal way. Indeed, it changes the way we think about these variables: institutions and ideas, rather than driving society, as many believe, merely facilitate its development. It also shapes the internal structure of society and economy. The relationship between the household, private, and public sectors depends upon the type of dynamic strategy being pursued as well as the stage reached in the strategic unfolding process. As shown in *The Ephemeral Civilization* (1997a: 408–9), the size and function of the American household changed considerably between the westward expansion (family-multiplication) strategy of the nineteenth century and the industrialization (technological) strategy of the twentieth century.

Strategic demand is also very different to the Keynesian concept of aggregate demand. It is more comprehensive, more central to the dynamic core of society, more active and dynamic. Strategic demand is the active principle in our model. Aggregate demand, on the other hand, is an ephemeral outcome of the dynamic process in general and of strategic demand in particular. Unemployment in this model is not determined by aggregate demand as such, rather both are jointly determined by strategic demand. Aggregate demand (in a simple two-sector model) is merely the gross addition to capital required by the unfolding dynamic strategy in an artificially designated period of 365 1/4 days, together with consumption expenditure over the same period made possible by the surplus generated by this strategy. And further, this is an outcome not of static or comparative–static equilibrium processes. Like an athlete running around a stadium, a seamless trajectory is traced out by a system that is only maintained by continuously throwing itself out of balance. This sequence of unbalanced lunges is masked by the appearance of systematic continuity. Only when something snaps – the hamstring of the athlete or the strategy of society – is the underlying reality revealed as the system collapses.

The dynamic-strategy model changes the perspective on John Maynard Keynes' analysis of the investment-demand schedule. As is well known, in *The General Theory* (1936) investment is largely determined by 'the state of long-term expectations'. Keynes argued that, as there were no longrun data concerning the rate of return on future investment, capital expenditures must be determined by some compulsive urge in human beings which he called 'animal spirits'. While Keynes regarded this as a 'psychological law', it was in fact no more than an admission that he was unable to explain why longrun investment took place. He shares this conclusion with Karl Marx (despite his reference to the 'underworld of Karl Marx, Silvio Gesell or Major Douglas' – Keynes 1936: 32), who also regarded investment by capitalists as compulsive and irrational. In contrast, the dynamic-strategy model is able to offer a rational explanation: investment is a response by investors to changes in both strategic demand and its close partner strategic confidence – to the unfolding of the dynamic strategy. Our dynamic-strategy model, therefore, solves the Keynesian dilemma of uncertainty by revealing the core dynamic mechanism in human society.

Where do supply forces fit into the dynamic-strategy model? The answer is that essentially they play a passive role. Population, capital (both physical and human), technology, and institutions respond to strategic demand through the incentives provided by **strategic inflation**. In the dynamic-strategy model, inflation, which is essential to the dynamic process, is a stable, non-accelerating function of economic growth. Supply-side forces are at their most important in the form of relative factor prices influencing the type of dynamic strategies and substrategies chosen and explored by materialist man. Obviously the opportunity cost of capital is an element determining the scale of investment undertaken, but the expected yield on that investment, determined by the unfolding dynamic strategy, is dynamically far more important. While it is true that, at a given point in time, investment and the rate of return are an outcome of hypothetical demand and supply schedules for financial capital, over the longer term it is strategic demand that determines both the supply of funds (as well as the institutions that provide them) and the expected yields. In the longrun, therefore, strategic demand creates its own supply, and not the other way round as explicitly stated by the old neoclassicals (Say's Law) and implied by the modern neoclassicals.

THE DYNAMIC OUTCOME – ECONOMIC FLUCTUATIONS

The dynamic-strategy model is capable of explaining fluctuations in economic activity, together with stagnation, crisis, and collapse in human society. Strategic demand is the pivotal feature of this explanation. Fluctuations of different wavelengths, which tend to converge towards means of 3 to 10 years, 20 to 60 years, and about 300 years, are largely the result of fluctuations in strategic demand. In turn this is due to the fact that the unfolding of the dynamic strategy does not occur smoothly.

As demonstrated in *The Dynamic Society* (1996) and *The Ephemeral Civilization* (1997a) there is a hierarchy of investment programmes in a viable society. At the lowest level are the individual investment projects that mature in anywhere between a few and a dozen years; then there are the dynamic substrategies that rise and fall over a period of a few generations (of 40 years); and finally there are the full dynamic strategies, involving a sequence of substrategies, that rise and fall over a period of about a dozen generations (or 300 years). Moderate short-term fluctuations are experienced when the life spans of individual investment projects coincide through the cohesive mechanism of strategic imitation; severe and prolonged depressions can emerge during the time interval between the exhaustion of a major substrategy and the emergence of its replacement; and stagnation, crisis, and collapse can result from the failure to replace an exhausted dynamic strategy. Essentially, it will be argued in Chapter 14, longrun growth takes place endogenously through waves that are driven by successful dynamic strategies and substrategies rather than through regular cyclical activity. While the surging waves appear to possess some regularity over time, the hiatus between them varies according to the unpredictable time taken to replace old with new substrategies and strategies. Where replacement is impossible the hiatus is infinite, as the society in question collapses.

It is the exhaustion of a dominant dynamic strategy, therefore, that should be of most concern to any society. The ultimate outcome depends on the ability and good fortune of a society to replace an exhausting dynamic strategy with a new strategy. Societies in the ancient world, such as Greece and Rome, were unable to replace their exhausted strategies of commerce or conquest and, as a consequence, stagnated, declined, and eventually collapsed. On the other hand, Western Europe was able to replace its exhausted conquest and commerce strategies from the late eighteenth century with the technological strategy (that gave rise to the Industrial Revolution) and, thereby, to renew its vitality. The reason, as discussed in *The Dynamic Society* (1996), was, as we shall see, largely a matter of timing. The significance of this to our own time is that there is evidence, mainly in terms of the pressure on natural resources, to suggest that the current technological strategy will probably face exhaustion during the twenty-first century. Supply-side variables play only a passive role in the fluctuating way in which a dynamic strategy unfolds and is replaced.

THE MECHANISM OF STRATEGIC STRUGGLE

A distinguishing feature of the dynamic-strategy model is its ability to explain the dynamics not only of the economy but also of sociopolitical structures. In particular, the model can demonstrate and explain the interaction between economic and political forces. This is important because it places economics in a realistic power structure, and because it provides insights into politically relevant economic policies.

While the dynamic-strategy model can explain sharp directional changes and reversals in political institutions, other models, such as currently fashionable evolutionary theory, cannot. The superficial appearance of evolution in Western civilization since AD 800 – such as the emergence of democratic political and legal institutions – has depended upon the fortuitous strategic sequence of conquest→commerce→technological change. As explained in *The Ephemeral Civilization* (1997a), the normal sequence in history has been the conquest→commerce→conquest sequence, which in the case of ancient Greece and medieval Venice led to a sharp reversal of the growing democratization of political and economic institutions. The only reason that conquest did not replace commerce in Western Europe during the late eighteenth century is the one of timing mentioned above and discussed in Chapter 11. This reversal of political development cannot be explained by other economic models.

The central mechanism by which strategic demand is converted into political change is the **strategic struggle** for control of the dominant dynamic strategy that is the source of income and wealth. It is important to realize that this strategic mechanism bears no relation to the flawed class dialectic developed by Karl Marx. In my model the competing societal groups are strategic groups not class groups. They are characterized not by ownership of the means of production but by investment, both physical and human, in the dominant dynamic strategy. Hence my strategic groups, which cut across Marx's classes, include strategists (or profit-seekers) both old and new, non-strategists (coerced workers and dependents), and antistrategists (or rent-seekers) both conservative and radical. A measure of the difference between Marx's system and mine is that the post-Industrial Revolution 'classes' of capital and labour are, in the dynamic-strategy model, both members of the 'new strategists' who historically were pitted against the 'old strategists' (the merchant/landowners) rather than against each other. While workers and industrialists differ over the distribution of the strategic surplus, they are united in their support of the new technological strategy. This is why a proletarian revolution in a viable technological society was never a possibility. The enemy of the technological society is not the worker but the radical antistrategist – the Bolshevik, the Maoist, the Nazi – who is determined to eliminate the new strategist and his dynamic strategy, for rent-seeking purposes.

All societies contain representatives of these strategic groups, which are involved in a continuous struggle for influence or control over the ultimate source of income and wealth. The relative strength of these groups differ through both space and time according to the nature and stage of development of the dynamic strategy being pursued. It is not, however, a simple progression over time as the evolutionary model might be expected to claim, rather it is a complex function of strategic change. Indeed, over the entire history of human society, the ratio between strategic groups has passed through a complete circle from the high ratio of strategists to nonstrategists existing in hunting societies, to a very small ratio in ancient and medieval conquest societies, to a modest ratio in commerce societies, and to a high ratio once more in technological societies.

In a corresponding way, political institutions have changed from early forms of team democracy in hunting societies, to oligarchies and dictatorships in ancient and medieval conquest societies, to limited democracy in ancient and pre-modern commerce societies, and universal democracy in technological societies. The power transfers reflect the changing relative wealth and, hence, demand for strategic control by various economic groups in society. The pathways of these power transfers is rarely smooth, as the old strategists, who rise to power on the surging wave of a traditional strategy (such as conquest) that is now exhausted and beginning to ebb, refuse to hand over control to the new strategists being swept into power by an emerging strategy (such as commerce). Invariably this strategic struggle has led to civil wars and revolutions, which have typically been won by the new strategists. But on occasion, when the new strategists do not have the economic power to over-whelm the old strategists quickly (as in Russia in 1917), the radical antistrat-egists (Bolsheviks) may hijack the revolution and eliminate the strategists both old and new. To prevent potential strategists from re-emerging, the antistrat-egists establish a command system that is also capable of extracting rent from the luckless population. Yet while the command system is an excellent instru-ment for oppression and rent extraction it cannot compete in the race for growth with strategic societies and, hence, it is ultimately swept away. Clearly this model has implications for the present and future.

It is not hard to see why political institutions emerge to support and facilitate the unfolding of the dominant dynamic strategy. Or why economic policy favours the ruling strategic groups. Political institutions, like all other institu-tions and organizations, are driven by strategic demand. Of course, there are times when institutions are out of sympathy with the objectives of strategists, particularly during an antistrategic regime, but within a surprisingly short time this anomaly will be removed and even the most unsympathetic regimes will be swept away. Yet it is just as true of democratically elected political parties in advanced democracies that commit major errors of policy judgement. Political institutions exist to serve the needs of the dynamic strategists.

STRATEGIC POLICY

The policy implications of the dynamic-strategy model differ dramatically from those of orthodox neoclassical theory that have been applied throughout the developed world. Also, it will be argued that strategic policies can be expected to counter the dangerous tendency of contemporary policy to undermine the longrun viability of Western democracies. While general principles and broad proposals are discussed, no attempt will be made in this book to formulate specific policies as these will vary according to national, even regional, circumstances.

Strategic demand provides a new central policy principle, namely to maximize the sustainable exploitation of strategic opportunities. But it should be emphasized that this is not equivalent to the optimum growth path idea, because such a path can be identified neither in prospect nor retrospect. This new general principle replaces, for the purposes of dynamic analysis, the artificial supply-side construct of social welfare. As argued below, Pareto optimality owes its existence to the absence of a theory of dynamic demand in neoclassical economics (or indeed in orthodox economics as a whole). In the dynamic-strategy model the **strategic test** replaces the Pareto efficiency test. Efficiency of production and distribution is, therefore, secondary to strategic development. Also the strategic test displaces the 'Wicksell test' advocated by constitutional economists because it provides the ultimate and measurable basis for 'unanimity and consensus'. It is a test relevant to the longrun as well as the shortrun.

The strategic test concerns the effectiveness of a policy in facilitating the exploitation of strategic opportunities. And the measure of this effectiveness is the rate of growth of real GDP per capita. If the rate of economic growth is significantly lower than that achieved by a particular society during a comparable period in the exploitation of an earlier substrategy, or is significantly less than that of other societies pursuing similar technological substrategies, then it is probably not maximizing the sustainable exploitation of its strategic opportunities.

What subsidiary objectives arise from the central strategic principle? Basically, that other issues such as economic stability and external and internal balance should not conflict with the exploitation of strategic opportunities. More specifically this means that governments should provide positive strategic leadership, and that inflation should be regarded as a natural outcome and essential element of the dynamic process. Stability will not be a problem for any society that is successfully pursuing a viable dynamic strategy.

The main economic problem in the mid-1990s is not price instability but slower and less continuous economic growth and higher rates of unemployment. In part this is due to a hiatus between the exhaustion of the technological substrategy employed so effectively by the USA and Europe between the Second World War and the early 1970s and the emergence of a new substrategy. But it is also due to the 'stability cult' in OECD countries, which is responsible for undercutting the revival of strategic demand. Each time our economic athlete gets to his feet, his legs are kicked away by governments pursuing deflationary monetary and fiscal policies. This orthodox policy approach, which is undermining the longrun viability of the developed world, must be reversed. And soon.

CONCLUSIONS

The dynamic-strategy model, therefore, makes strong claims to explain the dynamics not only of the economy but also of the political vehicle by which it is carried forward. These ideas will be explored in greater detail in the chapters that follow. Naturally the model can only be regarded as provisional until it has been tested repeatedly against real-world facts and against the claims of competing theories. Already these ideas, derived from historical study, have been tested against a great deal of real-world evidence. They have been through the only real laboratory available to the social scientist. And the dynamic-strategy model appears to outflank its competitors, not only by its more general nature but also by its real-world relevance. But only time will tell.

Part II
Dynamic Approaches

3 Growth Theory

The history of economic thought since the time of Adam Smith (1723–90) shows a continuing if sporadic concern with the theory of economic growth. This interest should come as no surprise, because it is obvious that we live in a dynamic world. What is surprising, however, is that very little real progress has been made in the field of economic dynamics relative to that of economic statics over the past three centuries. Growth theorists are still unable to claim that they can explain the dynamics of human society.

The reasons for this relative backwardness are twofold. In the first place, economic theorists have attempted to employ the method, laws, concepts, and theoretical tools from social statics in a very different field of study that requires entirely new methods, laws, concepts, and theoretical tools. Social dynamics, it is argued in Chapter 5, requires the inductive rather than the deductive approach. In the second place, growth theorists have failed to recognize the real **dynamic form** of growing societies. This has led them to impose an analytical 'shape' on their growth models – convergence to either the 'stationary state' or the 'steady state' – that is artificial, totally unrealistic, and deforming. But this is not meant to deny the empirical contribution made to the understanding of the growth of real societies that has been stimulated by this unrealistic theory. To demonstrate these views I will briefly review the classical, Keynesian, Solow–Swan, and 'endogenous' growth models.

THE CLASSICAL MODEL

The growth models of the classical 'school' were developed to analyse the dynamic forces thought to underlie the British economic system of the early nineteenth century. David Ricardo (1772–1823) and Thomas Malthus (1766–1834) were the main contributors to this model, which involves one sector, agriculture (although this can be expanded to include additional sectors), three factors of production (land, capital, and labour), and three socioeconomic groups (landlords, capitalists, and workers) competing with each other to enlarge their shares of the social surplus.

Although in longrun equilibrium, the analytical economy is busily operating to satisfy the objectives of the economic agents who are rewarded according to the productive resources they own: with landlords appropriating rent, capitalists earning profits, and workers receiving subsistence wages. It is like a stationary motor vehicle with its engine running, yet to be thrown into gear. The dynamic mechanism is activated by an exogenous shock, perhaps a

25

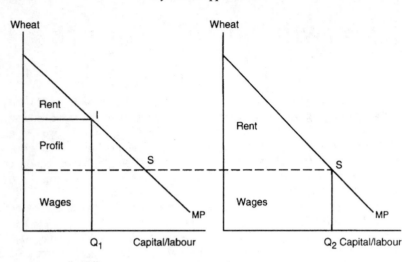

Figure 3.1 The classical model of growth and distribution

Notes: 1. An increase in the combined input capital/labour (in response to profits)
from Q_1 towards Q_2 will reduce the marginal product of the variable input.
Profits fall and rents rise, while wages remain at subsistence level.
2. This process will continue until the marginal product has fallen to S, the
stationary state, where it is equal to the subsistence wage, and profits have
been eliminated.
3. The particular interest of this model is that it has been traditionally used to
characterize the Middle Ages and to explain the alleged lack of growth. It is
also often used by naïve environmentalists.

discovery of new resources, a trade bonanza, or the introduction of a new
production technique. The purpose of the classical model was to show
how the economy could handle this injection of growth, which merely
involves convergence to a stationary equilibrium – the so-called 'stationary
state'.

Central to the process of convergence to equilibrium is the accumulation
of capital which is stimulated by increasing profits. Only capitalists invest
their surplus, because landlords devote their rents entirely to unproductive
consumption, and workers use their wages entirely for subsistence. Following
an exogenous injection of growth, the sequence of causation is: profits
rise→funds are invested in capital equipment, possibly embodying new techniques of production (resulting in further division of labour)→the demand
schedule for labour (MP_L in Figure 3.1) shifts to the right→nominal wages
rise→population increases→the margin of cultivation is extended→diminish-
ing returns are encountered→production costs rise→profits are reduced
while rents increase→the rate of capital accumulation and population
growth declines and even falls absolutely→the economy eventually reaches

the stationary state. The movement from one equilibrium position to the next, *at the same level* of real GDP per capita, is complete. Hence, while there is an increase in real GDP per capita in the immediate term of a generation or so, there is no longrun economic growth. Figure 3.1 provides a simplified diagrammatic explanation of this process. Classical economists such as J.S. Mill (1848: Bk IV, ch. VI) welcomed the prospect of the stationary state because it would replace the struggle for 'material improvement' with the achievement of 'moral improvement'.

A major problem with the classical model, which J.S. Mill (1806–73) was supporting as late as the mid-nineteenth century, is that it bore no relation to the world in which it was created. Despite living through the Industrial Revolution, Malthus and Ricardo completely underestimated the role of technology and commerce in counteracting the convergence to static equilibrium. This is probably why they made no attempt to make technological change endogenous to their system. They even incorrectly believed that their model reflected the past in which aristocratic landlords were unproductive and only the middle-class businessmen were entrepreneurial. This view, which has recently been disproved (Snooks 1993: 206–30), has been widely influential. It is a fundamental problem that highlights the need to base theoretical models on real-world processes.

The central feature of the classical growth model is, as we have seen, convergence to equilibrium. It is a feature that the classical model has in common with all deductive growth models. Equilibrium in the classical case involves the stationary state, whereas in the Keynesian and neoclassical growth models it involves the steady state. The fascinating question is: Why has the concept of equilibrium held such sway over growth theorists? I believe that the answer to this question explains not only the fundamental nature of growth models but also the reason they provide such little insight into real-world dynamics. Apart from the mathematical convenience of the equilibrium concept, it provides the dynamic form for the deductivist model. This dynamic form provides a structure for the growth model, and analytical meaning for theoretical growth. But, of course, form, structure, and meaning in deductive models are completely artificial and bear no relationship to reality. They are the outcome of a supply-side economics.

The simple fact is that real societies do not exist in a static equilibrium, nor do they converge to either a static or a moving equilibrium. But in the absence of any information about the dynamic form of the real-world growth process, some sort of arbitrary dynamic form must be imposed on a deductive system to give it coherence and analytical meaning. The problem, however, is that there are probably hundreds of different dynamic forms that could be imposed; the steady state is just one of them. Yet there is another way. In this book the real-world dynamic form is revealed and employed to provide a realistic growth model that endogenizes and explains all the arbitrary assumptions of deductive growth theory.

Later attempts were made to resolve some of the problems inherent in the classical model, particularly concerning the role of technological change and the nature of the dynamic form. Karl Marx (1818–83) and Joseph Schumpeter (1883–1950) were the chief among these.

Marx's growth model was a variation on the classical theme. While Marx accepted the importance of capital accumulation and its relationship to profits (although to the *rate* rather than the *size* of profit as in the classical model), he saw a greater role for technology, which he regarded as the main agent of change in the capitalist system. But he rejected the classical relationship between wages and population expansion, and substituted arguments about 'the reserve army of labour' and changing labour-force participation rates.

Despite these modifications to the classical model, the outcome of Marx's system was much the same. Although Marx's capitalists attempt to maintain profits through embodied technological change, the growing capital intensity of production (owing to the labour-saving nature of innovation) reduces the profit rate, places increasing pressure on wage rates, increases unemployment, and finally causes the capitalist system to collapse after experiencing increasingly severe fluctuations. At first glance, Marx's system appears to be influenced by an understanding of history, but on closer inspection it becomes obvious that reality has been subordinated to ideology (Snooks 1998: ch. 3).

One feature of Marx's model is particularly puzzling. Why, when capitalists invest in embodied technological change to maintain their viability, do profit rates decline? The short answer is that Marx built his model to achieve that outcome, just as Harrod built a model to achieve instability and the 'new' growth theorists built models to achieve positive longrun growth. We can see this from a brief review of the main equations in Marx's system. The value of a firm's output is given by

$$y = c + v + s \tag{3.1}$$

where y is output, c is the value of capital depreciation plus raw materials (both valued by their labour content), v is the wages bill, and s is 'surplus value' or profit (that is, a measure of worker exploitation, as total value added is due entirely to the efforts of labour). And the rate of profit is

$$p = s/c + v \tag{3.2}$$

where p is the rate of profit, s/v is the 'rate of surplus value' or the 'rate of exploitation' that Marx assumed constant. Now, as s/v is constant, any increase in c in equation (3.2) will lead to a decline in the rate of profit p.

Marx also attempted to give analytical meaning and structure to this system through his 'dialectical materialism' schema. This was a philosophical/political mechanism of class struggle that was inspired by Hegel's dialectical triad of thesis, antithesis, and synthesis. It was an entirely arbitrary dynamic form, owing nothing to historical reality, that Marx imposed on his model. Technological change is not really the agent of change in Marx's dynamic system because it is subordinated (as can be seen in part in equation (3.2)) to the teleological process of class struggle that its author was determined would lead to communism as the end of the historical dynamic process – the final stationary state. Despite the many theoretical insights in Marx's work, his dynamic model constitutes a backward step from the classical model because the dynamic form he substituted for convergence to equilibrium was pure fantasy.

Schumpeter began with the classical growth model and attempted to extend it in a number of ways by giving greater attention to historical reality than to the metaphysical invention of Marx. In *The Theory of Economic Development* (first published in 1912) Schumpeter's analysis begins with a discussion of economic activity in the normal state of equilibrium. He outlines 'the circular flow of life' in which all economic activity is repetitive, undergoing an endless and predictable routine. In this longrun equilibrium all factors of production are fully employed and are paid their marginal products. This is the province of economic statics. Economic growth occurs only when this longrun equilibrium is disturbed. Schumpeter (1949: 64) explains:

> Development... is a distinct phenomenon, entirely foreign to what may be observed in the circular flow or in the tendency towards equilibrium. It is spontaneous and discontinuous change in the channels of flow, disturbance of equilibrium, which forever alters and displaces the equilibrium state previously existing. Our theory of development is nothing but a treatment of this phenomenon and the processes incident to it.

Disequilibrium, then, is the subject of economic dynamics.

The disturbance of equilibrium is caused by innovation embodied in new plant and equipment. As in most growth theory before the 1980s, this technological disturbance, which generates extranormal profits, is treated as exogenous. It occurs only when the social climate is conducive to the appearance of a sufficient flow of 'New Men'. Once innovations, for whatever reason, are introduced by the 'New Men' or pioneering entrepreneurs, extranormal profits encourage a host of imitators to follow suit, leading to the emergence of a 'cluster' of complementary innovations. In response to this innovative activity there is a burst of investment financed by credit expansion that leads to price increases, structural change (from consumer to capital goods) and, after a lag, to increases in employment and output. Once innovation ceases, the continued expansion of investment (the 'over-investment' assumption) reduces profits to normal levels. New investment ceases, the price level falls, and recession emerges. Once more we are in longrun static equilibrium or the stationary state.

Schumpeter (1949: 235) explains that the innovation-led boom 'altered the data of the system, upset its equilibrium, and thus started an apparently irregular movement in the economic system which we conceive as a struggle towards a new equilibrium position'. His concept of innovation was rather broad, including new and better goods; new methods of production; the exploitation of new markets; the discovery of new sources of raw materials; and the rise of new types of organization. What he adds to the classical model here is the idea that convergence to static equilibrium takes place through a mechanism of boom and depression. Schumpeter is, in other words, concerned not only with the growth outcome but also with the process by which it was achieved. He argues that 'the boom... creates out of itself an *objective situation*, which, even neglecting all accessory and fortuitous elements, makes an end of boom, leads *easily* to a crisis, *necessarily* to a depression, and hence to a temporary position of relative steadiness and absence of development' (ibid.: 236). The boom, therefore, is a process of disequilibrium characterized by 'overproduction', 'skewness', 'the appearance of disproportionality... between quantities and prices of goods' as well as between old and new businesses and industries, and the growing menace of speculation (ibid.: 240–1). Depression is an inevitable outcome of the disequilibrium process, and

> the driving impulse of the process of depression cannot theoretically stop until it has done its work, has really brought about the equilibrium position... Nor will this process be interrupted by a new boom before it has done its work in this sense

owing to the uncertainties about 'new data' that make the 'calculation of new combinations impossible' (ibid.: 243).

This is the only orthodox growth model that is concerned with the growth *process* as well as growth *outcomes*. Why? Because it is informed by historical processes of change. As such it is the most successful and influential attempt in the history of economic analysis to use the deductive–inductive approach by employing historical observation to make the classical model more realistic. Not surprisingly it is the only growth model that has been successfully employed to reconstruct and interpret the *process* of economic development in real-world economies (see, for example, Butlin 1964).

In addition to making the classical concept of convergence to equilibrium more realistic, Schumpeter, in his later work *Business Cycles* (1939), also provides this basic model with a more plausible dynamic form. He provides it with a step-like set of equilibrium positions, which is like an escalator that regularly breaks down and has to be restarted on each occasion from an outside power source. Instead of steady convergence to a static equilibrium that is no higher on the real GDP per capita scale than all foregoing equilibria as in the classical model, Schumpeter views 'economic evolution' as a cyclical process that possesses an ascending, but irregular, trajectory. We are told that:

> To locate the points on our graphs which correspond to points of equilibrium...is from our standpoint the first and foremost task of time-series analysis...They mark the path of economic evolution as stepping stones mark the path across a brook...A line or curve through those points, or a band or narrow zone through those neighbourhoods, supplies a trend [the 'real trend'] that really has economic significance...this trend does not describe a phenomenon distinct from the cycle. On the contrary, since evolution is essentially a process which moves in cycles, the trend is nothing but the result of the cyclical process or a property of it...Real is only the cycle itself. (Schumpeter 1939: 206–7)

This evolutionary process consists of a hierarchy of long and short cycles (the 'Kitchen' of 3 to 4 years, the 'Juglar' of 7 to 11 years, and the 'Kondratieff' of 50 to 55 years) that trace out a 'real trend' rather than a 'statistical trend'. Yet, having made this important point, Schumpeter really only explains the fluctuations, not the whole 'evolutionary' process.

Schumpeter's dynamic form is considerably more realistic than that of other growth models, but it has serious limitations owing to the underlying classical model. The first of these arises from Schumpeter's retention of the convergence concept; and the second from the fact that growth is not a continuous, internally generated process, but is driven intermittently by an unexplained source of innovation. In the end, Schumpeter's model is no more dynamic than the classical system on which it was based.

THE KEYNESIAN GROWTH MODEL

Modern growth theory has emerged largely since the Second World War. The so-called Harrod–Domar growth model that appeared in the 1930s and 1940s was inspired by the revolutionary macroeconomic model fashioned by J.M. Keynes in *The General Theory* (1936). As persuasively demonstrated by Athol Fitzgibbons (1988), Keynes based his *General Theory* on the idea of flux (the origin of uncertainty) rather than longrun equilibrium, but he interpreted it in a static rather than a dynamic way. It was R.F. Harrod (1936, 1939, 1948) who, after working with Keynes on *The General Theory* throughout 1935, attempted to formulate a dynamic model. But he did so in neoclassical, equilibrium terms. In his turn, Keynes discussed (and published) Harrod's work on economic dynamics (Eltis 1987: 595–602). Harrod's objective was to translate what he saw as the central insight of *The General Theory* – the possibility of short-term equilibrium occurring below the full-employment level of national income – into dynamic terms. What we are interested in here is the fundamental nature of Harrod's model. As Domar's (1946, 1957) approach is similar, and subsequent, it will not be reviewed separately.

Harrod's dynamic model builds on the macroeconomic concepts of income, investment, and saving presented in *The General Theory*. Like Keynes, he does not attempt to provide any microeconomic underpinning. It is, therefore, a macroeconomic growth model. And as such it contrasts with the later microeconomic growth models of Solow–Swan and the new growth theorists, which are built largely from neoclassical production theory. But like the neoclassical growth theorists, Harrod was vitally concerned with convergence to, or divergence from, the steady state or equilibrium growth path. The source of longrun growth is exogenous to the model. According to Harrod (1948: 21–4), the motive force in his dynamic model is provided by two independent variables, population increase and technological change, which operate through the 'dependent' variable, capital stock. Basically he is interested in the conditions necessary to achieve the equilibrium growth path, and in what would happen if this steady state was not achieved.

Briefly, Harrod's argument is that in order to achieve the steady state, the actual rate of growth must equal both the rate of growth that economically rational entrepreneurs find satisfying (the 'warranted' rate), and the rate of growth that leads to full employment with no inflation (the 'natural' rate). Harrod's basic equation is

$$GC = s \tag{3.3}$$

where G is growth during a given period, C is the investment/increase in income ratio, and s is the average propensity to save. Equation (3.3) is merely a statement of the truism that *ex post* saving is equal to *ex post* investment. Equation (3.3) can be expressed as

$$\frac{\Delta Y}{Y} \cdot \frac{I}{\Delta Y} = \frac{S}{Y} \quad \text{or } I = S$$

where Y is income, I is investment, and S is saving.

Harrod's second equation expresses the equilibrium conditions for the steady state. This is his famous 'warranted rate of growth' and is written as

$$G_w C_r = s \qquad\qquad\qquad (3.4)$$

where G_w is the warranted rate of growth and C_r is the 'capital requirements' to achieve the warranted rate. In the steady state, or dynamic equilibrium, the actual growth rate and capital requirements must equal the rate of growth that just satisfies all entrepreneurs. If, however, G exceeds G_w, then C will be less than C_r, which will lead entrepreneurs to increase investment thereby causing G to move even further from G_w in the next period. This, Harrod argues, will lead to a cumulative movement of G away from the equilibrium growth path – a movement reinforced by the acceleration principle. This is Harrod's famous 'knife-edge' scenario.

Harrod's third equation concerns the natural rate of growth, which is really the potential full-employment rate possible with a given increase in technology and population. It is expressed as

$$G_n C_r = s \qquad\qquad\qquad (3.5)$$

where G_n is the 'natural' rate of growth. The significance of this equation is that if G_w is greater than G_n (owing to a sudden reduction in the growth of population or technology), it will be impossible for G to equal G_w, with the result that G will diverge cumulatively downwards from G_w, leading to deep depression. This system can also be used to analyse fluctuations owing to the different relationships between G, G_n, and G_w in different phases of the business cycle. Unlike Schumpeter's analysis of economic fluctuations, this is a highly abstract system.

Harrod made an important contribution to modern growth theory. In the first place he introduced the concept of the 'steady state' or equilibrium growth path. Despite the claim of some new growth theorists that 'although these [Harrod–Domar] contributions triggered a good deal of research at the time, very little of this analysis plays a role in today's thinking' (Barro and Sala-i-Martin 1995: 10), this concept has proven to be essential to all subsequent growth theory.[1] As I argue in this chapter, in the absence of any information about the real-world dynamic form, it is essential to impose an artificial structure upon deductive growth models. The steady state has been used for that purpose. Of course it is a totally arbitrary structure, which bears no relation to reality. The real dynamic form, as discussed in Chapter 10, is provided by the unfolding dynamic strategy rather than a hypothetical pathway that fulfils the expectations of entrepreneurs.

The other main contribution to economic dynamics made by Harrod, which is also denied by the new growth theorists, is the attempt to construct a macroeconomic growth model. In this book it is argued that realistic growth models are more likely to be constructed from macroeconomic concepts and variables. Unfortunately the Keynesian foundations that Harrod employed are not sufficiently extensive to build a successful dynamic model. And the reason for this is that Keynes was concerned only with shortrun proximate determinates of investment, saving, and income, rather than the longrun ultimate causes. What he treated as exogenous 'psychological laws' or 'propensities' – the propensity to consume/save, the 'state of long-term expectation', and the 'motives to liquidity preference' – should be treated as endogenous variables in a general longrun dynamic model. This can only be achieved through the historical method, because only the historical method can detect the role of dynamic demand.

NEOCLASSICAL GROWTH MODELS

The main methodological characteristic of the neoclassical growth model is that it has been constructed from the corpus of static microeconomic theory. Rather than asking what real-world economic dynamics looks like and how it can be modelled, the neoclassical growth theorist only wants to know how existing production theory can be used to generate an outcome that can meet a technical definition of growth. These are two very different approaches that generate very different economic growth models.

It is hard to escape the conclusion that the approach chosen by neoclassical growth theorists is very limiting. And deforming. Why should static production theory have anything to say about real-world dynamics and, even if it did, why should we expect it to be all-encompassing, useful, or even particularly sensible? It would be a remarkable coincidence if it were. Surely J.S. Mill (1843) was correct when he argued that 'social statics' and 'social dynamics' are two entirely distinct fields with different methodologies. They cannot be mixed together as the growth theorists propose. Yet there is no discussion of this major problem in the growth theory literature. It is merely assumed by mainstream economists that there is no alternative to the approach adopted by neoclassical economists. What is discussed in the literature, although this has been ignored and forgotten by mainstream economists, is that the usefulness of the neoclassical production function is severely limited owing to its precarious foundations (Robinson 1953–4; Harcourt 1972).

There are two main versions of neoclassical growth theory, the Solow–Swan model developed in the mid-1950s and elaborated over the following decade, and the 'new' or 'endogenous' growth model that has been developing since the mid-1980s. Economic growth in the Solow–Swan model is generated by a disturbance – such as a war, depression, or drought – that leads an economy to converge towards its own 'steady state' or dynamic equilibrium. This is similar to the nature of growth in the classical model involving convergence to the 'stationary state', or static equilibrium. In reality, this convergence in both cases is merely a process of economic recovery from a natural or man-made crisis. The Solow–Swan model, like that of Ricardo–Malthus, is unable to explain real or longrun growth. In both models longrun growth can only be generated by exogenously determined technological change. The 'new' growth model starts with the Solow–Swan version and attempts to endogenize technological change in order to model longrun growth as well as convergence to this dynamic equilibrium rate. The argument in this chapter, however, is that they have only been able to endogenize technological change by borrowing inductive ideas from outside the neoclassical system. This leads to more realistic results, but only at the expense of creating a hybrid model that will hardly appeal either to neoclassical purists or to realists.

The Solow–Swan model

By reviewing the way the Solow–Swan model is constructed we can explore its fundamental nature. The model is, as we shall see, constructed largely from neoclassical production theory within a general equilibrium framework. This has a number of implications: that essentially it is a microeconomic model of growth; that it is a supply-side model in which supply creates its own demand (a 'dynamic' version of Say's Law); that economic growth is a result of the structural conditions of production; and that it is concerned with outcomes rather than processes. In other words, the Solow–Swan model is an attempt to show how growth *outcomes* can be generated from a model based on static microeconomic theory, rather than to model the dynamic *processes* of real societies.

The distinction is important. Just because static production theory can be used to build a model capable of generating outcomes, which at first sight have the appearance of growth, does not mean that it can explain real-world dynamics. While this approach might be able to isolate some elements relevant to economic growth, it would be surprising if it had much relevance to reality. Indeed, as will be shown, the neoclassical approach focuses on only one very limited aspect of dynamics – convergence to the 'steady state' – and even this is only relevant to technologically advanced societies. It might be able to explain recovery from temporary crisis, but it is not able to explain longrun economic growth.

The simple Solow–Swan model is based on a closed economy with a Robinson Crusoe-type producer/consumer who owns all the resources, who controls the production process, and who consumes part of the output and saves the rest. There are just three fundamental equations in the model: the production function, with two inputs of capital and labour; the investment function; and the labour function. Of these the most important is the production function, because minor differences in the assumptions underlying the production function produce entirely different models of economic growth. Hence it is possible to generate a range of very different growth models merely by changing the set of arbitrary assumptions about the nature of production.

The main defining characteristics of the Solow–Swan production function are: each input exhibits positive and diminishing marginal products; the production function generates constant returns to scale; and as each factor approaches zero its marginal product approaches zero and vice versa. A popular production function of this type is the Cobb–Douglas production function that can be expressed as:

$$Y = AK^\alpha L^{1-\alpha}$$

where Y is output, A is technological change, K and L are capital and labour respectively, and α and $1 - \alpha$ are returns to the factors of production. It can be expressed in intensified form as:

$$Y = Ak^\alpha$$

The contribution made independently by Trevor Swan (1956) and Robert Solow (1956) was to employ a limited form of this type of production function. They assumed that as technological change is exogenous to the model, the production function can be written:[2]

$$Y = F(K, L) \tag{3.6}$$

or in intensive form

$$y = f(k)$$

The fundamental dynamic equation for the Solow–Swan model is derived from the change in the capital stock over time. This depends heavily on the assumption that the saving rate is exogenous and constant. Change in capital stock is given by

$$\dot{K} = I - \delta K = s \cdot F(K, L, t) - \delta K \tag{3.7}$$

where $\dot{K}$ is the increase in capital over time. This can be expressed in per capita terms by dividing equation (3.7) through by L (labour)

$$\dot{k} = s \cdot f(k) - (n + \delta) \cdot k \tag{3.8}$$

In equation (3.8), $s \cdot f(k)$ is the saving rate and $n + \delta$ is the effective depreciation rate for the capital/labour ratio. This has been expressed graphically in Figure 3.2. Basically the Solow–Swan model suggests that the steady-state capital/labour ratio (k^*) is determined by the intersection of the investment and depreciation functions. The steady state occurs when the variables K, Y, C, and L grow at constant rates and, hence, *per capita quantities do not grow at all!* This is why the Solow–Swan model cannot explain longrun economic growth.

The 'dynamics' of the Solow–Swan model are illustrated in Figure 3.3. This figure is based on the transformation of equation (3.8) into growth-rate terms by dividing through by k. In this figure the growth rate of k is given by the vertical distance between the investment curve $s \cdot f(k)/k$ and the effective depreciation line $n + \delta$. Where the 'initial' capital/labour ratio ($k(0)$) is less than the steady-state level (k^*) the growth rate is positive, and where it is greater than k^* the growth rate is negative. In both cases there will be a convergence to the steady-state equilibrium, with the rate of change being inversely related to the distance between the initial and equilibrium levels.

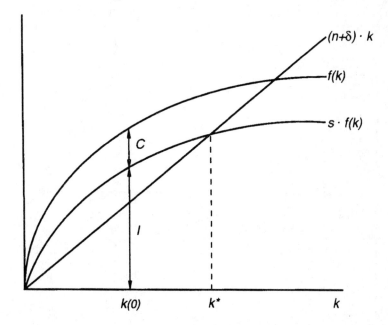

Figure 3.2 The Solow–Swan model

Notes: $k(0)$ is the initial level of the capital/labour ratio (owing to a disruption of some type), k^* is the steady-state level, I and C are the levels of investment and consumption and $f(k)$, $s \cdot f(k)$ and $(n + \delta) \cdot k$ are the production, investment, and depreciation functions.

These 'dynamic' outcomes flow directly from the assumptions underlying the neoclassical production function – diminishing returns to capital – and the Solow–Swan model – a constant saving rate. Hence, when the capital/labour ratio (k) is relatively low, the average product $(f(k)/k)$ is relatively high, which, owing to the assumption of a constant saving/investment rate, leads to a relatively high gross investment rate $(s \cdot f(k)/k)$ and a high growth rate $(\dot{k}/k)$. The growth outcomes of the Solow–Swan model, therefore, depend critically on the assumptions its authors were willing and able to make about the nature of production and saving.

Technological change can be introduced into this model without changing its steady-state nature, but only by making a number of even more unrealistic and limiting assumptions. The first of these is that technological change is driven by exogenous forces; the second is that technological change is 'labour-augmenting' (in that it raises output in the same way as the stock of labour); and the third is that technological change occurs at a constant rate. If these assumptions are made, the analysis of convergence to the steady state is the same as before.[3] The only difference is that the per capita variables of capital, income, and consumption grow in the steady state at the *assumed* rate of technological progress. Of course, all this is pointless because technological progress and, hence, longrun economic growth, remain unexplained.

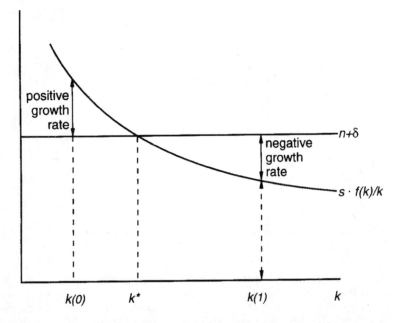

Figure 3.3 'Dynamics' of the Solow–Swan model

A more interesting approach to technological change in the Solow–Swan model is that by John Hicks in *Capital and Growth* (1965: ch. XVI). As a given equilibrium growth path is based on the assumption of a given technology there will be a family of equilibrium pathways associated with different technologies. In this 'traverse' model, Hicks envisages a society moving from one pathway to another as technology changes rather than just converging continually to a single pathway. This was Hicks' attempt to endow deductive growth theory with a more realistic dynamic form. As we shall see in Chapter 10, even this fails. He also discusses the conditions under which the equilibrium pathway becomes an optimum pathway for planning purposes. These conditions include the desire and ability of society (as a single person) to maximize some sort of social welfare function and to be able to correctly predict the way in which the various factors of production and technology change over time. Needless to say this is totally unrealistic and, for the inductivist, unnecessary.

A model analysing convergence to the steady state is not really a dynamic model. The convergence concept is concerned not with the longrun improvement in material living standards, but merely with recovery from some sort of crisis such as war, depression, or drought. Accordingly it is not valid to employ the Solow–Swan model to explain or predict the nature of convergence of longrun growth rates between nations, as many applied economists have attempted to do. To reiterate something that appears to have been forgotten by some applied economists, Solow–Swan convergence is concerned with recovery from crisis, while global longrun growth rates reflect more fundamental dynamic forces usually associated with technological change.

The applied convergence literature shows that evidence (see Figure 3.4) on global growth rates does not confirm the hypothesis that poor nations, which are further from some sort of notional steady state, will grow more-rapidly than richer countries. Only when similar countries, such as those in Western Europe or regions within the same nation, are examined does a strong inverse relationship between 'initial' income level and annual growth rate of real GDP per capita emerge.[4] These contrasting results are explained by growth theorists in terms of similar production functions, saving rates and, hence, steady-state conditions in closely related countries and regions of the same country. Only through allegedly holding constant the different steady-state conditions throughout the world, by including the proxies of human capital in their regression equations, are growth theorists able to conclude that 'the cross-country data support the hypothesis of conditional convergence' if not absolute convergence (Barro and Sala-i-Martin 1995: 30). In effect this is an admission that they cannot explain the pattern of growth outcomes at the global level using the Solow–Swan model – the model does

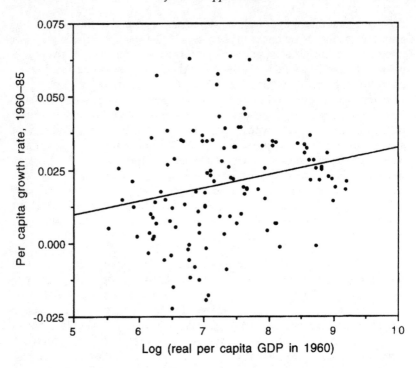

Figure 3.4 Convergence of GDP across countries: growth rate versus initial level
of real per capita GDP

Notes: For a sample of 118 countries, the average growth rate of GDP per capita from
1960 to 1985 (shown on the vertical axis) has little relation with the 1960 level of
real per capita GDP (shown on the horizontal axis). The relationship should be
negative. Hence, absolute β convergence does not apply for a broad cross-
section of countries.

Source: Redrawn from Figure 1.6 in Barro and Sala-i-Martin (1995:27) with permis-
sion of the McGraw-Hill Companies.

not predict different steady states. Hence, the Solow–Swan model is unable
to explain either real-world dynamic *processes* or even real-world dynamic
outcomes. As we shall see, the models constructed by the new growth
theorists attempt to resolve this difficulty by proposing models of technological diffusion. The problem with this solution is that these models have been
borrowed from development economists and historical economists.

In contrast to this disability of the Solow–Swan and, even, endogenous
models, the dynamic-strategy model developed in this book explains real-
world growth *outcomes* as well as dynamic *processes*. The dynamic-strategy

model suggests that the absence of an inverse relationship between income level and growth rates at the global level is due to the pursuit (or non-pursuit) of different dynamic strategies and substrategies; and that the existence of the inverse relationship within a group of closely related countries, or within the same country, is due to the different timing in the adoption of the same dynamic substrategy. In the case of those countries pursuing the same technological substrategy the 'strategic followers' grow more rapidly than the 'strategic pioneers' because of the lower costs of adopting an existing substrategy than in applying it, together with the steady supply of new techniques and institutions owing to the existing reservoir of successful ideas. Multiple regression analysis using human capital and income level explanators is also consistent with the dynamic-strategy model. Human capital can be thought of as a proxy for different dynamic strategies. While the Solow–Swan model attempts to explain growth outcomes in terms of the type of production function and saving rate adopted by the nations of the world, I attempt to explain it in terms of their dynamic strategies and substrategies. The dynamic-strategy model has the critically important advantage that it can explain dynamic *processes* as well as growth *outcomes*.

Some growth theorists believe that Solow–Swan convergence is a reasonable approximation of actual growth outcomes because it takes 'several generations' of say 50 to 70 years or even more to reach the steady state (Barro and Sala-i-Martin 1995: 38). But in fact economic history shows that recovery from crises such as depressions, droughts, and wars is completed within relatively short periods of time. Recovery from major depressions, such as those of the 1890s and 1930s, took less than a decade; and even recovery from the loss of major wars by Germany and Japan took no more than a generation (or 25 years). Hence the observed catch-up taking place over 70 years or more is not part of a recovery process (convergence to steady-state equilibrium) but part of the transition to a new technological substrategy and, thereby, beyond the analytical capabilities of the Solow–Swan model, which implicitly assumes that a society's dynamic strategy is constant.

The 'endogenous' growth model

In the mid-to-late 1980s a number of growth theorists, including Romer (1986) and Lucas (1988), became dissatisfied with models of the Solow–Swan type that were unable to explain longrun growth. They decided to construct a new growth model in which technological change, the saving rate, and population change are endogenous. Initially called the 'new' growth theory, but now generally known as the 'endogenous' growth theory, it emerged as an extension of the Solow–Swan model. This step was not

taken earlier by neoclassical economists because the introduction of technological change violates the assumption of perfect competition, owing to the
generation of extraordinary profits by innovators, and requires the introduction of a more complex production function and ways of achieving equilibrium solutions. Realism, in other words, was constrained by the nature of
existing microeconomic theory. None of the new growth theorists appeared
to be aware that Nicholas Kaldor (1957) had, some 30 years earlier, developed a growth model that endogenized technological change using a
'technical progress function'.

The major contribution of the more recent growth models is the outcome
of treating technological change as endogenous. So far this development has
passed through two main stages. The first stage involved an attempt by
Romer (1986), Lucas (1988), and Rebelo (1991) to introduce technological
change in the form of learning-by-doing as an unintended consequence of
investment. Yet this was not really a theory of technological change. In
the learning-by-doing models, which were inspired by Arrow (1962) and
Sheshinski (1967), pioneering discoveries immediately 'spill over' to the entire
economy through an entirely unrealistic instantaneous diffusion process.
The advantage of this assumption is that monopoly profits do not arise
and, hence, the earlier competitive framework required to determine the
equilibrium rate of technological change can be retained. But the outcomes
are not Pareto optimal because they can be improved through appropriate
policy. Nevertheless, the 'knowledge spill-over' assumption leads to increasing returns that overcome the tendency for diminishing returns to capital
accumulation in the Solow–Swan model, generating longrun growth at a
growing rate. Of course, this assumption is highly unrealistic for at least
two reasons: technological diffusion takes place gradually in reality not
instantaneously; and innovation requires intentional action by economic
agents investing in research and development (R&D).

Romer (1986) attempted to demonstrate the plausibility of the increasing
returns assumption by reference to four sets of data: those used by growth
accountants over the past century or so to demonstrate that output has
increased more rapidly than inputs; those used by growth theorists showing
convergence within groupings of closely related nations, but divergence
between these nation groups; those used by economic historians to show
that US growth rates increased between 1800 and 1980; and those data that
suggest 'a general pattern of historically unprecedented growth for the world
economy is evident, starting in the last part of the 1800s and continuing to
the present' (ibid.: 1001–2).

Elsewhere (Snooks 1993: 84–7) I have responded to this interpretation of
history in two ways. First, it is quite clear from US data over the past
two centuries that growth rates did not increase in a secular manner, but
fluctuated widely (even after smoothing). This problem is exacerbated because

Romer has taken the data at face value, failing to make any adjustment for the fortuitous coincidence of the expansionary impact in the USA of the Second World War in the 1940s and the 'golden age' in the 1950s and 1960s, which I claimed were 'historically abnormal and may never occur again in such a combination'. The slower growth of the past 20 years, which Romer did not take into account, would appear to provide some support for this evaluation.

Interestingly, more recent interpretations of the longrun evidence by growth theorists (Barro and Sala-i-Martin 1995: 6, 34) have stressed not that growth rates are increasing, but that they show 'no secular tendency to decline' and 'that the long-term experiences of the United States and some other developed countries indicate that per capita growth rates can be positive and trendless over long periods of time'. Needless to say, unlike the early Romer, these growth theorists are looking to reality for support of growth models that assume constant rather than increasing returns to scale. It is fascinating that theoretical economists are always convinced that the assumptions they make are supported by evidence of reality. Barro *et al.* also miss the essential point that there is no simple longrun trend, because growth rates fluctuate widely over long periods of time (see Figure 10.4, p. 139) owing, I argue, to the unfolding and substitution of dynamic strategies and substrategies.

The second criticism of Romer's empirics is that economic growth in Western Europe, let alone the world, did not begin in 1800 as Romer obviously believed at the time. Economic growth, in other words, is not a modern invention. Indeed, growth as measured by real GDP per capita is not just an outcome of technological change even when broadly defined. This blind spot is a major limitation of growth models based on neoclassical production theory.

The second stage in the development of endogenous growth models began in the late 1980s and early 1990s with the introduction of theories of R&D and of imperfect competition by Romer (1987, 1990), Aghion and Howitt (1992), and Grossman and Helpman (1991). In these models, technological change is the outcome of deliberate investment in R&D to achieve monopoly profits. The outcome of R&D investment is positive longrun growth, but only for as long as this investment continues. Owing to the generation of monopoly profits, the outcomes are not Pareto optimal and these models are usually accompanied by policy prescriptions for improving outcomes through taxes and subsidies.

One way of endogenizing technological change is, as Romer (1990) has done, by analysing its operation through an expansion in the variety of producer or intermediate goods. An increase in product variety is used as a proxy for innovation. Firms are motivated by anticipated monopoly profits to invest in R&D with the objective of discovering new intermediate products.

The production function adopted as a basis for the R&D model specifies diminishing marginal productivity for each input and constant (rather than increasing) returns to scale for all inputs together. The form of the production function for firm i employed by Romer (1987 and 1990) and others is

$$Y_i = A \cdot L_i^{1-\alpha} \cdot \sum_{j=1}^{N} (X_{ij})^{\alpha} \qquad (3.9)$$

where $0 < \alpha < 1$, Y_i is output, L_i is labour input, and X_{ij} is the employment of the jth type of specialized intermediate good. Technological change is introduced in the form of 'expansions' in the intermediate good N, and can be expressed, in terms of equation (3.9), as

$$Y_i = A \cdot L_i^{1-\alpha} \cdot N \cdot X_i^{\alpha} = A \cdot L_i^{1-\alpha} \cdot (NX_i)^{\alpha} \cdot N^{1-\alpha} \qquad (3.10)$$

Now, if the increase in NX_i takes the form of a rise in N for given X_i, diminishing returns do not arise and endogenous longrun growth occurs. Hence, endogenous longrun growth arises from this particular property or *assumption* of the production function.

The expansion of product variety is usually treated within a deterministic framework, in which investment in research leads to a regular flow of new product types. In turn this generates a smooth growth path. This assumption about dynamic form is made because growth theorists have no idea what shape the supply of technological discoveries will take. They have no strategic-demand function of the type employed in this book. As the neoclassical supply-side approach is formless, its advocates are forced to make a series of arbitrary assumptions. For example, Barro and Sala-i-Martin (1995: 216) tell us: 'Since we are primarily interested here in the determinants of longterm growth, we assume a deterministic R&D process in which cyclical elements are not present'. In reality, longrun growth proceeds not along a trend path (or indeed along a steady-state equilibrium path), but via waves determined by the unfolding of the dominant dynamic strategy and its substrategies.

While the introduction of endogenous technological change is a major advance from the Solow–Swan model, the method employed lacks conviction. Technological change is an arbitrary addition to the growth model because it does not possess a realistic sense of purpose. Why do individuals bother to invest in risky R&D when they could indulge in speculation or rent-seeking? And will they continue to invest in R&D forever, or will they finally be satisfied with their achievements and thereafter consume all of their income? The neoclassical model cannot tell us. There is no overall dynamic theory of why investors bother to invest. There is no endogenous driving force. The new growth theorists have advanced no further than J.M. Keynes, who told us in despair that investors invest because of their animal spirits. In this book I provide a realist theory of investment.

What appears to concern some growth theorists (ibid.: 237) is that while the R&D model can 'explain' longrun growth in individual countries, it cannot explain conditional convergence. Owing to the scale effects – larger nations can better afford the fixed costs of innovations – larger nations should grow faster than smaller nations. As this prediction is not borne out by evidence of global growth rates, the new growth theorist is tempted to borrow ideas about national leadership and catch-up through imitation from economic historians, rarely acknowledged, like Alexander Gerschenkron (1962). This is a departure from the method, normally followed quite rigorously, of deriving results deductively from the existing body of neoclassical theory. The greater pragmatism of some new growth theorists, while it may be applauded by some empiricists, is unlikely to receive the approval of core neoclassicists. Theoretical models begin to lose their coherence when they can be applied to reality only with the support of *ad hoc* ideas borrowed from elsewhere. It is like a Gothic cathedral that only holds together because it is supported by a series of flying buttresses.

Finally it should be briefly noted that the new growth theorists have also made progress in endogenizing the saving rate and population change in the neoclassical growth model. The saving rate is endogenized by including a model of the household in the Solow–Swan optimizing framework. Using the approach pioneered by Ramsey (1928), Barro and Sala-i-Martin (1995), for example, derive a complex consumption function rather than adopting the implicit linear consumption function of the Solow–Swan model, which is a special case of the former. They suggest that the saving rate varies with capital stock per capita. Also it is possible to model the demographic variables – such as migration, fertility, and mortality – that influence population change, together with the forces that influence the labour-force participation rate. Of course, what is gained in modelling realistic detail in this way is lost in intuitive simplicity. At the end of all this endogenizing we have a complex model that can only be grasped intuitively in its details and only through the computer in its overall implications. This is always a problem with models that cannot see the ultimate for the proximate causes – the wood for the trees.

Not all orthodox economists are convinced by the real-world implications of the endogenous growth model. Some have questioned the optimism of the prevailing growth theory, which assumes that economic growth will continue indefinitely. John Pitchford (1995a), for example, has reintroduced classical concerns about whether technological progress will continue to outpace the exhaustion of natural resources. While it is a concern that he has long held

(Pitchford 1960; 1974), in the absence of real-world information about this matter it is impossible, as he admits, to model with any certainty.

Pitchford develops a simple model in which learning-by-doing and population are endogenized. With this model he shows that it 'is possible to generate the endogenous growth theory result of growing per capita output from exhaustible resource effects', but that 'eventually per capita output will fall' owing to the exhaustion of natural resources (Pitchford 1995a: 9). By extending this model 'it is also possible to derive the same results where renewable resources are important for production'. He concludes that the model generates 'a growth process which looks like that of endogenous growth', but involves a convergence to equilibrium rather than equilibrium growth. The outcome is the stationary state. Hence, it is a model in the tradition of Malthus, Ricardo, and Mill. As I will attempt to show, however, real-world economic growth is not a matter of convergence to equilibrium, and the reason is that it is the outcome of the exploitation, exhaustion, and replacement of dynamic strategies rather than natural resources.

Development economists also have reservations about the ability of the neoclassical growth models to explain recent growth experience. These economists are concerned to observe the real-world growth paths of nations and groups of nations, and to 'explain' this in statistical terms. Basically they employ the comparative method. Two examples will suffice – Angus Maddison (1995) and Steve Dowrick (1995).

Maddison has taken a longer-term approach to growth than most orthodox economists by marshalling the GDP, capital stock, and population estimates of a large number of countries over the period since 1820 and arranging them into seven regional categories – Western Europe, Western Offshoots, Southern Europe, Eastern Europe, Latin America, Asia and Oceania, and Africa. His objective is to 'explain' the changing levels of real GDP in terms of its *supply* determinants of capital, labour, and technological change. This is the 'sources of growth' approach developed by Denison (1974). While it conveniently sorts out the relative importance, in a statistical sense, of these supply determinants – which Maddison calls the 'proximate' determinants – it completely neglects dynamic demand, and it does not lead to the development of a realist dynamic model. Maddison (1988) appears to favour an institutionalist model of economic performance, probably of the Douglass North (1981) variety.

Dowrick, like most development economists, focuses on the comparative growth performance of a wide range of nations during the past generation or so. More influenced by the growth theory literature, he focuses on growth rates, rather than levels, of real GDP per capita and productivity. Nevertheless, he is concerned that the neoclassical growth models provide a poor description of the actual growth-rate paths of nations and groups of nations since the Second World War. Rather than converging directly to the steady state as the theory suggests, average growth rates for most global regions appear to pass through a number of phases resembling a cubic function. Dowrick (1995: 7) explains: 'It is possible to view a substantial part of the development over the past 40 years, in particular the growth experience of the Asian, European and OECD economies, as following a common development path of take-off, acceleration and subsequent maturation and slowdown'. Starting from a lower level, growth rates accelerate to a peak of about 5 per cent per annum, and then slow down until they reach about 1–2 per cent per annum. He regards this as 'a highly stylised description of the post-war pattern of development' (ibid.: 16–17). Hence, the steady state in the second half of the twentieth century was not achieved, according to Dowrick, by nations or groups of nations until they had gone through a process of acceleration and deceleration. While Dowrick does not claim any universal applicability (nor could he, owing to the atypical experience of the 1950s and 1960s) of this growth-rate pattern, he does use it to evaluate the performance of individual nations during this particular historical period. This is, I believe, an attempt to provide modern growth analysis with a more realistic dynamic structure. Unfortunately it has not led to the development of a realist dynamic model. Interestingly, the terms and concepts he employs come from W.W. Rostow's discredited *Stages of Economic Growth* (1971).

What is the future of the neoclassical model? Will the endogenous growth model exhaust itself by the end of the 1990s, just as the Solow–Swan model did by the end of the 1960s? Some new growth theorists are optimistic about their future. We are told:

> Probably because of its lack of empirical relevance, growth theory effectively died as an active research field by the early 1970s, on the eve of the rational expectations revolution and the oil shocks...
> The recent growth research has attracted interest from economists in a wide variety of fields. Conferences on growth have participation from specialists in macroeconomics, development, international economics, theory, history, econometrics, and industrial organization. We think that the effective combination of theory and empirical work will sustain this broad appeal and will allow growth theory to survive this time as a vibrant field. We do not expect the growth theory of the 1990s to suffer the same fate as the growth theory of the 1960s.
>
> (Barro and Sala-i-Martin 1995: 12–13)

In my opinion they are wrong. The endogenous model will suffer exactly the same fate as the Solow–Swan model and for the same reasons, one empirical and the other theoretical. The empirical reason concerns the fatal flaw within the neoclassical growth model both old and new – its emergence from static neoclassical production theory, which is an inadequate foundation for sustaining interest in the resulting distorted models of societal dynamics. They are distorted by their focus on outcomes rather than processes; on supply rather than demand (strategic demand, not consumer demand); and on the mechanics of production rather than the pursuit of strategies. Association with empirical work will not extend their life because it is only concerned with evidence of growth outcomes, which has already been largely exploited, and because even this evidence has highlighted the deficiencies of the theory. Also by embracing *ad hoc* methods of theorizing, via ideas from development and historical economics, its theoretical robustness has been diluted, and its appeal in the eyes of neoclassical theorists has declined.

The theoretical reason for predicting that the new growth theory will exhaust itself during the early years of the twenty-first century concerns the nature of intellectual activity. Intellectual activity like societal dynamics traces out a trajectory of innovation and imitation, as existing and potential researchers look for ways of maximizing their career prospects. During this process, the opportunities for participation in a research programme are explored and ultimately exhausted. Once exhausted, existing and potential researchers look for other research programmes that can support their careers. The new growth theory is particularly vulnerable to this process of development and exhaustion because of its flawed structure. As will be argued throughout this book the structure of production is determined by the process of economic growth, not the other way round.

CONCLUSIONS

There are two major problems with orthodox growth theory that severely limit its application to the real world. The first of these arises from the inescapable fact that classical and neoclassical growth models have been constructed from static microeconomic concepts, particularly those from supply-side production theory. I argue, in the tradition of John Stuart Mill, that it is not possible to develop a dynamic model from static concepts. Secondly, all growth models have been built around an artificial dynamic form because, using the deductive approach, they have no information about the real dynamic form. This, I argue, can only be obtained from systematic observation of the unfolding dynamic strategy. Both of these limitations arise from the supply-side approach adopted by an orthodox economics that has no sense of dynamic demand.

There has to be another way to develop a dynamic theory, otherwise we will never be able to realistically model dynamic processes. Some of those dissatisfied with the orthodox approach claim we should borrow theoretical concepts from evolutionary biology and sociobiology. But, like J.S. Mill, I think we should restrict deductive modelling to social statics and adopt the inductive method for social dynamics. These suggestions are examined in the following two chapters.

4 Evolutionary Theory

Owing to the unsatisfactory nature of neoclassical growth theory, a growing number of economists have sought new dynamic insights from beyond the boundaries of their own profession. These insights they claim to have found in the deductive models of evolutionary biology. It is asserted that evolutionary theory provides a better understanding of the complexity of economic reality. And, as if to sanction their approach, they generally refer to Alfred Marshall's comment in *Principles* (1920: xii) that 'the Mecca of the economist lies in economic biology' – a mythical place he never attempted to visit.

To survey the approaches adopted by those who have actually set out for 'Mecca', I have divided the field into two quite distinct groups – those of 'evolutionary institutionalism' and of the 'new evolutionary economics'. Evolutionary institutionalism, which includes the work of Thorstein Veblen, Friedrich Hayek, Douglass North, and their disciples, focuses on the evolution of societal rules; whereas the new evolutionary economics, which includes Richard Nelson, Sidney Winter, and their followers, focuses on the evolution of 'routines' that primarily involve techniques of production. Hence, the former focuses on institutions (rules) and the latter on microeconomic organizations (social activities).

The question that needs to be addressed is whether the evolutionists of either or both types have provided a better understanding of the complexity of economic reality than the orthodox school. In answer to this question I argue that the economic evolutionists have merely swapped one supply-side deductive model for another, without any appreciable improvement in the understanding of the overall dynamic process. Indeed they have muddied the waters somewhat by introducing the erroneous evolutionary concept of institutional irreversibility. As shown elsewhere (Snooks 1997) institutional change is capable of performing complete reversals and, therefore, is not evolutionary at all. Further, the economic evolutionists have attempted to replace the existing artificial dynamic form in the neoclassical growth model – the equilibrium growth path – with equally artificial devices such as 'routinized behaviour' (Veblen 1899), punctuated equilibria (Hodgson 1993), and path-dependence (Nelson and Winter 1982; North 1990). While these artificial dynamic structures are necessary in a supply-side economics, they have no place in a realist dynamic theory. But this is not to deny that much valuable detailed research has been conducted by the evolutionists into economic relationships that do not bear on the overall dynamic mechanism. Often the theoretical structure is merely a convenient excuse for fertile empirical research.

EVOLUTIONARY INSTITUTIONALISM

Veblen and institutional evolution

Thorstein Veblen viewed the emergence of institutions, which he saw as the central focus of economics, in evolutionary terms. He argued that instincts, habits, and institutions in human society can be compared with genes in biology and that they are involved in a Darwinian process of selection. He claimed that 'an evolutionary economics must be the theory of a process of cultural growth as determined by the economic interest, a theory of a cumulative sequence of economic institutions stated in terms of the process itself' (Veblen 1919: 77).

While Veblen does not specify the precise mechanisms nor the criteria of the institutional selection process, he does claim that institutions are the equivalent of genes in biological evolution and that human agents are involved in 'purposeful behaviour'. A sense of this viewpoint can be gained from the following extract from Veblen (1899: 188):

> The life of man in society, just like the life of other species, is a struggle for existence, and therefore it is a process of selective adaptation. The evolution of social structure has been a process of natural selection of institutions. The progress which has been and is being made in human institutions and in human character may be set down, broadly, to a natural selection of the fittest habits of thought and to a process of enforced adaptation of individuals to an environment which has progressively changed with the growth of the community and with the changing institutions under which men have lived. Institutions are not only themselves the result of a selective and adaptive process which shapes the prevailing or dominant types of spiritual attitude and aptitudes; they are at the same time special methods of life and of human relations, and are therefore in their turn efficient factors of selection.

We are also told that these institutions, or habits of thought, are conservative and resist any fleeting forces of change. Veblen (ibid.: 190–1) states that 'men's present habits of thought tend to persist indefinitely, except as circumstances enforce a change. These institutions which have been so handed down, these habits of thought, points of view, mental attitudes and aptitudes, or what not, are therefore themselves a conservative factor.' It is this conservatism or 'social inertia' that enables institutions to be treated as the equivalent of genes in biology. A major force in overcoming this conservatism is, for Veblen, the 'purposeful action' of 'man' motivated by 'idle curiosity'. Veblen (1934: 80) tells us, 'by selective necessity he [man] is endowed with a proclivity for purposeful action'.

Though Veblen's work contains a number of suggestive comments of this type about what an evolutionary institutional economics might involve, it was not sufficiently substantial to challenge the neoclassical economics of his day. Only those desperately searching for the roots of a possible future school of evolutionary economics (Hodgson 1993: 136–8) would wish to read much into these tantalizing comments. Yet these suggestions warrant further exploration. They include the positive role for human agents, the concept of habits of thought, and Veblen's model of decision-making. Veblen's positive role for human agents is generally regarded as being non-Darwinian.

While the idea of a positive role for decision-makers does contrast with the role played by individual organisms in the neo-Darwinian interpretation of natural selection – the so-called 'modern synthesis' – in my opinion it is not inconsistent with Darwin's original position. As argued in *The Ephemeral Civilization* (1997a: ch. 5), Darwin's theory of natural selection, which involves a desperate struggle for existence by a multitude of individuals, provides a powerful driving force in Darwin's analysis. Individuals survive because they possess an intellectual or physical advantage which becomes more general in the population as they go on to reproduce. It is but a short step, and not inconsistent with Darwin's theory, to argue that individuals actively exploit any physical or intellectual advantage that they possess in this struggle for existence. Certainly in human society this is a deliberate and conscious process. Where Veblen does differ critically from Darwin is in his rejection of the struggle for survival as a rational process.

Veblen's concept of 'habits of thought' has a similar conservative function to that attributed by some to custom in pre-modern societies. Rather than pursue their material advantage, we are told, human agents follow traditional habits of thought and rules of behaviour. This is what I have called 'moral man' (Snooks 1993: 206–9; 1996: 150–63), who can be contrasted with neoclassical 'economic man'. Veblen appears to have opted for a version of moral man because of his distaste for the neoclassical assumption of economic rationality (Veblen 1904). Indeed, his version of institutionalism owed much to its historicist roots, mainly German, in its rejection of orthodox deductive theory based upon the concept of economic rationality, in its substitution of the metaphor of biology for that of physics, and in its focus upon societal dynamics. Yet he was rightly dismissive of historicism because it failed in its efforts to construct a body of theoretical work (Veblen 1919: 262–5). Anyway, Veblen (ibid.: 441) claims:

> Under the Darwinian norm it must be held that men's reasoning is largely controlled by other than logical intellectual forces; that the conclusions reached by public or class opinion is as much, or more, a matter of sentiment than of logical inference; and that the sentiment which animates men, singly or collectively, is as much, or more, an outcome of habit and native propensity as of calculated material interest.

While this is understandable in those, like Veblen, born in the mid-nineteenth century, it is curiously myopic in those, like some modern institutionalists and economic evolutionists (Hodgson 1988: 57–144), who have the advantage of a mountain of evidence to the contrary. As will be discussed below, the attraction of the idea of routinized behaviour has much to do with the attempt by unorthodox supply-side thinkers to project order and stability on to the chaos of a world assumed not to possess a pattern of dynamic demand. This is a substitute for the mechanical notion of equilibrium in neoclassical economics developed by orthodox supply-side thinkers. Both Veblen and the neoclassicists have failed to realize that the attempt by humans to maximize material advantage is not a result of 'logical intellectual forces', but rather of genetically determined desires that are pursued rationally through a process of imitation. In turn this leads to the unfolding of the dominant dynamic strategy which provides human society with its dynamic structure.

Finally, we need to consider the model of decision-making implicit in Veblen's work. As we have seen, he rejects the central concept of economic rationality in neoclassical economics. Human agents do not possess perfect information, understanding, or computing abilities. Hence they are unable to maximize individual utility. Instead they rely upon customary habits of thought and rules of behaviour to interpret the information they receive and to respond to this information. Institutions, in other words, provide the framework for human decision-making; and this framework is conservative, changing only slowly, except when there is a clash between societies which causes institutions to change more rapidly. It is a model without dynamic form.

MODERN EVOLUTIONARY INSTITUTIONAL ECONOMICS

The neo-Veblenians

Recent attempts to build a new theory of evolutionary economics have been influenced by the old institutionalism. Particularly by Thorstein Veblen. Some (Hodgson 1988; 1993) have argued that Veblen's concept of institutions – conventional habits of thought and rules of behaviour – is the appropriate level for selection in a Darwinian model of evolution.

The chief characteristic of the evolutionary approach to institutional change is its supply-side approach. Institutions are formed, achieve a degree of stability, and occasionally change rapidly owing to an internal adaptive process. The key issue here is how stability and order emerge from the chaos of a world devoid of any demand-side pattern. The neoclassical supply-side response is that order emerges from a world in which individual decision-makers – who have perfect knowledge, perfect understanding, and perfect computing abilities – maximize their material advantage. This leads to the steady state, or equilibrium growth. But with the rejection of neoclassical economic man by the old institutional economics – which has its origins in the clash between historicists and deductivists in both Germany and England during the last quarter of the nineteenth century (Snooks 1993: 46–63) – what is to prevent the triumph of chaos?

The institutionalist response is that stability can be achieved in their model of change by assuming that human behaviour is dominated by habit and routine. In other words human action is subject to the rule of custom, such that individuals do not seek to maximize their material advantage, but rather they conform to the conventional way of doing things. Only in a world of habit and routine, we are told, are prediction and orderly decision-making possible. Veblen (1919: 241) tells us that 'institutions are an outgrowth of habit. The growth of culture is a cumulative sequence of habituation, and the ways and means of it are the habitual response of human nature to exigencies that vary incontinently, cumulatively...'. Taking up this idea, and uniting it with those about firm 'routines' by Richard Nelson and Sidney Winter (1982), Hodgson (1988: 132–3) claims:

> The critical point is that both routines and formal institutions, by establishing more or less fixed patterns of, or boundaries to, or regulations over, or constraints upon, human action, actually supply information to other agents. Such inflexibilities or constraints actually suggest to the individual what other agents might do, and the individual can then act accordingly. Whereas if these rigidities or 'imperfections' did not exist the behaviour of others could change with every perturbation in the economic system, and such frequent adjustments to behaviour might be perceived as random or chaotic.
>
> In other words, institutions and routines, other than acting simply as rigidities and constraints, play an enabling role, by providing more-or-less reliable information regarding the likely actions of others. Thus the habits and routines formed by some individuals enable the conscious decision-making of others. One consequence of this function of institutions is that in a highly complex world, and despite uncertainty, complexity and information overload, regular and predictable behaviour is possible.

Hence, the order and stability required for systematic decision-making comes from the rule of custom – from the supply side. In contrast, in this book it comes from imitation of the dynamic strategist – from the demand side.

But how do the evolutionary institutionalists explain the emergence of these convenient patterns of habit and routine? Veblen, as we have seen, thought that habits arose, in some sort of vague way, both from human instincts and human society – from genetics and culture. Hodgson discusses this issue more fully. Habits, he tells us, have emerged to 'help us deal with complexity and information overload' (ibid.: 128), which elsewhere he explains

> Given that fully conscious rational deliberation about all aspects of behaviour is impossible because of the amount of information and computational competence involved, human agents have acquired mechanisms for relegating particular ongoing actions from continuous rational assessment. These are commonly known as habits, and their high degree of relevance to our subject was emphasized by Thorstein Veblen in many of his works (ibid.: 124–5).

Curiously, this is the same explanation as that employed by Douglass North (1981; 1990), a leading exponent of the new institutional economics, which is rejected by Hodgson and other evolutionary institutionalists. Further, Veblen and followers like Hodgson believe that the spread of 'selected' habits and routines takes place through a process of replication similar to that described by Richard Dawkins in *The Selfish Gene* (1989: ch. 11).

How far have the evolutionary institutionalists come in the last century since Veblen's pioneering, but largely impotent, work? In a recent book promisingly called *Economics and Evolution* (1993), Hodgson merely restates, in Veblenian terms, a possible future basis for evolutionary economics. We are told that institutions, or conventional habits and routines, are appropriate units of selection; that routinized behaviour is necessary to bring order out of the chaos of reality; that, in imitation of Eldredge and Gould (1972), 'socioeconomic development' should be viewed 'as periods of institutional continuity punctuated by periods of crisis and more rapid development' (Hodgson 1993: 254); and that 'there should be a place in an evolutionary explanation for some freedom of will, but not in quite the same sense as the fully deliberating and choosing agent found in the rhetoric of economic theory' (ibid.: 229).

In order to provide a dynamic form for their supply-side deductive model, evolutionists of this ilk have, without explanation, adopted the 'punctuated equilibria' development path of modern historical biologists. This development path involves brief periods of relatively rapid change followed by much longer periods of stagnation. In addition to the unexplored issue of whether this genetic pattern is relevant to human society, there is the unrecognized problem that even in biology the punctuated equilibria concept at best applies only to genetic change and not to the wave-like development of life (Snooks 1996: ch. 4). The appropriate comparisons, if such comparisons must be made, are between genetic change and technological change (not

institutional rules), and between genetic/technological change and life/eco-
nomic change. This confusion emerges from a failure to explore systematically the historical nature of both life and human society.

It is not an exaggeration to say that the achievement of the Veblenian
evolutionary approach to economics is merely to import some inappropriate
deductive baggage into the discipline from evolutionary biology. It is
claimed, for example, that 'recourse to biological analogies, while they
need to be handled with great care, is probably the best strategy for moving
economics out of its restrictive and mechanistic patterns of thought, and
providing a basis for fruitful development at the fundamental level' (Hodgson 1993: 26). In this book I will argue that not only is this not the best
'strategy', but that it might even divert economics from adopting the
best 'strategy' (that is, tactic).

The new institutional economics

The new institutional economics involves an extension of mainstream deductive theory to accommodate some of the views of the old institutionalists.
Probably the two most important pioneering figures in the field of evolutionary
institutional change are F.A. Hayek (1899–1992) and D.C. North (1921–). As is
well known, Hayek comes from the neo-Austrian tradition and North from the
neoclassical tradition of mainstream deductive economics. They both emphasize different aspects of the old institutionalist school, with Hayek, like Veblen,
focusing upon a 'Darwinian' evolutionary process, and North, like John Commons (1934), opting for an historical process involving an interaction between
institutions and organizations. But recently there have been signs that North's
approach is becoming increasingly evolutionary. As we shall see, neither of
these branches of evolutionism has developed a dynamic form for their models.
Hence they are unable to provide any predictable structure for the dynamics of
human society.

Hayek and cultural evolution

Friedrich Hayek's work on the evolution of institutions stems from his over-
riding interest in the contrast between market and non-market ('socialist')
societies. As early as the 1920s Hayek believed that socialist systems could
not succeed because they outlaw markets that are the essential source of
information required for the effective operation of any society. Socialist
systems, he claimed, are a logical inconsistency. Only systems characterized
by 'spontaneous order', as in capitalism, have any chance of long-term
success. The fate of the former USSR appears to prove his point.

If the rational mind is unable to create the institutions required for the
successful operation of complex societies, how, Hayek asks, can we account

for the remarkable order that exists in capitalist societies? This, as will be discussed in Chapter 6, is a question that has long exercised the minds of imaginative economists, going back to Adam Smith (1723–90) and other seventeenth-century and eighteenth-century writers (William Petty, John Locke, Bernard Mandeville, Adam Ferguson, and David Hume). The answer, Hayek believes, falls 'between instinct and reason', and involves the evolution of institutional rules. These rules, which restrain the demands generated by animal instincts, are not foreseen or planned by the human intellect. Yet these rules are responsible for the emergence and viability of human society. Hayek (1988: 12) explains:

> What are chiefly responsible for having generated this extraordinary order, and the existence of mankind in its present size and structure, are the rules of human conduct that gradually evolved (especially those dealing with several [that is, private] property, honesty, contract exchange, trade competition, gain, and privacy). These rules are handed on by tradition, teaching and imitation, rather than by instinct...[and] often forbade him to do what his instincts demanded, and no longer depended on a common perception of events.

There is, therefore, a tension between instinct and rules – the 'restraints on instinctual demands' – that leads to an uneasy co-operation that will often break down under competitive pressure. This tension plays an important role in Hayek's view of human history: 'the conflict between what men instinctively like and the learnt rules of conduct that enabled them to expand... is perhaps the major theme of the history of civilisation' (ibid.: 18). As we shall see, the role of institutional constraints receives more effective examination by North.

Clearly Hayek's explanation of the evolution of institutional rules is not novel. Not only was it anticipated some six decades earlier by Veblen, it was probably influenced by Karl Popper (1972) as well as by sociobiologists such as Edward Wilson (1975). Nevertheless, it is an issue that Hayek had made his own – the so-called 'knowledge problem' – as early as 1948, and it dominated much of his subsequent work (Vanberg 1994: 316). Hayek adopts a simple neo-Darwinian explanation, which involves the adoption of institutional variations through a process of group selection which, if successful, become dominant in the 'rule pool' by an increase in the population of the innovating society that absorbs other less successful societies (this is very similar to the sociobiological mechanism of 'reproductive success' – see Snooks 1997a: ch. 5). Hayek (1988: 16) asserts:

> The various structures, traditions, institutions and other components of this order arose gradually as variations of habitual modes of conduct were

selected. Such new rules would spread not because men understood that they were more effective, or could calculate that they would lead to expansion, but simply because they enabled those groups practising them to procreate more successfully and to include outsiders.

This evolution came about, then, through the spreading of new practices by a process of transmission of acquired habits analogous to, but also in important respects different from, biological evolution.

Hayek's discussion of the role of economic agents is revealing, and is an outcome of the idiosyncratic neo-Austrian approach to reason and experience. Human agents are reactive rather than proactive. They do *not* calculate the benefits and costs of institutional change, which just occurs in a passive way through 'trial and error'. Mankind, in Hayek's vision, is trapped in a world where its instincts are frustrated and its intellect is useless. But Hayek's vision, which stubbornly refuses empirical assistance, is a prisoner of its own presumptions.

While in Hayek's mind the operation of civilization depends upon co-operation, exercised through institutional constraints, the evolution and maintenance of these rules depends upon competition. In his own words (ibid.: 26): 'Not only does all evolution rest on competition; continuing competi-tion is necessary even to preserve existing achievements'. Hence, while co-operation is required for stability in society, competition is required to maintain both the health of a society and its dynamic quality.

Hayek's approach to cultural evolution is deductive in the tradition of the new institutionalism, and it is peculiarly anti-empirical. Like his old friend Karl Popper, he believes that knowledge is the product of reason and not of experience. Hayek (1952: 143) explains: 'All we know about the world is of the nature of theories and all "experience" can do is to change these theories'. It is not surprising then that there is a shapelessness about Hayek's evolutionary model. Yet, like most hypothetical-deductivists, Hayek cannot resist the temptation to 'illustrate' the general relevance of his theory by employing specially selected, 'stylized' facts from history. And even these facts are concerned with the evolution of the ideas rather than the actions of mankind.

Hayek does little to advance our understanding of the evolution of institutions beyond the views of Veblen. Indeed, his emphasis on a passive selective mechanism, which relies very heavily upon the neo-Darwinian theory of evolution, is less realistic than Veblen's insistence upon a positive role for human agents. Despite opinion to the contrary, Veblen's emphasis on a more active role for individual organisms in evolution is more faithful to Darwin than is Hayek. Indeed, the passive role of human agents accepted by Hayek has more in common with the revisionist 'reproductive success' model of the sociobiologists. Further, as we shall see, his treatment of institutional con-straints is not as sophisticated or as persuasive as that by D.C. North. Finally, because Hayek fails to adjust these basic views in the light of historical experience – a possibility he refuses to accept – his theories take on a markedly unrealistic appearance.

Yet, the main problems with Hayek's theory of cultural evolution are similar to those of the institutionalist tradition as a whole. First, Hayek proposes a theory of the evolution of rules that is divorced from the real economy. Rules emerge not in response to a demand from those investing in the strategic infrastructure of society, as argued in this book, but rather because they are more successful than other rules in promoting 'reproductive success'. This is a rather passive, supply-side approach in the tradition of sociobiology, which provides little room for decision-makers. Hayek's agents are reactive rather than proactive. Second, as shown in *The Dynamic Society* (1996), the major theme in history is not the conflict between instinct and rules, but rather the competition between individuals pursuing different dynamic strategies and tactics. As demonstrated later in this book, rules are adopted and modified in order to facilitate these strategies and tactics.

North and path-dependence

The new institutional economics in history has been pioneered by Douglass North, who adopts a deductive approach to the subject. North begins with the neoclassical model and releases a number of restrictive assumptions that bring institutions into play. These include the assumptions that decision-makers possess perfect information, appropriate models of reality, and per-fect information-processing abilities. North argues that, as the information reaching decision-makers is fragmentary and costly, and as their conceptual models of the world are imperfect, exchange between individuals gives rise to transaction costs which call institutions – or rules of the game – into being. These rules can be either formal, such as those enshrined in the statute books, or informal, such as customs or traditional forms of behaviour. While North's work has been widely embraced, there are some institutionalists, such as Alexander Field (1991), who believe that his focus on transaction costs is far too narrow and who advocate a broader approach to economics and economic institutions.

North's views on the role of institutions in the dynamic process have changed significantly over the past three decades. Over that time he has moved progressively closer to a social-evolutionary approach. In *The Rise of the Western World* (North and Thomas 1973), it is argued that economic performance is determined by changes in institutions, and that institutional change is largely a function of population change (driven by plagues, wars, and other exogenous events) through its impact upon the labour/land ratio, at least until the Industrial Revolution when technology became the driving force. The main dynamic mechanism involves relative price changes that create incentives to construct more efficient institutions. North's explanation, in other words, is derived from the deductive neoclassical model which suggests that economically rational decision-makers will adopt the most efficient institutions available in the face of exogenous change. Hence, the persistence of apparently inefficient institutions, such as those in Spain during the pre-modern period, remained as a puzzle that North and Thomas could not solve. As North (1990: 7) later admitted: 'Such an anomaly did not fit into the theoretical framework'. But this was not the only problem (Field 1994). Why, for example, did markets continue to develop after population was halved with the Black Death of 1348 if population growth was the driving force behind the earlier growth of markets? Why was there no reversal in this process over the following century? At the time, he and Thomas attempted to explain away such anomalies in an unsatisfactory *ad hoc* way.

In *Structure and Change in Economic History* (1981) North developed a more sophisticated analysis of institutional change. He moved away from the simple neoclassical efficiency mechanism and closer to the old institutionalists, by developing a transaction-costs model that attempted to explain the differential economic performance of societies with both efficient and inefficient institutional frameworks. The perseverance of inefficient institutions is the outcome of leaders devising property rights in their own interests. But he fails to develop an encompassing model to explain why they do so. Further, North's deductive economic model changes abruptly from period to period. For the pre-modern period he adopts an augmented classical model, in which exogenous population growth runs into diminishing returns in the face of the fixed resource of land; and for the modern era he adopts an augmented neoclassical model, which assumes constant returns to scale and embodies a highly elastic supply curve for knowledge (ibid.: 60). Both variations are extended in an *ad hoc* way by theories about institutions and ideology because he believes that the original models cannot explain the totality of the progress of Western society. His aim, he tells us (ibid.: 7), is 'to fill out the gaps in the neoclassical model'. This model, which lacks cohesion, is discussed more completely elsewhere (Snooks 1996: 130–4). To 'illustrate' the general nature of this model North provided an interpretation of institutional change in Western civilization since the Neolithic Revolution. He did not attempt any formal testing of his model. But still a puzzle remained. Why, ultimately, did competitive pressure fail either to eliminate inefficient nations or to force these nations to adopt more efficient institutions? Why was it that all societies did not move to optimal institutional arrangements as predicted by neoclassical theory?

By the time *Institutions, Institutional Change and Economic Performance* (1990) was published, North believed he had the answer to this final puzzle.

It is an answer that involves three elements that are tacked on to the basic neoclassical model: a 'symbiotic' relationship between institutions and organizations; a path-dependence of the institution–organization interaction that leads to a 'lock-in'; and a feedback mechanism involving imperfect information and imperfect conceptual models. Much of the weight of his new approach rests on both the distinction made by John Commons (1934) some six decades earlier between institutions and organizations, and on the recent path-dependence literature. In other words he has abandoned, as Field (1991: 1000) has noted, the attempt to build a general model of rule variation.

According to North in the latest version of his model, institutions, in conjunction with the usual economic constraints, provide the economic opportunities in society, while organizations emerge to exploit these opportunities. In this interactive process, maximizing organizations alter the institutions that brought them into existence. This is a type of evolutionary model, inspired by neoclassical economics as well as (indirectly) Darwin, in which the selective device is 'adaptive efficiency'. Owing to different information processes – involving different costs of information and different conceptual models (cultures) – institutional change in different societies takes different evolutionary paths. This is a path-dependent process involving increasing returns and fragmentary information feedback which leads to institutional 'lock-in' that resists competitive pressures. It is North's explanation of why inefficient institutions can persist into the longrun. Hence, in searching for a resolution to the problem of sub-optimal institutional arrangements in some countries – a problem that has worried him for some three decades – North has moved a long way towards the evolutionary supply-side approach of the old institutionalists. Economic growth, he tells us, is an outcome of the interactive evolution between institutions and organizations. Once again dynamic form is shaped by supply-side forces.

THE NEW EVOLUTIONARY ECONOMICS

The new evolutionary economics is concerned more with the growth of microeconomic organizations and the 'routines' they employ than with the societal rules that influence their conduct. Its primary focus is on the process of technological and structural change within industries, and how these micro developments impact upon the macro aggregates of GDP, population, and economy-wide productivity.

The pioneering work in this field is usually identified as Richard Nelson and Sidney Winter, *An Evolutionary Theory of Economic Change* (1982); although Jack Downie, *The Competitive Process* (1958), is now seen as a precursor (Nightingale 1996). This work, which was a reaction against the 'mechanical' nature and lack of reality of neoclassical growth theory, found inspiration in the earlier work of Joseph Schumpeter (1942) and Herbert Simon (1947). Over the past decade the Nelson–Winter model has attracted a considerable following of economists not much impressed with the new endogenous version of the neoclassical model. To keep the exercise manageable, I will focus on the Nelson–Winter model; but the more recent literature follows their approach and is described in a number of good surveys (Witt 1993; Nelson 1995).

The Nelson–Winter model

In Chapter 3 it was argued that, owing to the supply-side nature of the neoclassical growth model, it was necessary to adopt an arbitrary dynamic form. This arbitrary dynamic form, which is the steady state or equilibrium growth path, is a major source of dissatisfaction with the neoclassical model for a growing number of economists. In a recent survey article on evolutionary economics, Nelson (1995: 68) argued that:

> Mechanical analogies involving a moving equilibrium in which the actors always behave 'as if' they knew what they were doing seems quite inappropriate. Most knowledgeable scholars agree...that the process must be understood as an evolutionary one.

Of course, evolutionary theory involves a different model of behaviour to that of rational choice, and it generates a different growth process. Nelson and Winter adopt a behavioural model strongly influenced by sociobiology, and they view the growth process as path-dependent. Like the new institutional economics, Nelson, Winter, and their disciples on the road to 'Mecca' have substituted path-dependence for the neoclassical equilibrium growth path.

The object of the Nelson–Winter model is to analyse the endogenous process of technological change. In this they are at one with the more recent endogenous growth theory, but the ways in which they attempt to achieve their common objective are markedly different. Rather than employ neoclassical production theory, Nelson and Winter look for inspiration to Schumpeter's *Capitalism, Socialism, and Democracy* (1942), where technological advance is treated as an outcome of the investments undertaken by competing firms. What they do not acknowledge is that Schumpeter borrowed this model from Karl Marx.

In the Nelson–Winter model, firms rather than individuals are the 'key actors'. While firms must be staffed by individuals, these individuals are 'interchangeable' and their actions are 'determined' by the firms that employ them. Individuals play a rather passive role. This is in the tradition of sociobiology, which also treats individual behaviour as an outcome of 'higher' forces: in the Nelson–Winter model it is 'routines' and in the case of the sociobiology model it is genes.

Through a process of selection and adaption determined by relative profitability in competitive markets, successful firms become the 'incubators and carriers of "technologies" and other practices that determine "what they do" and "how productively" in particular circumstances' (Nelson 1995: 68). These 'practices' are the 'routines' in the Nelson–Winter model. The economic environment – a market or set of markets – in which these firms operate is 'exogenously determined' and taken as 'given'. In other words, they completely omit any discussion of dynamic demand – what I call strategic demand.

Nelson and Winter employ the 'routines' concept as a substitute for the rational-choice model. They reject the neoclassical concept of decision-making individuals who understand the wider context in which they operate and who attempt to maximize their utility in the full knowledge of what they are doing, for the more robotic sociobiological model of behaviour. As Nelson (1995: 68) explains: 'The term "routine" connotes, deliberatively, behavior that is conducted without much explicit thinking about it, as habits or customs'. Yet, despite this robotic behaviour, firms are part of a dynamic process that somehow involves 'profit-oriented learning and selection'. While firms do not compare their routines with all possible alternative ones, they do attempt to pursue effective routines in order to compete with their rivals and meet pre-determined profitability targets. In this sense firms are claimed to act rationally if not optimally.

The routines followed by firms take place in historical rather than analytical time and are considered to be *irreversible*. There are three types of routines. First, there are the 'standard operating procedures', which determine what and how much to produce, given the firm's stock of fixed assets. Secondly, there are the investment routines, which arise from profitability rules. Finally, there are, we are told, the 'search routines' that are undertaken by firms to discover better products and processes in order to compete more effectively against rivals for market share and profitability. This involves both innovation and imitation. It is also seen as a rather conventional activity. In terms of the biological analogy, which is the shaping influence for the Nelson–Winter model, the routines are the genes and the firms are the phenotypes or individual life-forms. What the counterpart to human beings is in the world of biological evolution we are not told.

The Nelson–Winter model can be regarded as an example of 'population ecology' within the wider class of Darwinian evolutionary theory (Nightingale 1996). Its dynamic operation can be outlined briefly in terms of the three evolutionary principles of 'variation', 'heredity', and 'selection'.

For evolution – genetic/technological change – to occur, it is essential that 'individuals' in a population possess different characteristics. Without variation there can be no evolution for the population as a whole. In the case of a population of firms, variation of routines will influence efficiency and, hence, profitability. Where the firm environment is competitive, the most efficient firms generate the highest profit rate and greatest market share and, therefore, are likely to persist over time. Surviving firms are carriers through time of successful routines, providing the basis for successful operation in the future. This is the principle of 'heredity'. Those firms that fail to live up to their profit and market-share expectations are likely to invest in search activities to improve their performance. This involves imitation of more successful routines and/or the creation of new, more innovative ones. Those firms possessing ineffective or inefficient routines that cannot be improved, go out of business. This is the process of economic selection. In addition to this focus on firms, Nelson and Winter have developed an alternative model that analyses the technological trajectory where the population under study consists of techniques rather than firms. This is similar to the cultural evolutionary models of sociobiology (Snooks 1997a: ch. 5).

While Nelson and Winter do not focus on path-dependency, they regard it as part of their model – as being 'built into' it, as it is in all other models of this type (Nelson 1995: 73). Essentially the path-dependent process is seen as a growth path determined by supply-side forces in the form of 'dynamic increasing returns'. Dynamic demand plays no part in this supply-side process. For example, pure chance, like biological imitation, might provide a firm or technique with an initial advantage over its rivals, that in turn leads both to greater and more extensive experience in employing existing routines, and to unanticipated investment in further routine improvement. This endows the 'routine' with an increasing efficiency advantage over its competitors. Once on this evolving path, firms become locked into a supply-determined process. The supporters of path-dependence claim that it is an 'historical' process rather than an arbitrary and mechanical equilibrium process. But, in fact, path-dependence is innocent of the historical reality of either the unfolding dynamic strategy or strategic demand.

Evaluation of the Nelson–Winter model

There are a number of problems with the new evolutionary economics that should be highlighted here. First, the biological analogy just does not work. By making firms rather than individuals the 'key actors', Nelson and Winter have effectively eliminated the driving force that is absolutely essential for any dynamic process. This is an outcome of adopting the sociological model of the neo-Darwinians (sociobiologists) rather than the original economic model of Darwin. The neo-Darwinians have played down the role of competition and the struggle of individuals for survival (Snooks 1997: ch. 5). So it is with Nelson and Winter. In reality it is the individual rather than the group that struggles to survive and prosper, whether we are dealing with human or animal populations. In any case evolution is a mechanism that, at best, affects only one variable (genes/routines) in a wider dynamic process.

Secondly, Nelson and Winter employ a supply-side model in which the economic environment of firms is regarded as exogenously determined and is taken as given. By contrast, the argument in this book is that economic change is the outcome of an interaction between individuals and their physical and social environment. This occurs through the unfolding of the dominant dynamic strategy and the generation of strategic demand for a range of inputs including institutions and organizations. This raises our third point: rather than being the 'key actors' in the dynamic process, firms are merely organizations that have emerged in the technological era (since the Industrial Revolution) to facilitate the unfolding of the technological strategy. And this unfolding process has led to major changes in the size, structure, and nature of these historically specific organizations. Before the Industrial Revolution there were no organizations like the modern industrial corporation. Instead, the individual decision-maker, in responding to the physical and social environment, generated a strategic demand for entirely different strategic organizations, such as the family unit in hunter-gatherer societies, the military unit in conquest societies, and the family firm in commerce societies. Their model can make no claims for universal relevance.

Fourthly, as Nelson (ibid.: 70) admits himself, their model applies (at best) only to the economic sectors of society. As he explains:

> Within this class of models, 'profitability' determines the 'fitness' of technology and of firms, and firms are the only organizational actors. These observations call attention to the fact that this theory would seem to apply only to economic sectors where the market provides the (or the dominant) selection mechanism winnowing out technologies and firms. It is not well suited for dealing with sectors like medical care, or defense, where professional judgements, or political process, determine what is fit and what is not.

Nor indeed to the constantly changing sociopolitical system. This draws attention to the limited scope of the model. Like the sociobiological theory that they imitate, their model is unable to explain the complexity of cultural change. Insights are limited to the culture of modern industrial firms. In reality the activities of these non-economic sectors are not the outcome of political or professional matters but of strategic demand. As such they, along with the 'economic sectors', can be explained by the dynamic-strategy model.

Finally, the central path-dependency concept is no more convincing than the neoclassical 'steady state' that it was adopted to replace. Indeed, it is vague and lacks a predictable shape. Neither approaches provide a satisfactory dynamic form for a dynamic model. That must come from a realist analysis of dynamic demand.

CONCLUSIONS

The evolutionary approach to economic change is driven by its dissatisfaction with neoclassical economics and shaped by its willingness to borrow heavily from other deductive disciplines, namely evolutionary biology and sociobiology. Economic evolutionists seem to believe that the limitations of neoclassical economics arise from its 'mechanical' rather than its deductive nature. By substituting the organic analogy of biology for the mechanical analogy of physics, we are told, economics will become a more realistic science. Even if that were true, which it is not, evolution is only a partial dynamic theory. In biology it can, at best, explain only genetic change rather than the fluctuating fortunes of life, and in the social sciences it can explain only institutional change rather than changes in the entire society. What is needed in both cases, as discussed elsewhere (Snooks 1996: ch. 4), is a wider dynamic model that encompasses and transforms these partial supply-side mechanisms.

It does not seem to have occurred to economic evolutionists that the barrier to developing a satisfactory dynamic theory is to be found not in the metaphor employed, but in the scientific method adopted. Nelson (1995: 85–6), for example, claims:

> Many years ago Veblen (1896) asked, 'Why is Economics Not an Evolutionary Science?' In my view economics would be a stronger field if its theoretical framework were expressly evolutionary. Such a framework would help us to see and understand better the complexity of the economic reality.

Surely this complexity will only be understood if we directly examine the patterns of reality as a basis for developing an entirely new theory rather than borrowing one from elsewhere. In this way we will create our own more relevant models and metaphors – models and metaphors that arise from human experience rather than from physics or biology.

Yet it is possible to reject the evolutionary model as a dynamic explanation and to retain a high regard for much of the detailed theoretical and empirical work on technological change and the growth of the firm undertaken within this framework. The specialist often uses an intellectual paradigm merely as a justification for detailed research that is largely independent of it. This detailed research should be considered as the positive outcome of a flawed theoretical paradigm.

5   Strategic Theory

Strategic theory makes a new beginning in the social sciences generally and economics in particular. It is the first modern theory of longrun dynamics arrived at through induction. There have been earlier attempts to derive economic generalizations using the 'historical method' but none has succeeded. This was not, it will be argued, due to the hopelessness of the task but to a fundamental flaw in research design and to an unfavourable environment. In this chapter we will briefly review those conditions and suggest how a new beginning can be made.

EMERGENCE OF MODERN SCIENTIFIC METHOD

The conflict between the supporters of the inductive and deductive methods has a long history. Both methods have had their advocates throughout history but, until this century, empiricism has been dominant. While empiricism can be traced directly through Thomas Aquinas (1225–74) to Epicurus (342–271 BC), Aristotle (384–322 BC), and Heraclitus (most active 500–490 BC), there are good reasons to believe that it goes back to the very beginning of human society. On the other hand, deductivism was sometimes advocated by famous scholars such as Plato (428–348 BC). Some have found it difficult to understand that in the ancient world neither intellectual method led to the development of a systematic body of economic generalization (Schumpeter 1954: 53). This, I have argued elsewhere (Snooks 1993: 94–106), was because the lessons of history were employed as a basis for policy. Needless to say, all scientific endeavour involves the use of *both* induction and deduction. It is all a matter of degree. When I refer to inductivists and deductivists, I mean the *main* (not the only) source of their ideas are empirical and logical respectively.

Economic theory emerged in Europe during the seventeenth and eighteenth centuries on a growing tide of empiricism. This modern tide began with the work of Francis Bacon (1561–1626) and included major figures such as John Locke (1632–1704), George Berkeley (1685–1753), and David Hume (1711–76). And it reached its logical extreme in John Stuart Mill (1806–73), who argued that all knowledge, even mathematical inferences, are merely 'highly confirmed' generalizations from experience.

The history of empiricism exhibits two main features. One is the gradual elimination of any matter inconsistent with the central role of experience in generating either the inputs of knowledge, or of knowledge itself. But in the process there emerged a growing scepticism about the nature of reality. The other feature is the claim that induction is the only method by which know-ledge of reality can be constructed. Their views appeared to be demonstrated conclusively by the experimental–inductive approach to science attributed to Isaac Newton. It is not surprising, therefore, that the pioneering British economists – William Petty (1623–87), Gregory King (1648–1712), and Charles Davenant (1656–1714) – adopted the empirical method.

The modern deductivists trace their origins back to René Descartes (1596–1650), an innovative French mathematician, who claimed that the physical world was created as a rational system that operated according to a knowable set of universal physical laws. To understand these laws, he claimed, it was essential to develop a theoretical model capable of being expressed, analysed, and tested mathematically. But he rejected the inductive method advocated by Bacon and, instead, adopted the deductive method of rationalism. Descartes' grounds were that, owing to possible distortions in our sense perceptions, we can see the external world only imperfectly. The only certainty is that we are thinking beings and that we have been born with an inherent knowledge of the truth. Hence, reason rather than experience is the only way we can understand reality. Despite the fact that Isaac Newton in the empiricist tradi-tion succeeded, where Descartes and his followers failed, in developing the foundations for modern science, this rationalist doctrine was passed on to Leibniz (1646–1716) and then to Kant (1724–1804). Although Kant was later influenced by Hume concerning the origins of sense perceptions, he refused to accept the argument that all non-analytical knowledge must be derived from these sense perceptions. It is this deductivist tradition that increasingly influenced the development of economics after J.S.Mill (Snooks 1993: 15–44).

THE 'PROBLEM' OF BOTH INDUCTION *AND* DEDUCTION

It has become almost an article of faith in the social sciences that deduction is superior to induction, owing to the so-called 'problem of induction'. This problem arises from an absence of any 'rules of induction' and, hence, of a mechanical way to infer laws from empirical data. Accordingly, inductive generalizations can only be drawn from observation with degrees of prob-ability. It is claimed endlessly that the inductive method has no counterpart to the logical rules of deduction. Some more extreme deductivists like Karl Popper (1992: 145) even claim that 'as far as induction (or inductive logic, or inductive behaviour, or learning by induction or repetition or by "instruc-tion") is concerned I assert with Hume, that there is no such thing'. This, Popper claims, 'solves the problem of induction' – as induction does not exist, neither does the problem! For Popper, empirical evidence can not be used to frame hypotheses, only to refute them.

In their enthusiasm to reject empiricism, the deductivists have overlooked a problem with their own methodology. Popper (1965: 192) and his followers claim that scientific hypotheses are not derived from observed facts but are 'free creations of our own minds, the result of almost poetic intuition'. The starting point of a scientific hypothesis is not important, because those based on unrealistic premises will be weeded out by a process of falsification – a process he calls 'error elimination'. What makes a hypothesis scientific is not its origins but whether it is capable of refutation.

Popper was excessively optimistic about this 'scientific' procedure. As all economists know, very few theories are ever abandoned just because they can be refuted by real-world evidence.[1] They are merely surrounded by supplementary *ad hoc* arguments (as shown in Chapter 3) until more persuasive theories are developed – persuasive not on empirical but on logical grounds. Old theories never die they are just made obsolete by newer, equally un-verified, theories. Herein lies what I have called the 'problem of deduction' (Snooks 1998: ch. 2). There is no way of ensuring that deductive models are based on realistic premises or, even more importantly, that they encompass all the important parameters of reality.

To evaluate both the deductive and inductive methods on a comparable basis we must examine the *entire* process of theory construction. Although inductive inferences are not made using mechanical rules of logic, the process at least begins with a systematic examination of the real world. Accordingly, the inductive model has a good chance of being all-encompassing and relevant to the world in which we live. On the other hand, while deductive inferences are necessarily true in a logical sense, they are only as realistic and encompassing as the assumptions on which they are based. As fact is stranger than fiction, deductive assumptions inevitably fail to embrace the totality of reality. This is the **problem of deduction**.

When this wider perspective is employed, the balance shifts in favour of induction. Before I began this book I was of the opinion that the problems of induction and deduction cancelled each other out, and that both methods had an equal chance of revealing reality. But since comparing the deductive growth models with my strategic-demand model, it has become clear that by spinning models out of the human mind rather than out of historical experience, the most important defining characteristics of real-world dynamics have been totally overlooked. As suggested in Chapter 3, deductive growth theorists have no idea about the nature of dynamic demand or about the real-world dynamic form. Accordingly, they fail to model dynamic demand and they impose a completely artificial and inappropriate dynamic form (the equilibrium growth path) on their creations. This is an example of Popper's 'free creations' that, in more than two centuries, have not been challenged on empirical grounds when they clearly should have been. Despite Mill's argument in *Logic* (1843) some 150 years ago that the conclusion of a syllogism – a formal deductive argument – cannot contain more knowledge than is carried in its premises, orthodox economics remains a deductive science. Neoclassical economists are still attempting to create a theory of dynamics from static building blocks that are close at hand.

WHY HAVE THE DEDUCTIVISTS TRIUMPHED?

The rival approaches to political economy that were emerging in Western Europe during the seventeenth and eighteenth centuries came into open conflict in both Germany and Britain in the late nineteenth century. In the Germanic world of the 1880s the *Methodenstreit*, or battle of methods, was initiated by the Austrian deductivists led by Carl Menger (1840–1921) against the more established German historical school led by Gustav Schmoller (1838–1917); whereas in Britain during the 1870s and 1880s it was initiated by the historical school (mainly T.E. Cliffe Leslie and J.K. Ingram) against the better established deductive school (mainly Alfred Marshall). This decisive European battle, which has been discussed in detail elsewhere (Snooks 1993: 23–9, 118–29), was won by the deductivists. Over the following generation the various European historical schools gave up the attempt to develop an alternative body of economic theory and focused their attentions instead upon historical studies, while the deductive schools became the mainstream of the new academic discipline of economics, which displaced the old discipline of political economy. The outcome was an increasingly abstract and mathematical form of economic theory.

The intriguing question is why the deductivists had such a decisive victory. It is intriguing not only because it explains an important paradigm shift in the discipline, but also because it holds the key to any future paradigm shift. The answer is to be found in the comparative advantage of deductivists in the struggle for academic power; the missed opportunities of the historical school; and the cold-war hostility to historicism in the 1950s.

The comparative advantage of the deductivists

The methods of induction and deduction require very different skills. Induction demands skills that are less easily taught to graduate students and which take much longer to mature. In order to make theoretical generalizations from a close observation of the past (including the present), the inductivist must be able correctly to detect and measure patterns in reality, and to formulate causal relationships between the underlying variables. This requires the usual technical skills needed to master the existing theoretical and statistical techniques, but more importantly the rarer realist imagination needed to sort out complex real-world relationships.

While technical skills can be quickly acquired, realist imagination emerges only slowly. The only training for realist imagination is experience – long years of applying technical and historical skills to detailed evidence. In my professional judgement, realists will not reach the peak of their powers until they have had about 25 years of post-doctoral experience – in other words by the time they are about 50 years of age. But even with this experience only the few will undertake path-breaking work. As John Milton (1667) said: 'Long is the way and hard'.

The deductivist requires different skills. Of paramount importance are the technical skills of deductive logic, mathematics, and statistical technique. Unlike realist imagination, these technical skills can be taught quite satisfactorily to graduate students through well-structured coursework programmes and thesis work involving existing deductive models and data readily available on computer disk. The amount of experience required to achieve maximum performance in the exercise of these skills is substantially less than for the realist – certainly taking no more than a decade. By the time deductivists are in their early to mid thirties they have reached peak intellectual performance. In the case of both deductivist and inductivist this peak activity can be carried on for a decade or so before any decline becomes evident.

In these circumstances the deductivists have an obvious comparative advantage in the early stages of their academic careers, while the inductivists have a comparative advantage in their later years. Understandably, both groups will seek to maximize the opportunities provided by their comparative advantage. In the early part of their careers, the deductivists will gain relatively rapid peer recognition as they publish a larger number of 'leading-edge' articles in the 'best' journals. At this stage the deductivists will be regarded as the 'best' or most 'brilliant' people in the profession. Hence, they will possess an advantage in competing for tenure-track jobs, for promotion to full-professorships, and for control of the most powerful positions in their departments, universities, and profession.

If this process begins in any academic department with equal numbers of equally but differently talented people, it will take only a number of student generations before the proportion of deductivists will dominate. The obvious reason is that the deductivists will reach the top more quickly and will, quite naturally, encourage the selection of students and staff who have similar talents to themselves – who are, by their definition, the 'best' people. But, of course, what the 'best' students and staff are 'best' at is not reality construction but deductive theorizing. Even excellent inductivists are regarded as 'second-rate', and only survive in economics departments, if at all, because there is undergraduate demand for a few courses about the real world that can be safely left to the historicists.

The ageing deductivists, however, are often less secure in their assumption of superiority. At an age, say late 40s, when they are beginning to recognize that their best years are behind them, some notice the late flowering of a colleague who had for the past generation struggled for recognition on the margins of the economics profession. A few, like Kenneth Arrow (1986) and Robert Solow (1986), may even come to appreciate the insights of their historicist colleagues; may even recognize that they possess interesting skills; may even sense that if the right institutional support were provided these skills might contribute something central to the mainstream of economics as well as to that side-show called economic history. But by then it is too late. The deductivists continue to dominate the departments in which they early rose to authority, and the inductivists merely dream of missed opportunities.

Missed opportunities

Despite the comparative disadvantage of the inductivists, it seems to me that they have not made enough of their opportunities. This was as true in the past as it has been more recently.

A major mistake made by the historical school in the generation following the *Methodenstreit* of the 1880s was their complete repudiation of the tools of the deductivists. Like some evolutionists of the present, they made the mistake of believing that deductive economic theory, based on the assumption of *homo economicus*, is tainted and could not possibly be employed to analyse the recurring patterns in history. Cliffe Leslie (1888: 179) went as far as to claim that 'the abstract and *a priori* method yields no explanation of the laws determining either the nature, the amount, or the distribution of wealth'!

According to Cliffe Leslie (ibid.), the task of the real economist was to 'trace the connection between the economical and the other phases of national history'; and according to William Ashley (1913, I: xii), a second-generation historicist, it was 'to discover the laws of social development – that is to say generalizations as to the stages through which the economic life of society has actually moved'. They were intent, in other words, on discovering what J.S.Mill called the laws of 'social dynamics'. But in this they failed, largely because they neglected to use the analytical tools available to them from deductive economics. As they failed to understand economic motivation and the nature of economic processes, they focused on the wrong level of historical change – on superficial events and 'stages' rather than on the underlying economic mechanism. What they did not realize was that more than the general historian's expertise was required for this task.

More recently many of the descendants of the historical school – modern economic historians – have even abandoned the attempt to explain 'social dynamics'. Either they have lost themselves in the study of unconnected and unique historical events and institutions, or they have merely attempted to imitate the approach of applied economists using historical rather than contemporary data. Both groups appear to be toiling in the shadow of the defeat of inductivism at the turn of the twentieth century. While their work may be interesting in itself, modern economic historians have lost sight of the bigger picture once possessed by the pioneering historicists.

The great antihistoricist campaign

The antihistoricist campaign of the 1950s conducted by Karl Popper, Isaiah Berlin, Friedrich Hayek, and Ludwig Mises, transported the earlier debate between deductivists and inductivists on to an entirely new plane. While the *Methodenstreit* of the 1880s was fierce, it took place between real combatants on genuine methodological grounds. By contrast the antihistoricist campaign of the 1950s was a one-sided political assault against straw combatants on spurious methodological grounds. It was an entirely destructive assault, because its intention was to destroy historicism without constructing anything in its place. While the attack was publicly directed against the long-since-dead historicists, whose descendants had become inoffensive economic historians, its real targets were contemporary philosophical inductivists who challenged Popper's extreme form of deductivism (Snooks 1998: ch. 5).

The antihistoricist campaign was extremely effective because it destroyed the credibility of inductivism in a way that reasoned academic debate could never have done, and it set back the scientific search for the laws of social dynamics by a half century. It was little better than a political smear campaign which was intended to intimidate scholars who might be interested in demonstrating that the extreme deductivists were wrong. The antihistoricists made a deliberate attempt to associate historicism and its inductive method with totalitarianism of both the fascist and communist kind. Its success owed much to its coincidence with the half century that saw the costly defeat of fascism in Europe and the global cold-war struggle between democracy and communism. Exciting support against one's methodological enemies by charging them with complicity in the rise of totalitarianism and the suppression of liberty and democracy was an easy matter in this environment. Few potential historicists wished to be tarred with that brush. Only W.W.Rostow dared to brave the onslaught, but he had to qualify his *Stages of Economic Growth* (1971) with the disarming subtitle, *A Non-Communist Manifesto*.

This was a regrettable intellectual episode. It not only involved the unacceptable tactic of guilt by association, but also the explicit objective of these self-proclaimed champions of individual liberty and free thought to 'get rid of historicism'. Karl Popper regarded this as his 'war work' during both the hot and cold wars of the 1940s and 1950s. It is hardly a mitigating factor that this neo-Austrian circle of friends and colleagues subscribed to the mistaken view that ideas *per se* are responsible for political as well as economic outcomes and, hence, that the ideas of historicism were directly responsible for totalitarianism. The inherent danger in this belief is that in order to destroy totalitarianism it is necessary to destroy the ideas that you believe have led to it. This is hardly consistent with their entirely proper desire for individual liberty and free speech. But it achieved its objectives. It made a major contribution to the suppression of any desire to explore the possibilities of induction or historicism in the social sciences. Perhaps with the self-destruction of total-itarianism and the passing away of the extreme deductivists, the former hostility will dissipate.

A NEW APPROACH TO INDUCTION

Despite everything that has been written by the extreme deductivists about the non-existence of induction, I claim that it is possible to formulate an effective framework for the inductive process. The evidence for this is the usefulness of the inductive dynamic-strategy model employed in a series of books, including this one. Elsewhere I have proposed a four-step inductive procedure called the **quaternary system of induction** (Snooks 1998: ch. 7). The four steps are: the discovery of quantitative and qualitative patterns in reality called 'timescapes'; the construction of a general model to explain the whole class of timescapes; the application of the general model to particular historical episodes to derive specific dynamic models; and the derivation of a model of institutional change. This quaternary system goes a long way to resolving the 'problem of induction'. In order to clarify the method employed in this book these four inductive steps, if not inductive rules, need to be briefly outlined.

Timescapes

Timescapes provide pictures of the dynamic outcomes of human society over time in both quantitative and qualitative terms. The quantitative pictures show the trajectory and numerical relationships between important eco-nomic variables involved in the dynamic process – variables that include population, capital stock, land, real GDP, productivity, and prices. These timescapes are derived for periods that cover not only recent decades but also hundreds and even thousands of years (Snooks 1996: ch. 12). They reveal the **strategic pathways** of real-world growth processes, which in both the ancient and modern worlds have involved 'long waves' of about 40 years and 'great waves' of about 300 years. In the ancient world these patterns form part of a great circle of civilization's rise and fall, while in the modern world they are part of a linear process of rise and rise.

These pathways trace out the course of a society's unfolding dynamic strategy. The importance of this knowledge is that it enables us both to model dynamic demand and to determine the dynamic form of the real-world growth process. This can be obtained from no other source, certainly not from deductive logic. It is this real-world knowledge about dynamic demand and dynamic form that enables us to overcome the problems encountered by growth theorists over the past two centuries.

The qualitative pictures, which are even less familiar to economic theorists, are also important. They reveal the historical patterns of institutional change of an economic, political, and social kind. These qualitative pictures, developed elsewhere (Snooks 1997a: pt II), show quite clearly that institutional change is not an evolutionary process; rather it twists, turns, and reverses on itself in response to the unfolding dynamic strategy. It all depends on the strategic sequence. Although Western civilization has experienced a conquest→commerce→technological strategic sequence over the past millennium, this was purely fortuitous coming as it did at the end of the neolithic technological paradigm, when the only way forward was to engineer a new technological paradigm shift – the Industrial Revolution (Snooks 1996: ch. 12). Greek civilization, which flourished during the middle period of that paradigm went through a conquest→commerce→conquest strategic sequence. Accordingly institutions changed not in a linear way but by doubling back on themselves.

What then is the significance of charting these timescapes or dynamic pathways? It is twofold. First, we are provided with a dynamic form both for the fundamental growth process and for the process of institutional change. This will be employed in developing models of both economic and political change. Secondly, this procedure provides an all-encompassing dynamic framework. It ensures that we do not completely omit, as deductive growth theory does, a major – indeed *the* major – variable such as **strategic demand** that is generated by the unfolding dynamic strategy. What timescapes cannot be used for is to predict the future, which is the old historicist fallacy.

The general dynamic model

The general model is constructed inductively using the historical method. It involves an examination of the timescapes as a class, together with historical material concerning human motivation, to explain in a general way why a society emerges, grows, stagnates, declines and, sometimes, collapses. It is a model concerned with the ways in which human decision-makers attempt to achieve their objectives in a large number of economic environments, why and how these ways are eventually exhausted, and why a previously successful society falters. It is a model that possesses universal validity as it can be used to explain the dynamics of human society throughout space and time once the specific fundamental conditions are known. This model is presented in *The Dynamic Society* (1996: 391–401).

Specific dynamic models

While the general dynamic model can explain growth and decline in general terms, it must be informed by particular historical conditions in order to suggest specific models that can explain the dynamics of individual historical eras such as our own. It is a procedure that can operate at a number of levels – that of entire technological paradigms (such as the palaeolithic, neolithic, or modern) or that of substrategies within individual paradigms (such as the microelectronic substrategy within the modern technological paradigm).

To develop these specific models we need to explore three sets of fundamental societal conditions. We need to know whether we are dealing with an open or closed society, as the degree of external competition is crucial. We need to know the degree to which global resources are fully employed, given the prevailing technological paradigm. And we need to know the nature of a society's dynamic strategies and substrategies. The way these conditions are employed is discussed in *The Dynamic Society* (1996: 401–13).

Modelling institutional change

The dynamic-strategy theory can be used to explain institutional change. As shown in *The Ephemeral Civilization* (1997a), institutional change is not an evolutionary process. It can only be satisfactorily explained as a response to the unfolding dynamic strategy. If the strategic sequence doubles back on itself so will institutional change. This understanding was arrived at only from a close study of human history over the past ten thousand years. As discussed in Chapter 10, an unfolding dynamic strategy generates a changing strategic demand for a wide range of inputs including facilitating institutions and organizations. The central mechanism by which strategic demand is converted into institutional change is the **strategic struggle** analysed in Chapter 15. This mechanism involves a struggle for control of the sources of national wealth between the old and new strategists (profit-seekers), the conservative and radical antistrategists (rent-seekers), and the nonstrategists (dependants).

Until the end of his long life, Karl Popper (1992: 147) maintained that 'sensible rules of inference do not exist'. This was hardly a sensible judgement. My quaternary system of induction can be regarded as a comprehensive framework within which real-world dynamic models can be developed with a reasonable degree of clarity and precision. While it will not eliminate disagreements over interpretation of real-world data, it does produce interesting results that are open to informed criticism. And most importantly this inductive system, unlike the deductive method, enables us to include all the important explanatory variables involved in the real-world dynamic process.

This was how the central concept of strategic demand was discovered. In the end the proof of the pudding is in the eating.

CONCLUSIONS

While the deductivists have dominated the discipline of economics since the turn of the century, there are good reasons for believing that the inductivists will make a comeback in the near future. The earlier deductive victory was decisive at the time but not necessarily permanent. After dominating the field for almost a century, the deductivists have still to show that they can develop the important field of social dynamics. Clearly they regard social dynamics as an important area of study: as Robert Lucas (1988) tells us, 'once one starts to think about [economic growth], it is hard to think about anything else'. Orthodox economists have invested heavily in growth theory, particularly in the 1950s and 1960s, and again since the mid-1980s. But they still cannot satisfactorily explain the dynamics of human society. It is time, therefore, for another approach. And there are good reasons for believing, along with J.S. Mill in the 1840s, that the successful approach will take the form not of evolutionary or institutional economics but of historical economics. The early historicists lost an excellent opportunity to develop social dynamics a century ago, owing to a fundamental flaw in their research design, and later possibilities were torpedoed by the political attack of the antihistoricists. With a new research design and the demise of antihistoricism, a renewed inductivist offensive may well be successful. If it is, we could shortly see a paradigm shift taking place in the economics discipline.

Part III
Dynamic Order

6 From the Invisible Hand to No Hand at All

A central issue in economics is what type of economic system will maximize economic growth. This has preoccupied economists from the time of Adam Smith to today. Should we rely on the outcomes of individual decision-making, or should we intervene in some way? But this simple question overlooks the complexity of reality. How is it possible for individuals pursuing their own self-interest to unintentionally create orderly institutional structures that not only operate surprisingly efficiently but generate relatively high rates of economic growth? Why is it not possible to devise more effective dynamic institutions? So far the answers provided by even the most imaginative economists have been less than persuasive.

The answers given to these questions have varied quite considerably over the past two centuries. Adam Smith, who was the first political economist to treat this issue as central to his societal system, introduced the concept of the 'invisible hand' by which individuals pursuing 'self-love' were guided to create institutions that restrained their selfish desires in order to promote the emergence of liberty and economic growth.[1] For this purpose Smith constructed a system in which the driving force of self-love was constrained by the Stoic virtues embodied in the 'impartial spectator', an instrument of divine forces. In other words, Smith, like the ancient philosophers, constructed his political and economic system on moral foundations.

Owing to the obviously unscientific nature of Smith's solution, other economic thinkers have attempted to develop less mystical systems. Friedrich Hayek, who revived the eighteenth-century idea of 'spontaneous order', attempted to take God out of the equation. According to Hayek the emergence of spontaneous order is a product neither of the mind of God nor of man. Rather it is the outcome of an evolutionary process that falls somewhere 'between instinct and reason'. All attempts to develop man-made economic systems, he argues, are doomed to failure. At the same time John Maynard Keynes, who saw reality as an unknowable state of flux, argued that order arises from this chaos because human beings act out their 'animal spirits' and follow social conventions.

While Hayek and Keynes removed God, they have not really removed the mystery – a matter that causes unease among modern economists. Constitutional economists like James Buchanan reject the idea that it is impossible for the mind of man to develop new and better 'constitutional rules'. Instead they look back selectively to the political economy of Adam Smith and propose an examination of the working properties of alternative sets of rules or constraints. The neoclassical solution to this embarrassing, unresolved problem is to pretend that it does not exist. Instead, beginning with Léon Walras (1834–1910), they have focused on a mathematical analysis of the interactions in a static self-ordering system. Apart from providing mathematical proofs of the existence of general equilibrium, neoclassical economists have abandoned any attempt to explain how and why spontaneous order emerges in free enterprise societies. The general equilibrium system just is. This static system abstracts from the hand of both God and man.

THE INVISIBLE HAND

It is not possible, as Athol Fitzgibbons (1995) elegantly demonstrates, to understand Adam Smith's *Wealth of Nations* (1776) without first reading his *The Theory of Moral Sentiments* (1759) and his lectures on jurisprudence.[2] Smith's objective was 'to define a set of laws, a constitution in the widest possible sense, that would permit Britain to benefit from liberalism without triggering the fearful process of long-run cultural degeneration' (Fitzgibbons 1995: 14). To do so he analysed the moral and political rules that would be required by a liberal and durable society, and used these as a basis for his study of the resulting economy. Any conflict between morals and wealth could be resolved through a more just legal system. Hence, Smith began his task by establishing the moral requirements of a modern state and the institutions needed to establish them, and only then did he examine the nature of a dynamic economy. This is the very reverse of the methodological procedure discussed in Chapter 5.

In *Moral Sentiments* Smith began with the belief that, while self-love provided the 'principle of motion', it would not lead to social cohesion (Skinner 1987, IV: 360). Natural man, therefore, needed the guidance of an invisible hand. Smith argued that the invisible hand operated through the 'impartial spectator', which is the instrument of the Stoic god – the god-in-the-world rather than the Christian God in heaven. Hence the Stoic virtues – self-command, prudence, justice, and beneficence – that were planted in the breast of every 'reasonable' man, placed a constraint on desires and enabled the construction of just laws. Justice, according to Smith (1776/1961, II.ii: 3–4), 'is the main pillar that upholds the entire edifice'. Only if the impartial spectator were denied by the leading individuals in a particular society would the laws of the jungle, rather than justice, prevail.

Smith argued that the fortunes of any society depended on the moral principle it pursued. He divided history into four stages – prehistory, Greece, Rome, and medieval Europe – and claimed that each stage passed through a sequence from democracy to monarchy to aristocracy. Each of these societies was based on a dominant principle: democratic society pursued 'utility', and experienced liberty and stagnation; monarchical society pursued 'authority' and reaped nihilism and economic growth; and aristocratic society pursued 'virtue', and achieved social cohesion and stagnation.

Because each of these dominant moral principles was insufficient to achieve both liberty *and* economic growth their host societies eventually declined culturally and collapsed, to be replaced by more resilient societies. Smith believed, therefore, that both the rise and fall of human societies was due to the inherent potential and the fatal flaw in the moral principle they adopted. Only in a society that was able to combine all three moral principles could both liberty and economic growth be successfully achieved. Such a society, Smith believed, was Britain in the mid-eighteenth century. Owing to its institutions of monarchy, aristocracy, and democracy, Britain was able to achieve economic growth, social cohesion, and liberty. This moral hybrid-vigour, Smith claimed, would prevent the collapse of the British Empire. Smith's objective, therefore, was to discover the moral 'principle' that he thought governed human society.

Most modern economists are familiar with Adam Smith's model of economic growth, which has at its core a process of capital accumulation financed from the surplus (or profits) received by capitalists (workers were too poor and landowners too self-indulgent to save), which made possible increased efficiency through the growing division of labour and to the widening of markets. Few, however, are aware of, or care to investigate, the moral basis of Smith's theory of economic growth. An exception is Athol Fitzgibbons (1995: 146–8) who argues that Smith developed a 'moral theory of economic growth' in which 'justice' provides a framework conducive to capital formation; 'prudence' is the basis for saving needed to fund investment ('capitals are increased by parsimony, and diminished by prodigality and misconduct' – Smith 1776, I: 358); and 'self-command' is required to undertake risky capitalist projects that generate economic growth.

Clearly Adam Smith's societal system was not completely scientific. And as such it was attacked by his friend David Hume, who wanted to analyse society and develop laws without recourse to moral principles. Hume was more in touch with the new spirit of the modern world than Smith. And, for the same reason, modern economists usually ignore Smith's *Moral Sentiments* together with the later sections of the *Wealth of Nations*.

There are two features of Smith's system that require comment: the distinction he makes between 'self-love' and 'self-interest'; and his use of what I will call a 'moral sequence' to explain the changing sociopolitical structure of human society. First, the distinction between self-love and self-interest, like many of Smith's concepts, has no empirical foundation. Smith argued that self-interest was the outcome of self-love modified by virtue, the bonding agent in human society. But what is self-love? It is a mythical quality of mankind rather than an operational economic concept. As the objective of mankind is to survive and prosper – something etched in our genes (Snooks 1997a: chs 2, 5) – and as co-operation as well as competition is required to achieve this, self-love as a guiding principle would have led to the extinction of our species. Thus, self-interest rather than the mythical self-love is the genetically determined attitude of mankind to life. What role, therefore, is left for virtue? This begs the question about non-human animal life: as they do not pursue virtue how are they able to convert self-love into self-interest? Smith's distinction, therefore, is entirely artificial.

Secondly, what are we to make of Smith's 'moral sequence' associated with the rise and fall of human society? While no modern economist would accept such an argument, I raise the matter because it is the very reverse of the 'strategic sequence' (Snooks 1996: ch. 12; 1997: ch. 3) that I treat in Chapter 16 as central to my dynamic-strategy model. In my *inductive* model, the rise and fall of societies, together with their institutional and moral character-istics, is the outcome of the adoption, development, exhaustion, and replace-ment of the dominant dynamic strategies. Smith's *deductive* system, which begins with the outcomes of my *inductive* system, entirely reverses the real-world process. If we substitute 'dynamic strategy' for 'moral principle' and 'strategic confidence' for 'virtue', our systems would possess broadly similar features, although Smith's confusion over cultural and economic outcomes would remain.[3] The possibility of reversing the real-world sequence is an ever-present danger with the deductive method. But the important point is that the role of strategic demand in my system eliminates the need for Smith's mystical 'impartial spectator' in generating **dynamic order**.

SPONTANEOUS ORDER

Like Adam Smith, the neo-Austrian economist Friedrich Hayek (1899–1992) treated the co-ordination problem as central to his conception of economics. The complex order of human society, which is greater than could be consciously planned by individual decision-makers, was called 'spontaneous order' by Hayek. He was concerned to discover how this order came about and what caused it to fail periodically. While Adam Smith was largely concerned with why, Hayek was mainly interested in how, the co-ordination of human society occurred. Not surprisingly, Hayek rejected Smith's belief that human institutions were the result of divine intervention. Even though institutions are not the result of the intention of God or man, Hayek thought they arose from human action in the pursuit of self-interest.

Hayek's entire approach to economics was determined by the co-ordination problem. His published work in the fields of price, capital, and monetary theory was designed to explain co-ordination and its periodic failure. This approach even provided the foundations for his business-cycle theory. Central to his explanation of spontaneous order is the role of markets as a process of discovery and information by which the co-ordination of human activities is achieved. It was this realization that led Hayek to claim, as early as the 1920s, that a centrally determined system could not succeed because it was unable to generate the information required to formulate central plans.

If the rational mind was unable to create the institutions required for the successful longrun operation of complex societies, how did the remarkable order attained by free enterprise societies emerge? As shown in Chapter 4, Hayek claims that these rules, which constrain the demands generated by animal instincts, are not foreseen or planned by the human intellect. But why have these constraints on desire evolved if they are not imposed by God – or at least been demanded by men inspired by divine virtue – as in Smith's system, and if they are not desired by men? Hayek's answer, as we have seen, is that they have evolved in a Darwinian manner. He adopts a simple neo-Darwinian explanation that involves the adaption of institutional variations through a process of group selection under competition which, if successful, become dominant in the 'rule pool' by an increase in the population and power of the innovative society. The more populous society absorbs the less successful societies.

There are a number of difficulties with this evolutionary hypothesis. First, it assumes that the success of societies depends only on the evolution of rules. But what about success in war, commerce, and technological change? As I show in *The Dynamic Society* (1996) and *The Ephemeral Civilization* (1997a), these dynamic strategies are far more important than rules (that merely facilitate these strategies) in the survival and prosperity of societies. Secondly, it is purely a supply-side argument. There is no sense here of the more powerful forces on the demand side. In an effort to make the idea of spontaneous order scientific, Hayek has rejected Smith's demand-side argument (the demand for virtuous institutions by individuals inspired by the Stoic god), but has failed to find a substitute. Accordingly he has fallen back on a rather tenuous supply-side hypothesis of an evolutionary nature.

In the next chapter I will argue that the demand variable that both Smith and Hayek needed but were unable to find is **strategic confidence** generated by a successful dynamic strategy. Strategic confidence can account both for the emergence of co-ordination and for its periodic failure.

THE TAMING OF CHAOS

Anyone who has carefully read John Maynard Keynes' *The General Theory* (1936) will be aware of the state of uncertainty that underlies that masterful analysis. As is well known, the heart of *The General Theory* is Chapter 12, which is concerned with 'the state of long-term expectation'. Here Keynes discusses the forces underlying investment, which is the main determinant of national income and 'effective demand'. Here we encounter a world of uncertainty where it is impossible to calculate the likely return on investment and, hence, of positive human action. Keynes (1936: 149) tells us:

> The outstanding fact is the extreme precariousness of the basis of knowledge on which our estimates of prospective yield have to be made. Our knowledge of the factors which will govern the yield of an investment some years hence is usually very slight and often negligible.

The contrast with the subsequent rational expectations theory is refreshingly stark.

Yet, we know that year after year, generation after generation, and even century after century, investment over a vast range of activities is undertaken and that great civilizations rise and flourish. If the world is so uncertain, why is this so? Keynes' response, which is ultimately unsatisfactory, is twofold. First, he speculates that it 'can only be taken as a result of animal spirits – of a spontaneous urge to action, and not as the outcome of quantitative benefits multiplied by quantitative probabilities' (ibid.: 161). Secondly, he asserts, this action is directed by 'convention', and 'the essence of this convention...lies in assuming that the existing state of affairs will continue indefinitely, except in so far as we have specific reasons to expect a change'. For Keynes, this is how order emerges from the chaos of reality.

Yet, even a careful reader of *The General Theory* will not be aware of the philosophical foundations of Keynes' theory of uncertainty. For revealing this we are indebted, once again, to Athol Fitzgibbons (1988). In his book, *Keynes' Vision* – based on his subject's extensive unpublished writings – Fitzgibbons tells us that Keynes rejected the neoclassical notion of general equilibrium, because he 'recognized that change is of the essence', and that the economy 'is in flux because of uncertainty over the future' (ibid.: 121). Keynes, we are told, believed that humanity lives in a 'twilight of probability', that consequences 'are generally lost in the river of time', and that the economy is a cross-section of chaos (ibid.: 24, 116). It is a world-view based upon a 'metaphysical vision' that was derived from the philosophies of David Hume, G.E. Moore, Plato, and Edmund Burke.

The chaos in Keynes' world – a chaos tamed by reason, intuition, and pragmatism – is, I will argue, an outcome of seeking reality through philosophy rather than history. *The General Theory* has pre-modern philosophical (ethical) origins, in that it is built upon metaphysics. It succeeds brilliantly, only because it is a triumph of pragmatism over philosophy. But it has its blind spots. Ironically, the person who gave us a theory of static effective demand was unable to see the encompassing role of dynamic strategic demand. That requires beginning with reality rather than ethics.

THE ENLIGHTENED INTELLECTUAL

While constitutional economists like James Buchanan have adopted the libertarian ideas of Hayek, they reject his argument that the mind of man is unable to design institutional arrangements that operate more effectively than those that arise spontaneously. Yet Buchanan (1987: 586) embraces the Austrian school's emphasis on methodological individualism, which regards individual choice as the basic unit of analysis and treats 'collectivities', or social groups, merely as the outcome of individual choices and actions. This explains the rejection by constitutional economists of any positive role for governments in pursuing national objectives. Governments, we are told, should exist only to facilitate private enterprise by protecting individuals and property rights and by enforcing privately negotiated contracts. The problem, they tell us, is that governments will always be tempted to do more!

Further, Buchanan argues that the ultimate source of social value resides exclusively in individuals. In the absence of any sense of strategic demand, it is this belief that provides the constitutional economist with the criterion to evaluate policy proposals and outcomes. This is imperative because they have rejected the Pareto efficiency criterion as not being empirically grounded. All change, therefore, is to be evaluated in terms of the revealed preferences of individuals, or at least in terms of what intellectuals consider these preferences to be. This is discussed further in Chapters 15 and 17.

Where Hayek and Buchanan part company is over the ability of mankind to frame alternative sets of political rules. Buchanan (1987: 587) claims that 'the ultimate purpose of analysing alternative sets of rules is to inform the choice among these sets'. He is confident that the constitutional economist can effectively offer 'guidance to those who participate in the discussion of constitutional change'. Unlike Hayek, therefore, Buchanan is convinced that the intellectual has an important proactive role to play in resolving problems of market efficiency. In this, Buchanan self-consciously looks back to the classical political economy of Adam Smith. Yet in doing so he has abandoned Smith's concept of 'divine demand' and has substituted the supply-side concept of the enlightened intellectual operating in the interests of all other individuals in society. Whether they like it or not.

GENERAL EQUILIBRIUM THEORY

General equilibrium theory is a neoclassical response to the co-ordination problem. While Léon Walras (1874–7) made the major contribution to this form of analysis, it was independently discovered by H. Gossen (1854), W.S. Jevons (1871), and Carl Menger (1871). But this form of analysis will not detain us long because it is essentially a static rather than a dynamic system.

General equilibrium theory is a self-ordering system involving interactions between its component parts that are best expressed in mathematical form. It does not concern itself with why or even how spontaneous order emerges or periodically fails, only with what form the interaction takes, how it reacts to exogenous shocks, and whether the existence of general equilibrium can be proved mathematically. It is a tool limited to the analysis of comparative–static rather than dynamic issues (despite recent attempts to introduce dynamic elements), because it assumes that all individual decision-makers are in equilibrium and that tastes, technology, population, and other resources are constant. But, of course, these are the very factors involved in the longrun dynamic process. General equilibrium theory is merely used to determine the outcome of exogenously determined changes in these variables within a comparative–static framework. Further, as noted in Chapter 1, the general equilibrium model can only be used, even for comparative–static analysis, in the shortrun, because it implicitly assumes that the dynamic strategy is unchanged. The interesting and central dynamic issues struggled with by Smith and Hayek are neatly sidestepped by the neoclassical economist.

CONCLUSIONS

While it is generally acknowledged that the co-ordination problem is a central issue in economics, deductive economists from Adam Smith to modern neoclassicals and new political economists have failed to provide a convincing explanation of its existence. In the following chapter it is argued that this is because the deductive method is unable to detect the presence of strategic confidence generated by the unfolding dynamic strategy. The presence of this critical, demand-side variable can only be encountered through the inductive method. With the exception of Adam Smith, who felt comfortable including the demand for virtue arising from a Stoic god, all the rest have adopted a supply-side approach that is incapable of explaining the nature of the remarkable dynamic order of human society.

7 The Strategic Principle of Dynamic Order

Spontaneous order is an unsatisfactory concept. It needs to be reinterpreted both in terms of its meaning and its causation. It will be argued that the purpose of a self-ordering society is not to achieve some political or moral end such as liberty or virtue, but to enable its members to maximize the probability of survival and prosperity. Ironically the instrument by which survival and prosperity are achieved is also the unwitting source of the self-ordering system. This principle of societal order is the unfolding dynamic strategy.

Survival and prosperity are achieved through the successful pursuit of a dominant dynamic strategy. In order to facilitate this pursuit it is necessary to develop institutions and organizations that necessarily involve placing constraints on individual behaviour. This is one of the costs of material advancement that are outweighed by the benefits of economic growth. The resulting co-operative behaviour is motivated not by virtue or chance, but by **strategic confidence** that is generated by a successful dynamic strategy.

Ours is a dynamic rather than a static world. As the dominant dynamic strategy unfolds, changes are induced both in **strategic demand** for a wide range of inputs including institutions and organizations, and in strategic confidence concerning the future. While the strategic unfolding continues and society prospers, strategic confidence remains high, generating trust and co-operation between individuals at all levels of society and stability in its institutions. But when this unfolding falters owing either to structural reasons or to strategic exhaustion, confidence will decline, causing a deterioration in former trust, co-operation, and institutional stability, and, hence, in societal order. In other words, the changing nature of societal order, which is best viewed as dynamic order, is determined from the demand-side by an unfolding dynamic strategy. This is the strategic principle of **dynamic order**.

THE REAL NATURE OF INSTITUTIONS AND ORGANIZATIONS

The basic argument in this chapter is that institutions and organizations that are at the heart of a self-ordering system emerge and change in the longrun primarily in response to changing strategic demand generated by an unfolding dynamic strategy. Only their superficial, ephemeral forms are shaped by what I have called relative institutional prices. Hence, in a competitive environment, strategic demand for both institutional and organizational support will be met in the most efficient way possible at the time in response to the relative costs of various possible alternatives that reflect factor endowments and prior historical developments. This has been demonstrated exhaustively in my recent book *The Ephemeral Civilization* (1997a).

Societal rules, both formal and informal, will be established and constantly altered to carry out the dynamic strategies by which decision-makers attempt to maximize their chances of survival and prosperity. These rules are required, as argued in Chapter 9, in order to economize on that scarcest of resources, the intellect. Similarly, societal organizations of all types – economic, political, social – also respond largely to these dynamic strategies, rather than to institutions as new institutionalists like Douglass North (1990) argue. The incentives to which organizations respond, therefore, are to be found in the strategic opportunities rather than the opportunities provided by institutions. Societal rules do not provide opportunities or incentives of their own volition, they merely communicate the opportunities generated by the fundamental dynamic forces. There will, of course, be a degree of interaction between these demand and supply forces, but causality flows overwhelmingly from the former to the latter. Also rules do not evolve in a Darwinian manner as Friedrich Hayek (1988) argues.

It is in the process of **strategic imitation**, by which the vast majority of decision-makers emulate the action of the successful strategic pioneers, that societal rules are employed. Institutions are needed to economize not on information but on intelligence. Rules are required also by those who attempt to achieve their objectives through order and control. Hence the rule-makers are the strategic followers and the apostles of order, while the rule-breakers are the strategic pioneers. As the former constitute the vast majority of decision-makers, rules are essential to the dynamics of human society even though they are purely derivative of it.

While these variables will be modelled more fully later in the chapter, enough has been said to provide a framework for categorizing institutions and organizations in order to see how institutional change occurs. Institutions and organizations are dealt with together here because both respond to strategic demand in similar ways, and because the new institutionalist focus on institutional rules is too narrow. They are jointly determined by strategic demand, and any *independent* interaction between them is relatively minor.

Strategic institutions

Strategic institutions are those formal and informal rules of conduct that are required to support the emergence and development of the dynamic strategies of family multiplication, conquest, commerce, and technological change. These institutions, which operate at both the macro/micro and national/regional levels, cover the full societal spectrum of economic, social, and political activities. They include the economic and political systems; the rules by which business is conducted; the way goods, services, and factors of production are bought and sold; the way business is financed; the rules of monetary supply; the way property rights are allocated; the way politics is conducted; and the way people interact at a social level. The type of dynamic strategy pursued by a particular society has a characteristic and predictable impact upon all these institutions.

In simple societies the demands made upon intellectual faculties are *relatively* light and, hence, the role of formal rules is relatively unimportant; informal rules and custom are sufficient. As the society becomes increasingly complex, **strategic costs** (interpreted by institutionalists as transaction costs) will rise with the increasing demands made upon intellectual resources. This will lead to the growing importance of formal institutions or rules. This is not, as Mark Casson (1991: 3) has argued, a result of declining 'mutual trust'; nor does it endanger the viability of that society. What endangers society is the exhaustion and non-replacement of the dominant dynamic strategy. This leads directly not to a reduction in trust, but to a decline in strategic confidence. It is the decline in confidence in the prevailing strategy by decision-makers that leads to a loss of trust and societal order.

The variable nature of society's strategic institutions have been discussed in detail in *The Ephemeral Civilization* (1997a). The four main dynamic strategies generate demands for different types of societal rules, in order to facilitate very different approaches to the eternal pursuit of survival and prosperity. A few examples will suffice to illustrate my point. As far as the economic and political system is concerned, a conquest strategy will lead to central economic and political control by a military strongman (king or dictator) because of the monopoly of economic ownership; the commerce strategy will see the emergence, owing to a more widespread ownership of economic resources, of a regulated market system with a wider political franchise which, depending on the era, will range from elected merchant princes in democratic city-states to parliamentary systems with an upper middle-class franchise in nation-states; and the technological strategy results in a market system with a parliamentary democracy based upon universal franchise owing to the universal system of economic democracy. While this set of relationships between the dominant dynamic strategy and the economic and political system is not entirely precise at the detailed level, it is quite clear in bold outline. The same is true of the different systems of exchange of property rights, law, and of social intercourse.

These relationships are not accidental. Different strategies can best be implemented with different economic and political systems. A society that switches from a commerce or a technological strategy to a conquest strategy, for example, will see the emergence of a new ruling elite; it will experience significantly less freedom of political or economic expression; control over its rules of exchange will pass from private (free markets, private monopolies, guilds) to public (forced labour, plunder, state distribution) control; its property rights will change from a widespread (or even universal) to a restrictive and authoritarian basis; and its democratic rules of social exchange will be replaced by autocratic decree. Changes of this nature can be seen throughout the historical record, as in the case of Carthage (after 300 BC) and of Greece (after 338 BC) as they turned increasingly from commerce to conquest; and in the case of Germany and of Japan after the mid-1930s as they turned from the technological to the conquest strategies. These reversals, which were due to changing dynamic strategies, cannot be explained by evolutionary institutionalism. The same is true of more minor institutional changes taking place in modern society in response to the development and replacement of technological substrategies.

Strategic organizations

As in the case of institutions, the various dynamic strategies call forth a set of characteristic and predictable organizations. In *The Ephemeral Civilization* (1997a) I divide strategic organizations into two main categories – major strategic organizations, and support organizations. The major strategic organizations are those demanded by decision-makers to implement and expand society's dominant dynamic strategy. For societies pursuing the family-multiplication strategy this involves the kinship teams required for hunting and gathering; for those pursuing conquest it covers military and imperial organizations; for those pursuing commerce it includes trading and financial organizations together with state naval and foreign service organizations; and for those societies pursuing the technological strategy it encompasses industrial and commercial organizations together with a comprehensive state bureaucracy.

Any society changing its dominant strategy would also need to change its major strategic organizations. A society, for example, switching from commerce to conquest – such as Athens during the Peloponnesian wars – would gradually replace its commercial organizational structure with a military structure; while a society switching from commerce to technological change – such as Western Europe between the eighteenth and nineteenth centuries – would replace its commercial structure with an industrial system. And we could expect to see a massive change in our present organizational structure if, under pressure from an eco-dictator, the technological strategy collapsed and, by default, was replaced by the conquest strategy (Snooks 1996: ch. 13). In this event the industrial–commerce complex would be subordinated to a military–imperial system. The effect would be similar to that achieved partially in both Europe and Asia in the 1930s and 1940s which saw the emergence of dictators pursuing irrational objectives such as racial purity.

Support organizations also depend upon the type of dynamic strategy pursued by any society. The nature of education and training, the type of manufacturing concerns, the character of research and development, and even the forecasting methods employed (compare the non-scientific forms employed in both Nazi Germany and ancient Rome) depend on the dominant strategy. Once again this can best be seen in a society switching its dynamic strategy. With a shift from commerce to conquest – which can be seen in Carthage in the third century BC or Greece in the fourth century BC, or Venice in the early sixteenth century – the support organizations shift from a preoccupation with the development of skills and the manufacture of products required in trade to a focus on activities needed for war. This was also experienced in Western democracies during the Second World War.

Quite clearly, the strategic and support organizations of society depend upon the opportunities and incentives generated not by institutional constraints as argued by Douglass North and other new institutionalists, but by its dynamic strategies. And changes in these organizations are driven not by forces on the supply side favoured by these institutionalists, but by the forces of strategic demand generated by an unfolding dynamic strategy. The role of supply forces – relative institutional prices – is limited to considerations of organizational design.

CHANGES IN INSTITUTIONS AND ORGANIZATIONS

The key to understanding institutions is the realization that they can only achieve the objectives of those who employ them if they are relatively stable. It is not possible to conduct business successfully if the rules of the game, such as property rights and market regulations, are constantly changing. Continuous revolution, as the Chinese discovered in the 1960s and 1970s, is bad for business. Institutions, therefore, are of no use unless a degree of stability can be attained. But we know that they do change over time. The argument developed in *The Dynamic Society* (1996) and *The Ephemeral Civilization* (1997a) is that this change in the longer term is driven by strategic demand and shaped by relative institutional prices. As we have seen, dynamic demand changes when, and only when, there is a change in the fortunes of a strategy. Hence, those periods of relative stability in society's institutions reflect the stability of strategic demand rather than the stasis that, we are told by the evolutionary institutionalists, is supposed to characterize the Darwinian process of institutional change. Relative institutional prices, which are the costs of alternative institutions that can be adopted to facilitate the dynamic strategies, change owing to changes in economies of scale and technology that arise from the dynamic processes of the real economy.

Strategic demand

Strategic demand for institutional and organizational structures is, as indicated above, generated by the dynamic process of the real economy. It is an outcome of the major dynamic strategies of family multiplication, conquest, commerce, and technological change. This is the 'fundamental law of institutional change' (Snooks 1998: ch. 10). Shifts in strategic demand occur due to the changing fortunes – or unfolding – of the dominant dynamic strategy, and to the transition from one strategy to another. In turn these developments depend upon changes in relative factor endowments and in the wider competitive environment. As will be seen in Chapter 11, strategic demand is very different to the orthodox concept of aggregate demand, which is merely an outcome of the dynamic system at any point in time. Aggregate demand, which can be thought of as 'static demand', is both narrower than and derivative of strategic demand.

We need to consider both the nature of strategic demand and the forces that cause it to shift over time. Changes in institutions and organizations are achieved by human agents wanting to invest in the dominant dynamic strategy and needing to establish stable rules and organizations to do so. The demand for relevant organizations is quite straightforward. Individuals form associations with each other – such as trading, financial, shipping, insurance, industrial, and military organizations – to enable investment in, and the operation of, the dominant dynamic strategy. The demand for institutions, however, is more complex because the procedure involved is less direct. To change the formal strategic rules it is necessary to influence those who hold political power. This can be achieved either by tempting or pressuring the political leaders. Temptation can be exercised by giving the political leaders a share of the strategic profits either through bribery or through legal business arrangements. Political pressure is exercised by lobby groups who threaten to divert the political support of their strategic backers to the political opposition. The struggle for strategic control of the sources of wealth is tackled in Chapter 15.

Institutional supply

While the primary dynamic mechanism generates a changing demand for institutions and organizations to facilitate the objectives of materialist man, their design is shaped by supply-side forces. Basically these forces involve costs associated with the range of feasible rules and organizations that could be employed in any particular society to meet the change in strategic demand. The forms chosen will depend upon which of the available alternatives meet the prevailing strategic demand most efficiently and hence maximize material advantage. This 'law of institutional economy' (Snooks 1998: ch. 10) takes into account past decision-making and the general cultural context. In other words, the most efficient institution or organization 'available' to a particular society at a point in time is not necessarily the most efficient form available in a timeless sense. While a society's history of decision-making does not lock it into a particular development path, as many under the influence of recent ideas about 'path-dependence' claim, it does affect the costs of alternatives.

Within the limits provided by the strategic-demand framework, changes in institutions and organizations will also occur as relative institutional prices change. These prices change whenever there is a change in technology broadly conceived to include ideas relevant to the structure of human society. But even these changes depend upon the primary dynamic mechanism. Enough has been said about the supply side, as this has been discussed at length in the works of the new institutional economics. Yet a new perspective and orientation that gives pride of place to strategic demand is required in institutional analysis. Until now we have lacked a persuasive account of the demand side.

Only strategic demand can, for example, solve the puzzle in Douglass North's work of why apparently inefficient institutions persist in the longer term. The model developed here suggests that inefficient institutions persist in societies where formerly successful dynamic strategies have been exhausted, or where dynamic strategies have never been successful. In these circumstances of *strategic* failure, the most profitable *tactic* for the ruling class is rent-seeking. And this rent-seeking generates a demand for tactical instruments – rules and organizations – that are, in comparison with societies employing successful dynamic strategies, relatively inefficient. Rent-seeking is a tactic rather than a strategy because it aims not to increase prosperity through the growth of real GDP per capita but merely to redistribute wealth more inequitably.

While the institutions associated with rent-seeking might seem inefficient to the successful dynamic strategist, they are effective instruments in the hands of either failed strategists (as in many Third World societies today), or dedicated antistrategists (as in the former USSR or in Communist China) in their attempt to gain a greater share of existing wealth. This model can, therefore, effectively account for the differences in institutions, organizations, and economic performance between England and Spain in the premodern period, or between developed and Third World countries in the late twentieth century, that have puzzled North (1990: 113–17). Spain's earlier successful conquest strategy had been exhausted by the early seventeenth century and, in the competitive circumstances of the time, could not be replaced with the commerce strategy so effectively used by England throughout the sixteenth and seventeenth centuries. This produced in Spain a level of performance and an efficiency of structure that compared unfavourably with England's, particularly as the exhausted commerce strategy in the eighteenth century gave rise to the technological strategy we know as the Industrial Revolution. The Spanish ruling elite, however, was able to use new and existing institutions quite effectively in redistributing wealth in their own favour and in maintaining the existence of a less efficient economic system. North's explanation, that Spain's poor performance was the result of its culturally determined inefficient institutions, is not at all persuasive. It is not valid to use the coincidence of poor performance and 'inefficient' institutions as evidence for the institutional hypothesis for societal dynamics. Both are jointly determined by the dynamics of the real economy. The same is true for the continuing contrast between First and Third World nations.

CONCLUSIONS

The principle of dynamic order that has shaped human society throughout history is the unfolding dynamic strategy, which generates changes in both strategic demand and strategic confidence. As strategic demand changes so does society's main institutions and organizations; and as strategic confidence changes so does the level of trust and co-operation in society. Dynamic order, therefore, is demand-determined and demand-driven.

This dynamic-strategy approach resolves the difficulties encountered by deductive economists in explaining the self-ordering nature of human society. Strategic demand replaces the demand for virtue in Adam Smith's societal system. And in doing so it rescues the problem of co-ordination from the swamps of mysticism. Also it demonstrates the limitations of the supply-side approaches of institutional evolutionists (Friedrich Hayek and Douglass North), the new evolutionary economists (Nelson and Winter), and the neoclassical general equilibriumists.

Part IV
The Driving Force

8 The Passive Nature of *Homo Economicus*

One of the central problems with orthodox growth theory is that it lacks an endogenous driving force. This is the legacy not only of the attempt to construct a dynamic model from pre-existing static production theory, but also of the use of an unrealistic and inappropriate model of human decision-making. These two issues are closely related. While the concept of *homo economicus*, which requires economic agents to make unerringly rational decisions, *may* be an appropriate assumption for shortrun static theory, it is a liability when modelling longrun dynamics. Even the modifications suggested by psychologists (bounded rationality), institutionalists (transaction costs), and evolutionists (passive selectivity) do not render *homo economicus* suitable as the driving agency in dynamic theory. But then neither does neoclassical production theory provide appropriate building blocks for such an enterprise. In this chapter I will outline the orthodox theory of human decision-making and how this has led to the omission of an endogenous driving force.

ORTHODOX MODELS OF HUMAN DECISION-MAKING

The conventional wisdom includes the neoclassical rationality model, the bounded rationality model, the new institutional model, and the evolutionary model. None of these, it will be argued, provides an effective basis for a general theory of longrun dynamics.

The neoclassical model

Neoclassical growth models are, as shown in Chapter 3, based on pre-existing microeconomic (largely production) theory. In order to employ neoclassical production functions in growth theory, it is necessary to retain the simplifying assumption of economic rationality. Only by abandoning microeconomics would it be possible to adopt a more realistic model of decision-making – a model that will provide the essential driving force in longrun dynamics.

The model of decision-making underlying all orthodox economics is intuitively attractive but fundamentally mistaken. It is widely assumed, at least by academics and intellectuals, that decision-makers possess mental models of the way the world – or at least that part of it that concerns them – works, that they exhaustively collect relevant information about alternative courses of

99

action, and that they efficiently process the data in the light of their models. In this manner, we are told, each and every economic agent is able to make choices that will maximize their utility as consumers, profits as producers, and net income as owners of the factors of production. Although this research model is widely accepted it is just not borne out by reality.

In particular, the neoclassical model of human behaviour is based upon the extreme assumptions that the average decision-maker possesses a *true* model of the way the world works, that he or she possesses *perfect* information, and that he or she is able to use the model and the data to *quickly and correctly* assess the probable outcomes of various well-known alternative options. This optimizing approach is adopted not because it is a realistic model of human behaviour, but because it enables the mathematical solution of economic theories based on it. It is concerned not to explore the process by which decisions are made, but merely to predict choice in the future.

This has long been the case in neoclassical economics. Yet more recently the Young Turks in the discipline have extended the assumption of economic rationality from the way economic agents respond to objective circumstances in the world around them to the subjective way they see the future. Since the mid-1970s the notion of rational expectations – popularized by the influential articles of Thomas Sargent and Neil Wallace (1975), Stanley Fischer (1977) and Robert Lucas (1976) – has come to dominate orthodox economic thinking. The roots of this concept can be found in the work of John Muth (1961) and, of course, Friedman (1968) and Phelps (1968). Rational expectations is a simple yet seductive idea; that economic agents are able not only to understand the world around them but also to anticipate what will happen in the future and to take pre-emptive action. While rational expectations is only an assumption with no supportive evidence, it has been employed widely throughout the economics discipline. In particular it has been employed to analyse the alleged inflation–unemployment relationship, namely that, while unexpected inflation temporarily lowers unemployment below its natural rate, expected inflation has no impact on unemployment. A corollary to this is that only unexpected price increases lead to increases in output.

Neoclassical economists have failed to take seriously J.M. Keynes' argument in *The General Theory* (1936: ch. 12) that, as investors base their decision-making on the 'state of long-term expectation' and, as there are no data about the future, neoclassical mathematic models are useless. Keynes' suggestion, however, that investment decisions are based on 'animal spirits' really amounts to saying that he has no idea what they are based on. He just treats it as an untested psychological law. In Chapter 9, I have developed a realist model of individual behaviour that dispenses with both the superhuman elements of economic rationality and the entire concept of rational expectations; and in Chapter 10, I examine data on the growth–inflation relationship that refutes the rational expectations hypothesis.

But those economists who are concerned less with theoretical elegance and more with reality have been critical of the neoclassical model. They have demanded a more realistic model of decision-making in order to attain greater precision in explaining and predicting economic behaviour at both the macro and micro levels. Two different approaches have emerged from this dissatisfaction: the bounded rationality approach of Cyert and March (1963), Simon (1956, 1982), and Williamson (1975); and the new institutional economics approach of Hayek (1988) and North (1990). Advocates of both approaches are also more concerned with the *process* of decision-making than those in the neoclassical paradigm.

Bounded rationality

The bounded rationality approach attempts to identify the 'cognitive' limitations of the decision-maker – which includes limitations of knowledge and computational ability – and to incorporate this into the analysis. It is, therefore, an approach concerned not only with the outcome of decision-making as in the neoclassical model, but also with the process by which decisions are made. Various models of bounded rationality have been constructed by relaxing one or more of the restrictive assumptions made in the neoclassical model. Justification for these procedures usually concerns laboratory-based psychological research (Hogarth 1980). This research suggests, in the first place, that the major expenditure of time and money in the decision-making process occurs in the search for and evaluation of various possible courses of action, rather than in making the final decision once the various alternatives are known. Neoclassical theory merely assumes that the alternatives are known and fixed from the beginning. In the second place, psychological research suggests that strong cognitive limits – in the form of real-world recognition and understanding – apply when evaluating the likely consequences of various alternatives. Third, the neoclassical assumption of utility maximization, or economic rationality, is unrealistic because it assumes computational abilities well beyond the capacity of the average decision-maker.

The best known response to these issues is the 'satisficing' approach of Herbert Simon (1956). Simon stresses the difficulties involved in making optimal choices owing to the complexity of computational problems, even when electronic computers are used. As he says: 'The complexity of the world is not limited to thousands or even tens of thousands of variables and constraints, nor does it always preserve the linearities and convexities that facilitate computation' (Simon 1987: 244). Accordingly, Simon argues, when the decision-maker is unable to optimize, or when the costs of doing so are too high, he will choose a 'satisfactory' rather than an optimal alternative. In this way only some of the constraints required for optimization will be satisfied. This Simon calls 'satisficing', in contrast to the neoclassical 'optimizing'. While the outcome of this decision-making approach may be satisfactory, there is no guarantee that a better solution could not be achieved by employing an alternative sub-optimal technique.

The important question here is: How does the decision-maker arrive at a satisfactory solution? What are the criteria for a 'satisficing' outcome? What is the process involved? Owing to his training in psychology and computer science it is probably not surprising that Simon ignores history, which is the real laboratory of economics, indeed of the social sciences as a whole, and turns to another deductive discipline in the behavioural sciences, psychology. Simon (1987: 244) says:

> Psychology proposes the mechanism of aspiration levels: if it turns out to be very easy to find alternatives that meet the criteria, the standards are gradually raised: if search continues for a long while without finding satisfactory alternatives, the standards are gradually lowered. Thus, by a kind of feedback mechanism, or 'tâtonnement', the decision maker converges toward a set of criteria that are attainable, but not without effort.

This 'aspiration-level' mechanism involves, we are told, much simpler computations than the neoclassical optimization procedure.

Yet this approach is not without its costs, both for the decision-maker and the economic theorist. The decision-maker has no way of knowing whether he or she has made the correct choice. There will always be a nagging concern that a better deal could have been made, together with an anxiety that someone may undercut him or her at any time. These costs, which may adversely affect the outcome of decision-making, are the consequence of a model in which choices are made by individuals in isolation from each other. A more realistic model, which eliminates these costs, can (and, in Chapter 9, will) be derived from historical research. Despite Simon's (1987: 244) claim to the contrary, this psychological model is not a better explanation of 'what is known empirically of actual choice behaviour and of the computational limits of the human mind'. This model is the outcome of artificial experiments that do not encompass the full range of decision-making possibilities. In other words, the games that laboratory subjects are asked to play are not the games that they do play in reality. The experimental question asked is how individuals make decisions under certain controlled conditions, rather than how they do so in reality.

There are costs for the economic theorist in adopting the satisficing approach. And Simon readily acknowledges these. The theory based on this model of choice is not only less elegant than neoclassical theory, but the strength and variety of the theorems that can be derived from this version of rationality are significantly diminished. In particular it does not provide a satisfactory basis for growth models based on neoclassical production theory. Also, predictions about behaviour using the satisficing rather than the optimizing model are either less precise with the same amount of empirical data, or require a great deal more data to achieve the same degree of precision. Those following in Simon's footsteps need to gather considerable information about 'aspiration levels' and about the way decision-makers adapt to different circumstances. But it is precisely this type of data that is difficult for researchers to obtain, unless one is willing to accept the results of simple experiments undertaken in psychology 'laboratories' that take this model for granted. No doubt the economist's choice between the alternative satisficing and optimizing models will depend on his or her objectives. Neither, I will argue, is realistic in a dynamic setting.

It is important to understand the type of model of human thought and action that underlies this approach to economic rationality. Simon regards human beings as 'information processing systems', and the metaphor for such a system that emerges constantly from his writings is the digital computer. Simon tells us 'that human beings, in their thinking and problem solving activities, operate as information processing systems' (Newell and Simon 1972: 47). The process by which this is supposed to take place is described as follows:

> Human problem solving... is to be understood by describing the task environment in which it takes place; the space the problem solver uses to represent the environment, the task, and the knowledge about it that he gradually accumulates; and the program the problem solver assembles for approaching the task... the problem solver's program extracts some of the structural information that is embedded in the task environment in order to find solutions by means of a highly selective search through the problem space (ibid.: 867–8).

This may be the way in which game-players solve problems, although even chess players and chess-playing programmes fall back on moves that have been successful in the past – that is, on history. Certainly it is not the way the average decision-maker operates on a daily basis.

The new institutionalism

The new institutionalists have also attempted to render the neoclassical model more realistic by relaxing the assumptions about perfect information, complete conceptual models of reality, and perfect computing abilities. While they share Simon's view of human beings as information-processing systems, they look back to an older American tradition of institutional economics, rather than to psychology, for an alternative model of decision-making. They argue that as information available to decision-makers is fragmentary and costly, and as their conceptual models of reality are incomplete, exchange between individuals gives rise to transaction costs, which call institutions, or societal rules, into being. These rules can be either formal, such as the laws of the land, or informal, such as customs. Generally accepted rules, therefore, are employed to overcome the costs and uncertainties of living in an imperfect world.

Evidence of this view, however, is conspicuous by its absence. Not only are institutions required to facilitate exchange in an imperfect world, but the imperfect world is the foundation stone for the new institutional economics. Remove that stone and the central role of institutions in a dynamic society collapses. As demonstrated elsewhere (Snooks 1997a: ch. 4), although new institutionalists like Douglass North have used history to *illustrate* their theories, they have not – indeed cannot – use it to prove their theories.

A DRIVING FORCE?

There is no endogenous driving force in the growth models of orthodox economics. Economic agents, who are merely assumed to make optimizing or satisficing choices, are passive rather than dynamic. This reaches its extreme expression in the new evolutionary economics which, taking its lead from sociobiology, treats economic agents as little better than automatons. Orthodox economists believe that a viable society will gravitate towards the most efficient outcomes obtainable under prevailing conditions. This tendency to equilibrium results not from the driving ambitions and foresight of economic agents, but from the exercise of passively rational choices in a receptive world. *Homo economicus* is employed to create a rational self-adjusting world. It is like a clockwork world that has been wound up by an invisible watchmaker.

Classical and neoclassical growth theory

Classical economists such as Adam Smith, David Ricardo, and J.S. Mill thought that a viable economic system contains systematic forces that cause it to gravitate towards longrun equilibrium (Milgate 1987: 179–81). It was on this belief that Adam Smith's concept of natural prices – the level to which prices would tend in the longrun – was based. But this idea can be seen most clearly in the classical growth model in which economic change is identified with convergence to longrun equilibrium. This stationary state would, it was believed, be maintained until it was disturbed by an exogenous shock. There is no endogenous driving force in classical economics.

Neoclassical economists continued this preoccupation with equilibrium analysis, but increasingly came to focus on intertemporal equilibrium. This began with Alfred Marshall (1920: bk V), who distinguished between 'temporary equilibrium', 'short-run equilibrium', and 'long-run equilibrium' when analysing demand and supply, and was extended by Friedrich Hayek (1928), E. Lindahl (1929), and John Hicks (1939) before the Second World War, and by Malinvaud, Arrow, and Debreu after it (Milgate 1987: 182). While this changing conception of equilibrium, which possesses a sequential nature, undermined the classical view of a natural price, it did not alter the orthodox conception of economic change. There are two major examples of this idea of longrun gravitation to equilibrium – the natural rate of unemployment concept, and the neoclassical growth model. As is discussed in more detail in Chapter 13, the widely employed concept of the natural rate of unemployment (or NAIRU) was developed by Milton Friedman (1968) on the Smithian idea that in the longrun an economy will persistently gravitate toward its 'natural' or steady-state equilibrium rate of unemployment. It is a convenient assumption made by a supply-side paradigm to explain economic change without modelling dynamic demand. This is also the case, as discussed in Chapter 3, with orthodox theorizing about economic growth. The central feature of the neoclassical growth model is convergence to the 'steady state' – the equilibrium growth path. Economic growth in this tradition, therefore, is still seen as the gravitation towards an equilibrium generated by the underlying conditions of production, rather than the outcome of an endogenous driving force.

Even the 'new' growth theory lacks a realistic internal driving force despite its claim to have generated a number of 'endogenous' growth models. The attempt to endogenize technological change is based on assumptions made about the production process. Technological change, as outlined in Chapter 3, has been introduced into the neoclassical growth model, at first by assuming that learning-by-doing is an *unintended* consequence of investment, and later through unsatisfactorily explained investment in R&D. Technological change emerges in the extended neoclassical model, therefore, from assumptions made about the production process. Clearly there is no endogenous driving force in these supply-side growth models.

Keynesian growth models

John Maynard Keynes (1936) also challenged the classical concept of long-run equilibrium, but in a more fundamental way. He focused on the adjustment not of prices but of output and employment. By denying that the economy was gravitating inevitably to full employment equilibrium, Keynes was forced to consider the ultimate determinants of investment and consumption rather than just taking them as given. In his famous analysis of the marginal efficiency of capital, Keynes introduced the concept of 'the state of long-term expectation', which depended on the confidence of investors. Unable to explain this state of confidence, or 'spontaneous optimism', which defies 'mathematical calculation', Keynes accepted it as the outcome of a fundamental 'psychological law' embodying the 'animal spirits' of mankind. This was, in fact, an admission that he did not understand the ultimate driving force in human society. Yet, while unable to model the driving force, Keynes was at least aware that something more than the rational calculation of economic man was at work (something the rational expectationists subsequently forgot), and that it had more to do with biological desires than with intellectual ideas. Clearly he thought that economic agents were more than passive participants in the game of life. For the purposes of dynamic analysis, this was Keynes' most important contribution.

But when Roy Harrod attempted to draw out the dynamic implications of *The General Theory*, he completely overlooked this fundamental issue. Instead he analysed the more topical issue of the economy's failure to automatically gravitate towards the full-employment level of output. In order to focus on the special conditions required to achieve the full-employment equilibrium growth path – the steady state – Harrod assumed that growth was exogenously determined and was communicated to the economy through the impact of the 'independent' variables of population and technological change on the capital stock. In doing so he missed an opportunity to build on the major insight of *The General Theory* concerning the longrun determinants of investment. But, I suppose, that was inevitable in a profession dominated by deductivists. Accordingly, there is no endogenous driving force in Harrod's growth model.

By missing the major dynamic contribution of *The General Theory*, Harrod unwittingly led the way to a neoclassical takeover of dynamic theory. By focusing on the technical conditions for the steady state, he provided an opening for neoclassical economists to employ existing production theory to explore growth-related issues. The subsequent boom in publications on the neoclassical growth model discouraged any macroeconomic approach based on Keynesian insights about the driving force in human society.

Evolutionary models

Economists dissatisfied with neoclassical growth theory turned not to Keynesian insights but to evolutionary models in biology. In the main these dissenters have been attracted to the neo-Darwinian version rather than to Darwin's own model. While Darwin emphasized the 'struggle for existence' between fiercely competing individual life-forms, which he called 'the war of nature', the more fashionable neo-Darwinian, or sociobiological version, emphasizes the 'reproductive success' of individuals. Elsewhere (Snooks

1997: 98–101) I have argued this is a major distortion of Darwin's work, because it eliminates the driving force from the evolutionary process. It is this very feature that seems to attract those economists interested in evolution, largely because *homo economicus* is a passive rather than a dynamic decision-maker. This characteristic is evident in the evolutionary approach to institutional change taken by both Friedrich Hayek and Douglass North, but it dominates that by Richard Nelson and Sidney Winter.

Hayek (1988) views human progress as an outcome of the evolution of societal rules, or institutions. As we have seen, he adopts a simple neo-Darwinian explanation of institutional change, involving the generation of institutional variation through a process of group selection which, if successful, becomes dominant in the 'rule pool' by an increase in the population of the innovating society, which is thereby able to absorb other less successful societies (Hayek 1988: 16). This hypothesis is very similar to the sociobiological mechanism known as 'reproductive success'. Like the sociobiologists, Hayek employs a passive selective mechanism in his evolutionary system, despite all that he might say about competitive processes.

Douglass North (1990) in his later work also employs an evolutionary model, yet one inspired by neoclassical economics as well as Darwin (even if indirectly through the old institutional economists), in which the selective mechanism is 'adaptive efficiency'. This concept of evolution involves the adoption of more efficient rules under competitive pressures. Owing to different information processes – involving different costs of information and different conceptual models (owing to different cultures) – institutional change in different societies takes different evolutionary paths. There may be little rapprochement between these paths because, North claims, evolution is a path-dependent process involving increasing returns and fragmentary information feedback which may lead to institutional 'lock-in' that resists competitive pressures between nations. Path-dependence, therefore, involves non-reversibility which generally characterizes evolutionary processes. It is through path-dependence that North attempts to explain why inefficient institutions can persist in some countries in the longrun. There is little room for individual initiative in this impersonal evolutionary process. The absence of an endogenous driving force, in North's hypothesis, therefore, derives from both its neoclassical and evolutionary origins.

The new evolutionary economics pioneered by Nelson and Winter (1982) is closer to sociobiology than either Hayek or North. There is little room here for the driving nature of individuals struggling to survive and prosper. As outlined in Chapter 4, Nelson and Winter focus on organizations (firms) rather than individuals, and they see the process of innovation and imitation of 'routines' (equivalent to genes) as an outcome of something equivalent to 'reproductive success' in sociobiology rather than to 'natural selection' in the original Darwinian model. The world of new evolutionary economics, like the world of sociobiology, is robotic in nature, with individuals or groups of individuals operating in a highly constrained manner. Survival depends not on the aggressive pursuit in a highly competitive world of a freely chosen and successful dynamic strategy, but on being able to maximize its 'routines' (genes) in the routines pool (gene pool). Once again there is no driving force here, only a passive sorting device of organizational routines.

CONCLUSIONS

Modern growth theory lacks the most important element required by a general theory of dynamics, namely an endogenous driving force. There are three main reasons for this. First, growth theorists have adopted an unrealistic and inappropriate model of human decision-making. Secondly, these theorists have attempted to construct growth models from neoclassical production theory, which is based on the simplifying assumption of economic rationality. And *homo economicus* is a passive rather than a dynamic concept. Growth is seen as the adjustment process of a rational economic system rather than the outcome of an endogenous driving force in an uncertain and hostile world. Finally, the neo-Darwinian evolutionary theory adopted by those dissatisfied with neoclassical growth models is characterized by passive selective devices. Hence, modern growth theory has no real engine of change. A more realistic model of human decision-making is outlined in the next chapter.

9 The Dynamic Nature of 'Materialist Man'

The driving force in any dynamic model should arise from a realistic analysis of human motivation and decision-making. This can only be achieved by observing mankind in history rather than in the psychologist's laboratory. We need, therefore, to construct an inductive model based on extensive historical research. The intention in this chapter is to construct a more realistic model of human behaviour and to show how this can provide the endogenous driving force for a new theory of longrun dynamics.

This new model has three main characteristics. The first is concerned with motivation, the second with the decision-making process, and the third with the role of rules in decision-making. Briefly, the driving force in this model is the biologically determined desires of mankind; its objectives are to satisfy these desires by maximizing the probability of survival and prosperity; its process involves an interaction between the unfolding dynamic strategy and the investment decisions of strategic pioneers and their followers; and societal rules are an outcome not of the cost of information but of strategic demand and the costs of analytical thinking for a species which, despite its intellectual achievements, is essentially intuitive rather than cerebral in nature. Institutions, therefore, are employed to facilitate the dominant dynamic strategy and to do so in a way that economizes on the scarcest of all resources in nature – intelligence.

THE DRIVING FORCE

The nature of materialist man

An extensive study of the dynamics of human society, the results of which are presented in *The Dynamic Society* (1996) and *The Ephemeral Civilization* (1997a), make it clear that human decision-makers are not the passive sort embodied in the orthodox concept of *homo economicus*. And even less so of the type envisaged by the followers of sociobiology. In reality, decision-makers are driven by an intense desire to survive and prosper. This can be seen operating throughout the history of human civilization and, indeed, throughout the past two million years since the emergence of mankind. Elsewhere I have called this 'the law of human motivation' (Snooks 1998: ch. 8).

Historical analysis suggests that biologically determined desires – the result of genetic change over almost four billion years – are far more important than intellectual ideas in human motivation and, hence, in human behaviour. Indeed, human decision-making is driven not by intellectual objectives but by animal desires. John Maynard Keynes' intuition about the importance of 'animal spirits' is borne out by historical research. The desire to survive and, having survived, to satisfy our biological appetites is the driving force in society. In recognition of the difference between the passive decision-maker in orthodox economics and the dynamic decision-maker in reality, I draw a distinction between *homo economicus* and **materialist man**.

Of course, the human intellect does play an important role in the operation and progress of human society, but that role is limited to facilitating the satisfaction of our basic desires. In fact, as demonstrated elsewhere (Snooks 1997: 121–7), the difference in the pursuit of this objective between human and non-human species is not a matter of kind but a matter of degree. Human beings merely rely to a greater degree on the intellect to satisfy their genetically determined desires than other species because of their larger and more complex brains.

Intellectuals are loath to accept the primacy of desires as a driving force and the relegation of ideas to a facilitating device. Economists are no different. When discussing the relative importance of ideas and desires in determining the progress of civilization, economists, even of the calibre of J.S. Mill (1875, I: 257) and F.A. Hayek (1988: 12–18), always choose ideas. Why? A major reason, as suggested elsewhere (Snooks 1996: ch. 6), is that the status and wealth of intellectuals depends on their success in persuading the rest of society, or at least the ruling elite, that ideas are primarily responsible for the achievements of human civilization.

Intellectuals also find it difficult to accept the self-centred nature of human beings. They have a faith in the fundamental altruism of mankind, despite all the evidence to the contrary. It is a faith that rises above the ever-present exploitation, physical and psychological abuse, betrayal, abandonment, dishonesty, corruption, and theft not just in society in general but in the family in particular; and that rises above the exploitation and war between nations and even between regions or ethnic/political groups within nations.

The issue of altruism needs to be re-evaluated. According to general usage, 'altruism' is a principle for action by which an individual will deliberately attempt to improve the welfare of others even if it reduces his or her own welfare. Altruism, therefore, is an end in itself rather than a means to a different end. Hence, any act aimed at maximizing the welfare of self, but which in the process improves the welfare of others, cannot be regarded as altruism. To do so would be to confuse ends and means. If the end is the maximization of individual material advantage, and the means is co-operation with other individuals who also gain, then self-interest rather than altruism is the driving force. Much of the recent writing in economics has confused ends with means. Co-operation is not the same as altruism. This does not deny that some individuals are altruistic in the proper sense of the word, just that they are in a small minority.

Economists have long debated the altruism–selfishness issue. A relatively new element in this debate (Becker 1976; Frech 1978; Samuelson 1983; Bergstrom 1995) is the concept of 'kin selection' borrowed from sociobiology where it emerged about 30 years ago (Hamilton 1964). It is rather curious that some economists should take this idea from sociobiology rather than directly investigate the issue historically, because sociobiology is a science in which individual *behaviour* (rather than desires) is genetically determined owing to the mechanical selection process of differential reproduction (Snooks 1997: ch. 5). When applied to the social sciences, sociobiological theories generate models that provide no freedom of choice (for example, Bergstrom 1995).

A realist model of human behaviour

By using the historical method, I have been able to develop a more realistic model of human behaviour – the concentric spheres model – that is based on the notion of genetically determined desires and is consistent with individual freedom in both human and non-human species (Snooks 1994a: 50–1; 1997: ch. 2). It can be used to sort out the altruism–selfishness issue. In this model, the way in which an individual behaves in relation to other individuals depends not on the 'genetic distance' between them as in the kin selection model, but on the 'economic distance' or importance of other individuals or groups in maximizing the material interests of the self.[1] In this model, represented in Figure 9.1, the individual is at the centre of a set of concentric spheres that define the varying strength of co-operative relationships between the self and all other individuals and groups in society. The strength of the economic relationship between the self and any other individual or group – which is measured by the **economic distance** between them – will depend on how essential they are to the maximization of the self's utility. Those aspects of the self's objective function that require the greatest co-operation – such as the generation of love, companionship, and children – will be located on spheres with the shortest economic distance from the centre. For the typical individual, spouse and children will occupy the sphere closest to the centre, with other relatives, friends, workmates, neighbours, members of various religious and social clubs, other members of his or her socio-economic group, city, state, nation, and group of nations, occupying those concentric spheres that progressively radiate out from the centre. As the economic distance between the centre and each sphere increases, the degree of co-operation between them diminishes.[2]

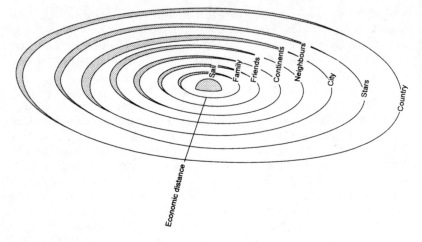

Figure 9.1   The concentric spheres model of human behaviour
Source: Snooks (1997a:30).

Underlying the concentric spheres model are two balancing sets of forces, one centrifugal and the other centripetal. The centrifugal force is the incessant desire of the self to survive and prosper – a desire that leads the typical individual to place himself before all others. This force provides individuals with ambition and competitive energy. The centripetal force (the economic gravity holding society together) is the need of self to co-operate with other individuals and groups in order to more effectively achieve its objectives, through the pursuit of the dominant dynamic strategy. It is through this interaction between competition and co-operation that the individual maximizes the probability of his or her survival and prosperity, and that social order is created from the primordial chaos. These forces find expression in the 'primary laws of history' (Snooks 1998: ch. 8).

But exactly what is it that enables self-seeking individuals to co-operate with each other? The usual answer is that it is something called 'trust'. This response, however, merely begs a further question: What generates trust? Institutionalists argue that trust is an outcome of the evolution of formal and informal rules that determine predictable and co-operative conduct. Yet no one has proposed an evolutionary model that can convincingly explain the changing nature of societal rules, particularly when sharp institutional reversals occur, as they do quite regularly in history.

The dynamic-strategy model presented in this book tackles the problem from a different and more realistic direction. It suggests that the reason chaos, which results from the breakdown of the centripetal force, does not occur in any given society is that it is successfully pursuing a viable dynamic strategy. This successful dynamic strategy leads to a workable network of competitive/co-operative relationships, together with all the necessary supporting rules and organizations. Individuals in this society, therefore, relate directly to the successful dynamic strategy and only indirectly to each other. It is not a matter of mutual trust as such – of having confidence in the nature of other individuals – but rather having confidence in the wider dynamic strategy in which they are all vitally involved.

Hence, it is not individual trust, but **strategic confidence** that keeps society from flying apart. What we know as 'trust' is merely derived from strategic confidence. And as the dynamic strategy unfolds, the nature of strategic confidence and, hence, trust changes in subtle ways. The dynamic-strategy model, therefore, can explain the nature of investor confidence that was left hanging in Keynes' *The General Theory* (1936).

Strategic confidence – the economic gravity of the concentric spheres model of behaviour – lasts only as long as the success of a society's dynamic strategy. Once the dynamic strategy has been exhausted and cannot be replaced, strategic confidence declines and, in extreme cases, vanishes entirely. And as strategic confidence falls, so too does social trust and co-operation, leading to the fragmentation of society as families turn in on themselves and, in extreme cases, as individuals begin to abandon even their families. This implies, in terms of Figure 9.1, the stripping away of the concentric spheres one by one until the self is left isolated, attempting to live by his wits alone. This announces the victory of centrifugal over centripetal forces and the destruction of the former society.

Strategic confidence, which is the outcome of a successful dynamic strategy, is communicated to the citizens of that society in two main ways. The first and most important mechanism involves a continuous increase in material standards of living. While this flow of material returns is maintained, so is strategic confidence. But once this stream is interrupted, confidence begins to decline. This is why Western governments that are inspired by economic-rationalist policies are playing a very dangerous game by deliberately disrupting growth through their deflationary policies in the hunt for a fictional enemy called inflation. The second, and less important, mechanism is the use of ideology to draw society's citizens into acceleration of the dominant dynamic strategy.[3] It is less important than the income mechanism because it is only effective, and then only in a reinforcing manner, when living standards are rising or, at least, not falling. Nonetheless it is a mechanism that is employed more extensively, yet less effectively, when the dominant dynamic strategy begins to fail.

THE STRATEGIC-IMITATION MODEL OF DECISION-MAKING

In reality there is little fundamental difference between the basic neo-classical model of decision-making and the bounded-rationality or institutional extensions of it. Both sets of revisionists accept the view that each decision-maker makes each and every decision in isolation by collecting as much information as is economically possible about the subject under consideration, by applying an appropriate conceptual model to that data, and by computing a rational outcome. The major difference between the parent neoclassical model and the various revisionist versions is reflected in the degree of perfection they are willing to assume about the responses of economic agents to the present and their foresight about the future. While the neoclassicists assume a perfect world, the revisionists assume a world that is less than perfect. Their response is merely to release some of the assumptions of the basic neoclassical model. But this is not the way to develop a better theory of human behaviour.

To develop a better theory we need to abandon the present view of human decision-making – developed by atypical individuals with a comparative advantage in abstract thinking – as a problem-solving process of information processing. Despite the inevitable protestations of scholars, human beings are not intellectual game-players of the digital computer variety. Also, the average person makes no attempt to model the world in his or her head. The only 'models' they possess are non-functional, such as conspiracy models (which ascribe their difficulties to various minority groups), religious models (which provide divine justification and support), or models of self-justification (which convert selfish motives into altruistic ones). And these survive largely because they are *not* confronted by information about reality. A comprehensive, rather than a selective, study of history demonstrates quite clearly that human decisions are just not made in that way. Ironically, even neoclassical economists abandon their models and rely on intuition when involved in national policy-making (Snooks 1997a: ch. 13). A better theory must be based not on psychology or institutionalism, but on historical experience.

Historical experience suggests that the decision-making process is imitative rather than isolationist, and is dualistic rather than holistic. While this cannot be established in the psychology laboratory, it can be observed in historical reality. Unlike the established models, it can explain the remarkable cycles of fashion – the bandwagon effect – in decision-making in all aspects of human life. Many have commented upon curious fashions in dress, diet, popular and classical culture, art, architecture, customs, rituals and ceremonies, technologies, religions, and lifestyles (Plato, *Republic*: paras 395–7; Schumpeter 1949; Mises 1958; Dawkins 1989). To this we can add the current fashion in OECD countries of economic policies that focus on price stability at the expense of unemployment and growth (Snooks 1997a: 498–503).

An understanding of these fashions is central to an understanding of how society works. This can be illustrated by considering an example with which we are all familiar – the way fashions change in relation to health. Because the objective in human society is to survive and prosper, the average person is highly anxious about the state of his or her health. Yet despite this critically important objective, the average person has no useful mental model about how the body works, and makes no attempt to collect detailed information about the effects of different foods, lifestyles, and exercises on human health. Instead, we follow the advice of recognized 'experts' (even when some of these are really quacks), and imitate the lifestyles of famous and successful individuals. Of course, the joke is that even the experts do not possess 'true' models or adequate information and, as a result, their advice is constantly changing. And as the advice changes so too do the lifestyles of our anxious health-conscious community. At one time we are told that dairy products are good for us and that vigorous exercise, unlike walking, is dangerous; then we are told that dairy products and mono-unsaturated fats are bad, polyunsaturated fats in abundance are good, and that jogging is essential; subsequently we are told to reduce our consumption of polyunsaturated fats in favour of mono-unsaturated fats and even dairy products, and substitute brisk walking for jogging; and at the time of writing the expert opinion is that any form of exercise, even in short bursts, is beneficial if the sum total comes to about 30 minutes a day (*Science* 1997: 1324–7). And so fashions in health ebb and flow as we imitate the famous and successful. The same is true of fashions in sexual attitudes, 'political correctness', religious and political movements and, of course, economic activity.

None of these fashions has been adequately explained in terms of the established models of decision-making. But they can be explained by the strategic-imitation model. In this model, the decision-making process can be divided into the pioneering and routine phases, with each part of the process being dominated by a different type of decision-maker – the strategic pioneer and the strategic follower. Each phase will be dealt with separately.

The pioneering phase

Investment in new ideas and projects is an extremely uncertain activity because little information of any kind about likely outcomes is available to the strategic pioneers, and it is a risky activity because of the high probability of failure for new ventures. As innovative ideas are without precedent, and as these ideas can change society in unpredictable ways, pioneers can only make informed guesses about likely outcomes. While they may use the limited information available to gauge the benefits and costs of what they are proposing, the pioneers operate more on intuition about outcomes and on faith in their own abilities. They have no foresight as assumed by the supporters of rational expectations. Individuals, mainly family and friends, supplying support in the form of financial and human capital do so because they share this belief in the pioneer's abilities. This is not an area of economic activity in which conservative financial institutions will want to be involved. They only finance routine decision-making.

The essential point to realize is that the **strategic pioneers** do not make their decisions in a vacuum. They work within the boundaries of an unfolding dynamic strategy, and respond to the changing incentives that it generates. In other words, the pioneers operate at the leading edge of the unfolding strategy and actively explore its economic potential. This involves the development of new substrategies which, within the technological strategy of the modern era, can be thought of as new **technological styles**. Hence, there is an interaction between the strategic pioneers and the unfolding dynamic strategy, which gives direction and meaning to their activities. While these activities are not random, many pioneers misread the signs and fail. Only a few succeed, but these provide the example for the many to follow. And it is this mass following that provides the driving energy for the strategic unfolding. The core of the dynamic-strategy model, therefore, is the interaction between the unfolding dynamic strategy and the strategic pioneers, which provides a dynamic structure that marks it off from other theories of economic growth.

The pioneers are few in number and even less significant in proportion to the total population of decision-makers. They are more ambitious, possess greater imaginative and intellectual skills, are prepared to take greater risks, have greater faith in themselves and, most importantly, have a greater perception of how the dynamic strategy is unfolding than the vast majority of routine decision-makers. They are driven by a greater abundance of biological desires that drive all life. When conspicuously successful, the pioneers are followed by large numbers of imitators. Needless to say, they are not always successful. Indeed, owing to the risks that attend untried ways, only a very small proportion of the pioneers are able to achieve their objectives. But, as the material rewards that fall into the hands of those who do succeed are very great, there is always a steady stream of those willing to test their ambitions, skills, and faith.

We are now in a position to discuss the mechanism by which successful pioneering decisions are made. There are two parts to this mechanism – the drive and ambition of imaginative risk-takers, and the competitive process of alternative investment projects. The pioneers invest most of their time not in the collection of information about alternative projects, nor in the development of conceptual models of reality, nor in the computation of optimal solutions, but rather in developing imaginative ideas that they *believe* will bring windfall gains and in demonstrating the successful outcomes of their ideas. These ideas may be arrived at from an awareness of the unfolding dynamic strategy achieved either through contemplation or, more likely, through a practical involvement in, or association with, a particular industry or activity. In essence, the pioneers provide the driving force required to propel their ideas and projects into the market place. And it is the market place of competing ideas and projects, shaped by the dominant dynamic strategy, that determines the outcome. Only a very small proportion of pioneers will successfully realize their material ambitions.

Success breeds success. The pioneers who get it right are provided with the rationale for what they have done. Successful feedback leads to further developments along the same lines. There is no need to examine alternatives while-ever individual pioneers are achieving the outcomes they desire. Only when the feedback is less favourable will they even consider alternative investment projects, and these will only be pursued if the benefits of the alternative exceed not only the costs of the new project but also the costs of scrapping the initial one. And this will probably only occur in the generation following the successful pioneering phase. By then the, initially pioneering, organization will have entered the routine phase of imitating the success of its forefathers or of others – unless a second-generation pioneer comes to the fore.

It is this pioneering mechanism – involving an intense competition between individuals pursuing competing ideas and projects – rather than the attempts by individuals to calculate the benefits and costs of alternative strategies that produces what might be regarded as optimal outcomes. In an important sense, the individual pioneers embody the alternative projects that the existing model either assumes to be given (neoclassical) or assumes that each individual attempts to determine and evaluate (revisionist). The effort of each pioneer is directed to the 'discovery' of a single project. Of course many of these projects will be duplicated or will involve some overlapping with other projects. What the pioneers require to become involved in this competitive process is not vast amounts of information and superhuman computing abilities, but rather great energy and imagination. They do not shop around for the best idea, they believe their idea is best. The market of competing pioneers, which is shaped by the unfolding dynamic strategy, will do the rest. It is from this competitive process that the most appropriate ideas will emerge.

The routine phase

Investment in routine ideas and projects by the **strategic followers** is characterized by far less uncertainty and by greater predictability than investment in entirely new ideas and strategies by the pioneers. After the pioneering phase, it is clear which projects are the most profitable. The successful pioneers, and their supporters, earn supernormal profits on their strategic investments. This provides, for the first time, positive information about the rates of return on investments in various alternative projects. The central question is how this information is used. In the routine phase, decision-makers do seek information but not of the kind envisaged by the traditional behavioural model. They do not seek detailed information on the costs and benefits of all possible alternatives. Rather they seek information on who and what is successful and why they are successful. Who is earning super-normal profits on what investments, and how can I get in on the act? Their aim is to imitate not the mechanism of digital computers, but the projects of the successful pioneers. This process, which I call **strategic imitation**, is based on the systematic observation of both human society and animal life in *The Dynamic Society* (1996) and *The Ephemeral Civilization* (1997a). It is one of the 'primary laws of history' (Snooks 1998: ch. 8).

Strategic imitation, of course, is more complex and interactive than this suggests, because once the followers apply imitated ideas to a commercial area, they will make further modifications of their own in the light of their own circumstances and experience. There are still many smaller battles to be fought, lost, and won in the attempt to work out the ideas of the pioneers for new environments. This will involve small changes and (lower order) innovations in response to slightly different economic and competitive environments in order to successfully (and sometimes unsuccessfully) apply these new ideas. The microeconomic process of strategic imitation, therefore, does involve scope for degrees of imagination and independence. It is an important characteristic of human nature that it is able to find scope for imaginative responses on even the smallest scale. This process of adaption has received considerable attention from others (Tunzelmann 1994; Magee 1997). But the important point to be made here is that the wider decision-making process has at its core an imitative mechanism.

This is not to say that some information on benefits and costs is not collected, just that it is collected to justify rather than to determine routine investment decisions. Such a procedure has three major advantages: it reduces the time taken to collect and process benefit–cost information; it provides the investor with additional confidence; and it is used to persuade conservative financial interests to make funds available for the enterprise. As the decision on what investment strategy to employ is made before any serious attempt to collect and process information, the difficulties involved in the formal benefit–cost calculation are reduced to manageable levels. The collection of data is highly selective, and the desired outcome is known in advance. The object of the exercise is to confirm decisions made on the basis of entirely different information – information about successful strategists and strategies. This confirmation provides additional confidence in the task ahead.

A major reason for at least attempting benefit–cost calculations is to obtain funding for investment proposals. This occurs in both the public and private sectors. More recently the public sector has, under pressure from taxpayers, adopted the procedure of commissioning feasibility studies on large public projects. These studies, however, are generally undertaken after, rather than before, major projects have been chosen. Their purpose is to justify rather than to determine public decision-making. And those undertaking the feasibility studies are chosen accordingly.

In the private sector, individuals and firms must convince financial organizations that the investment proposal is sound. These organizations have standard forms for roughly estimating likely income flows that are based upon the past financial performance of the individual or organization and on the value of any realizable assets. Even banks do not attempt to gather vast amounts of information nor do they employ complex computer models to calculate likely future returns on proposed investment projects. They merely look at whether or not this individual or firm has previously succeeded or failed and how successful others have been in the past when pursuing similar projects. In effect, this exercise is merely a formalization of the imitative procedure undertaken by all routine decision-makers. It does not attempt to calculate the benefits and costs of all alternative projects as required by the neoclassical and revisionist models.

The information required for strategic imitation is, in contrast to that required in the neoclassical model, readily available and is easily evaluated. We gain it from direct observation of those around us, from professional advice, from the media, and from books, magazines, and electronic sources. In the past the main form of imitation was through direct observation of local celebrities. While this was probably more important then than it is today in sophisticated societies, we are still only too aware of the *nouveaux riches* in our midst. Mankind possesses a primitive and unquenchable need to display the objects of material success. The intense desire to imitate the successful is matched only by an intense desire to display the fruits of success. It is true that imitation is the sincerest form of flattery. The only difference between sophisticated and primitive societies, apart from the scale of material success, is the way in which this interactive mechanism of display and imitation is effected. While in the past the main mechanism was word-of-mouth, today the media play a major role. Most of us gather a large proportion of our **imitative information** from the media which specialize in watching the rich and successful and in sharing this information, often in the most crudely voyeuristic form, to its readers and viewers. We are treated to a continuous parade of the successes to be imitated – and the failures to be avoided. This information is not the stuff of benefit–cost calculations, but of whom we should imitate if we are to be successful in life.

Popular books and magazines are also important sources of information for routine decision-making. Once again these sources supply not the type of information required to undertake benefit–cost calculations, but information about who or what should be emulated and how we should do so. This type of imitative information covers all aspects of our lives, not just investment decision-making. Hence it is a fertile source of data for the fashions that continually sweep through human society. By browsing the shelves of popular bookshops and newsagencies, we discover an almost endless range of specialized magazines and books on every facet of our lives at work, at home, and at leisure. We are shown who are the most successful in material terms, what their opulent lifestyles are like, and how we can imitate them in even the most modest ways. We are told about their businesses and investments; about their houses, gardens, swimming pools, and tennis courts; about their motor vehicles, yachts, holidays, clothes, hairstyles, lovers, children, and their various leisure interests. And we are told how to obtain some of these things for ourselves. These magazines and books are not just for entertainment. They are also for instruction – to enable us to imitate the successful. It is this information that feeds our desires and thereby fuels the driving force in human society.

Increasingly the imitative information obtained through popular books and magazines is being provided through computer software and international computer network systems. This has been called, somewhat extravagantly, the 'information superhighway'. I say 'extravagantly', because it is a function already provided through the media and popular books and magazines, and because its promoters like to give the impression that this information will be the basis for some sort of intellectual revolution. In fact, what the 'information superhighway' will provide in the main is popular entertainment and imitative information, not the type of intellectual information originally carried on the Internet. There is no mass market for hard ideas and facts, and there never will be. And, as an article in *Time* reported (3 July 1995: 38, 40), a recent survey suggests 'one of the largest (if not the largest) recreational application of users on computer networks' is trading in sexually explicit imagery! What will not receive pride of place on the 'information superhighway' is information that will enable subscribers to undertake detailed benefit–cost calculations of the type envisaged by the neoclassical model. Why? The answer is that there is little demand for this type of information, either in electronic or book/magazine form, precisely because materialist decision-making is not made in this way. But what the Internet has achieved is a revival of the role of word-of-mouth as a means of distributing imitative information; this time globally rather than locally.[4]

What is it that drives the followers to imitate the pioneers? There appears to be a genetically determined desire to do as well if not better than our neighbours, and the fear that if we do not run with the herd something nasty will happen (possibly perpetrated by the herd itself which mistrusts dissidents). This is something we share with all other species in nature. It is a central part of the desire to survive and prosper, which always emerges in competitive environments. In the case of our own species it amounts to good old-fashioned envy regarding the prosperity of others. Imitation comes easily and pleasurably to us. It is a natural outcome of one of our most conspicuous characteristics – mimicry. And, as discussed elsewhere (Snooks 1997: 122–6), it is a characteristic we share with other animal species. In childhood we learn through mimicry, in youth we amuse ourselves and our peers by mimicking others, and in our later years we laugh along with professional comedians whose stock-in-trade is mimicry. It has a more serious purpose, too, as the basis for human decision-making.

There is a darker side to the process of imitation that reinforces the natural desire to be part of the crowd. In every society there are some who react against the crowd. These are the dissenters, the original thinkers – those who dare to be different. They would appear to be less well adapted genetically to survive and prosper. And as such they will either be forced to conform or will be rooted out of society. Although the dissenters are always in a small minority, they are seen by the crowd as a threat to the survival and prosperity of the majority. This can be seen throughout history in the way society has turned against highly original thinkers like Socrates, Galileo, and Darwin; it can be seen in the widespread persecution of religious and political minorities; it can be seen in the vilification of individuals who speak out against prevailing attitudes on issues like race, sex, gender, and immigration; and it can be seen in the attempted repression by academic societies of original thinkers who challenge the conventional wisdom. This predictable intolerance works to strengthen the mechanism of strategic imitation.

In sum, what is the imitative process of decision-making? It comprises two elements. The first of these involves the immediate strategic followers who, in the pursuit of survival and prosperity, attempt to imitate the actions of successful pioneers. The second of these is the market of innumerable opportunists, all jostling for a share of the supernormal profits first generated by the pioneers. Only the most skilful or the most fortunate of the followers will reap more than normal profits – and even then only for a limited period – while some will fail completely. The eventual outcome for any society operating in a competitive international framework will approach the optimal, not because individuals were able to estimate that outcome, but because they followed the successful pioneers and were tested in the market place. There is, therefore, no place in this realist model for rational expectations.

The strategic-imitation model has more in common with the theory of J.A. Schumpeter (1939, 1949) than any other. The reason is, no doubt, that Schumpeter's theory of innovation and economic development also incorporates historical observation. Schumpeter argues that innovations emerge from an economy in equilibrium when the 'social climate' favours the emergence of 'New Firms' led by enterprising 'New Men'. Owing to the creation of monopoly profits, opportunistic imitators enter these new fields in 'clusters'. This leads to an upswing in economic activity that continues until the monopoly profits are driven down to normal levels and the supply of innovations dries up. These innovations include new goods, new processes, new markets, new resources, and new industrial organizations.

This was not the source of my strategic-imitation model. Indeed, there are important differences between us. First, the dynamic-strategy model incorporates a theory of decision-making (the strategic-imitation model) that is relevant to the entire society, whereas Schumpeter's model only attempts to explain why the class of 'New Men', who have a propensity to innovate, emerge, and why they are imitated by others. Secondly, the dynamic-strategy model attempts to explain the emergence and development of broad strategies and substrategies, while Schumpeter's model is really only an explanation of the upswing of the business cycle; it does not really explain the longrun growth rate (Higgins 1959: 137). Third, in my model the strategic pioneers respond to the incentives generated by an unfolding dynamic strategy, whereas Schumpeter's innovators emerge in response to a vaguely defined 'social climate'; my model has a dynamic structure that is lacking in Schumpeter's model. Finally, the dynamic-strategy model incorporates a theory about the fundamental reason for imitation in decision-making – which I have called **intellectual economizing** – and Schumpeter's does not.

THE ROLE OF RULES

What is the role of rules in human decision-making? The existence of rules is widely assumed to be evidence for the institutionalist argument about the costs of information. To the contrary, the theory of human behaviour developed here suggests that rules are evidence not of the costs of obtaining information, but of the costs of thinking. Decision-making rules, in other words, emerge from an attempt to economize on nature's most scarce resource – the intellect. The human race is the only species in the last four billion years that has had the capacity to think creatively but, I claim, even we are basically intuitive rather than intellectual in nature. We respond to desires rather than ideas. Ideas are only used by society, and then sparingly, to facilitate the achievement of our desires.

Despite the fact that modern man emerged at least 100 000 years ago, thinking is not an activity that comes easily to us. Systematic thinking can only be achieved after many years of training. While originality in highly formalized thinking – using symbols and a set of simple rules as in mathematics – can be achieved after 15 to 20 years of training, originality in less formalized thinking – the detection of complex relationships between variables in real-world processes – can only be achieved after about 40 years of intensive training. As abstract thinking is a very scarce resource most people develop routines and rules in order to conduct their daily lives. Even academics, who deal with ideas on a professional basis, go through much of their professional work and their daily lives using formal and informal rules. While intensive thinking may be undertaken when designing research programmes and in drawing conclusions from research results, the major part of scholarly activity involves routine data collection and highly repetitive experiments. And even much of the interpretation of evidence relies on mechanical rules of statistical inference, such as the diagnostic tests in econometrics. The old saying that research is 99 per cent perspiration and 1 per cent inspiration is not far from the mark. Even pure research relies heavily on the existing body of knowledge. Intellectuals, like everyone else, are forced to economize on this extremely scarce resource. We reserve thinking for any unfamiliar or critical problems that arise – yet even here we prefer to follow others who have successfully negotiated these problems rather than think about them ourselves – and we employ rules and custom, which are flexible rather than rigid, for the rest. There are parallels here with the way scarce brain cells are employed in nature. Animals at the top of the food chain (lions and tigers) are able to devote a higher proportion of their brains to the problem of survival than to the production of fatty acids by consuming animals (cattle and sheep) that specialize in this type of production.

Could artificial intelligence (AI) be the answer? Although progress since the mid-1950s (the international conference on AI at Dartmouth College in 1956) has been much slower than expected, critical observers suggest that recent developments have been encouraging and that the 'goal of a general artificial intelligence is in sight, and the 21st-century world will be radically changed as a result' (Lenat 1996: 18). While this will certainly help us to economize on that scarce resource, 'natural intelligence', it will not radically change the way we make decisions. We will continue to imitate the successful and will employ AI to gather imitative information rather than benefit–cost information, not only because there are no data about the future but also because we just do not make decisions as neoclassical economists believe. AI will merely become an important instrument in the timeless process of strategic imitation.

Yet, despite the fact that intelligence is a very scarce resource, those who specialize in its development – scholars, academics, and intellectuals – receive no more than a modest return for their services. These specialists do not possess a relatively high marginal product as their services are not in great demand. Why? The answer is obvious. Despite the size of our brains, humans are not intellectual beings. We do not use complex systems of thought to make day-to-day decisions, and we do not pursue intellectual leisure activities. The size of the market for intellectual ideas and hard facts about reality, even in the most highly educated societies, is pathetically small. On the one hand, the best decision-makers are decisive 'men of action' who operate more on intuition than intellect, and on the other we prefer uncomplicated entertainment to intellectual pursuits. Certainly both our leaders (political and business) and our entertainers (popular culture and sport) receive much higher material returns than our intellectuals.

Little reflection is required to see why this is so. We need only think – briefly of course – about the way we spend our lives. How much intensive and sustained thinking is involved? At work we rely heavily on established procedures, generally established by others. Even if we were responsible for these routines, the thinking involved is restricted to the establishment phase. In such an environment, change, which causes us to re-evaluate and to solve new problems, appears burdensome. It possesses a significant cost. We do it reluctantly and only at all because of the pressure of competition. Without competition there would be little intensive or sustained thinking. This is what having a quiet life is all about – not having to think.

When we return to our homes in the evenings and weekends we are quick to turn our backs on the competitive pressures of our work environments and to engage in leisure activities that do not require systematic thought. We submerge ourselves in a variety of activities including craft work, listening to music, watching sport or other intellectually undemanding programmes on television, reading entertaining books, playing with the children, gossiping with other family members and friends, consuming intoxicating substances, or even meditating (that is, suspending thought). Where there is work in the house or garden to be done we give ourselves entirely to a well-rehearsed and unthinking routine. Our only frustration is when something goes wrong or some essential item has not been returned to its proper place – frustration because we are forced to rethink our routine. Even when shopping we delight in the familiar. If any supermarket owner wishes to infuriate his or her customers it is only necessary to completely rearrange the consumer goods on the shelves. We normally shop by routine and these changed locations cause a great deal of annoyance as it forces us to devise new ways of finding the goods we need. Thinking imposes a significant cost.

Leisure outside the home is spent in various ways, very few of which are very demanding intellectually. Some seek entertainment and diversion in cinemas, theatres, and sports arenas; some even engage actively in these entertainments; and some seek diversion through social interaction at public functions, private homes, public houses, and dance venues. We enjoy the release from intellectual activities. Once again in pursuing these leisure activities we crave the familiar. The unknown, the challenging, the unexpected can cause displeasure because these situations force us to think. Of course, there are those who have more adventurous personalities, and less demanding careers, but even these rare birds like to be in charge of any situation. They like to economize on thinking.

What we need to consider here is exactly who needs rules. There are three main groups who find rules, or institutions, attractive – the **strategists** in pursuit of profits, the strategic imitators, and the **antistrategists** in pursuit of rents. The strategic pioneers have only a limited need for rules, because they do not need to economize so heavily on things intellectual and because they have great confidence in their own ideas and abilities. They are convinced they can take on all comers, and win. They are the rule-breakers of society who find the conventional way of doing things impossibly restrictive. Those who seek rules are the strategic followers. They need rules to facilitate the dynamic strategy because they are forced to economize heavily on thinking and because they have little confidence in their own ideas. They are the rule-makers in society. When something goes wrong with their plans they believe someone else is to blame and that they should be compensated for their loss. Those who follow others are rarely able to accept responsibility for their actions. They even devise rules to be exercised through the courts of law to ensure this. They are able to do so because they – the strategic followers – are in the majority. A species that must economize so heavily on intelligence is not the type of decision-maker envisaged by supporters of rational expectations.

Secondly, the political representatives of the dynamic strategists use rules to encourage and direct the population to support their initiatives. This is the reason for the strategic struggle in society – so that the strategists can gain control of the instruments of policy to secure the sources of their wealth and income. Finally, rules are demanded by the antistrategists who pursue rent-seeking through the establishment of exploitative systems. The representatives of order, who are the rule-makers in society, wish to direct other individuals to support or comply with their objectives. This is achieved through formal rules, informal conventions, and centralized religion and propaganda. On the other hand, the representatives of chaos, who constitute the creative forces in society, attempt to break down these rules. There is, therefore, a strategic and tactical element in the rules of society.

CONCLUSIONS

Materialist man who, in a typically competitive environment, struggles to survive and prosper, provides the endogenous driving force required for a realistic theory of longrun dynamics. It is a dynamic principle motivated by biologically determined desires that can only be satisfied through the pursuit of an appropriate dynamic strategy. The resulting dynamic process involves an interaction between the unfolding dynamic strategy and the investment decisions of the strategic pioneers and their more numerous followers. At its core is a decision-making mechanism, called strategic imitation, whereby what is economized is the scarcest resource in nature – intelligence – rather than cost–benefit information.

At the same time the unfolding dynamic strategy generates the confidence – strategic confidence – required to form the necessary co-operative relationships in order to channel the energy of materialist man into an effective societal strategy. Institutions, therefore, are required to facilitate the dynamic strategy in a way that economizes on intelligence. The central concept of an unfolding dynamic strategy, which provides the dynamic form for our model, and the changing strategic demand to which it gives rise, are examined in the following two chapters.

Part V
The Dynamic Mechanism

10 A Realistic Dynamic Form

Orthodox economic dynamics employs a supply-side approach. This has had a characteristic impact on both the dynamic form of existing growth models and the explanation of the growth process. The contribution that might be made to this subject by a new demand-side approach has not even been contemplated. It is argued here that the dynamic form of a realistic growth model is the outcome of an interaction between strategic demand and the strategic response of supply-side variables. In this chapter I outline a realistic dynamic form for my model, and in the next I examine the concept of strategic demand and its interaction with strategic response.

Because the neoclassical growth model completely overlooks strategic demand, orthodox economists have found it necessary to transfer the concept of equilibrium from economic statics to economic dynamics in order to provide the model with a dynamic form or structure. As the steady state is merely an extension of static equilibrium, the dynamic form of the neoclassical growth model is entirely artificial. This places severe limitations on the use of orthodox growth models in understanding reality and in formulating sensible policy. If we are to understand the real-world process of change, we need to develop a growth model with a realistic dynamic form. But it is essential to stress that it is the underlying dynamic mechanism rather than the shape of the growth process that is important here.

THE STEADY STATE – AN ARTIFICIAL CONCEPT

In neoclassical growth models, the steady state, or equilibrium growth path, is an attempt to provide not only a structure for the growth process but also an objective for a growing society. It is a dynamic centre of gravity towards which an economy will automatically converge. The equilibrium pathway for the Solow–Swan model, which is determined by the nature of the neoclassical production function, and for those new growth models that retain the concept of the steady state, is shown diagrammatically in Figure 10.1. These models assume that the growth path is smooth and that the growth rate – which is determined exogenously in the Solow–Swan model and endogenously in the new growth model – is constant over time. This picture can be varied, but only by making a number of arbitrary assumptions. John Hicks (1965), for example, makes the point that for each state of technology there will be a different equilibrium growth path.[1] Accordingly, in reality a society will move or 'traverse' to a new pathway with each discrete change in technology. Apart

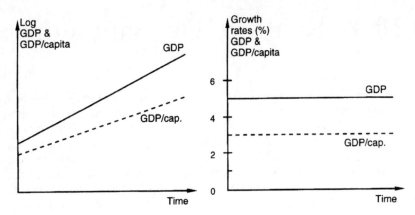

Figure 10.1   The neoclassical equilibrium pathway

Source: Based on text.

from making the point that convergence is likely to involve a movement to aseries of pathways rather than a single pathway, little is added to the Solow–Swan model. Any attempt to map these changes in pathways and growth rates would be pointless in the absence of real-world information, because Hicks does not provide a model to suggest how these 'traverses' would take place. It is the substance of the dynamic form, not its appearance, that is of interest. And, as suggested earlier, that substance is entirely artificial.

THE STRATEGIC PATHWAY – A NEW DYNAMIC FORM

A realistic dynamic form can only be derived by observing the way societies grow over the longrun. This is, of course, only one aspect of the larger objective of inductively deriving a realist dynamic model from historical analysis. We need to explain the underlying dynamic process as well as the dynamic pathway. To do so we need to draw a distinction between a 'time path' on the one hand and a 'dynamic pathway' as employed in this book on the other. A time path is merely the statistical profile of an unexplained variable over time, whereas a dynamic pathway – in this case the **strategic pathway** – is the embodiment of an explained dynamic process.

By observing the dynamic process in a large number of societies allocated in space and time, it is possible to derive not only a general dynamic mechanism but, at the same time, a general dynamic form. In turn this general model can be employed to analyse the growth of particular societies and to make certain predictions about growth in the future. To highlight the differences between the strategic pathway in reality and the steady state in the neoclassical growth model, diagrams similar to those in Figure 10.1 can be drawn in both the general and particular case.

But before we do, it is important to realize that the strategic pathway is not an optimum pathway as envisaged by Hicks (1965: 201–76). Without making a number of completely unrealistic assumptions – the maximization of a simple social welfare function and foreknowledge about changes in the supply 'determinants' of growth – it is not possible to define an optimum growth path. There is no way of knowing what that deductive fiction might look like or how the actual dynamic pathway might compare with it. It is merely an artificial construct of supply-side neoclassical economics which has been unable to model the demand-side forces that are driving human society. In reality there is no optimum, or even equilibrium, growth path, only a strategic pathway that unfolds as entrepreneurs explore society's changing strategic opportunities. The supply-side determinants of growth respond to the changing strategic demand that emerges from the unfolding dynamic strategy. In other words, the strategic pathway is determined by the dynamic interaction between a changing strategic demand and the strategic response of supply-side variables.

A dominant dynamic strategy unfolds not in response to teleological forces but to the action of individuals attempting to survive and prosper in a competitive world. In order to exploit strategic opportunities, individuals and their governments invest in the necessary infrastructure, plant and machinery, techniques, institutions, and organizations. And as the dynamic strategy unfolds, the living standards of the participants rise. This unfolding process continues until the strategic opportunities have been exhausted – the outcome of the 'law of diminishing *strategic* returns', which states that 'investment in a dominant dynamic strategy will ultimately experience diminishing returns, which will lead to a deceleration, and eventual cessation of societal dynamics' (Snooks 1998: ch. 8). This stage will be reached when marginal strategic revenue and marginal strategic costs are finally equated. It is important to realize that dynamic diminishing returns are experienced not on resources but on strategies.

This law encompasses the classical law of diminishing returns based upon the misleading assumption of a fixed supply of land (or natural resources). The classical version is a special case of this more general law as it is based upon conditions specific to a rare and restricted period in human history. While it has only occurred twice in the last 11,000 years on the cusp between two technological paradigms, we may be approaching a third occurrence. The classical economists focused upon a world of transition between an exhausted neolithic and, a yet to be realized, industrial technological paradigm. At this rare historical moment all former dynamic strategies – conquest, commerce, and neolithic technology – had been exhausted, and it appeared that the stock of natural resources was finite in an absolute sense. In fact the supply of natural resources depends upon the dynamic strategies of materialist man. Hence diminishing returns at the societal level are experienced not on natural resources but on dynamic strategies. The **strategic crisis** replaces the Malthusian crisis. Owing to their myopic historical focus the classical economists thought that the diminishing returns they actually detected were due to land being a fixed factor of production rather than to the exhaustion of the neolithic technological paradigm.

This dynamic law also resolves the difficulty inherent in the neoclassical version of diminishing returns which transfers the law from a situation where land is in fixed supply in the longrun to a situation where all factors of production are in fixed supply in the shortrun. While diminishing returns on fixed factors can only be established in the shortrun (because only in the shortrun can factors be fixed), it is only in the longrun, when substitution of factors can occur, that the concept has any operational significance. This dilemma is resolved when we see diminishing returns at the macro level as an outcome of exhausting dynamic strategies rather than either exhausting natural resources or fixed factors in the shortrun. The continued introduction of new technologies prevents the exhaustion of the modern dynamic strategy and hence prevents the emergence of diminishing returns at the societal level. (But, of course, diminishing returns occur on individual investment projects as those projects are exhausted.)

The general dynamic form

Figure 10.2 presents a generalized strategic pathway for Western civilization over the past millennium. There are significant differences between the general strategic pathway and the steady state. The most obvious of these is

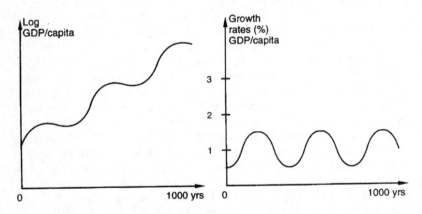

Figure 10.2 The general strategic pathway

Source: Based on text.

the wave-like pattern of the strategic pathway in contrast to the smooth equilibrium path of the neoclassical model. These great wave-like surges are, according to my detailed historical research, about 300 years in duration. Elsewhere, I have called them the 'great waves' of economic change (Snooks 1993: ch. 7; 1996: ch. 12). Attention here is focused on the waves of growth (the upswings) rather than on the complete 'cycles' (peak to peak) because, as explained in Chapter 14, these fluctuations are the outcome of a dynamic mechanism that generates wave-like surges separated by periods of hiatus, rather than systematic cycles. One of the insights of the dynamic-strategy model is that economic growth in any individual society is episodic.

What Figure 10.2 does not show, owing to its long time-scale, is the fact that these great waves consist of a series of 'long waves' of 20 to 60 years in duration. The latter should not be confused with the discredited Kondratief waves of 50 to 60 years. Without wanting to pre-empt the discussion in Chapter 14, let me say that the length of these waves, both 'great' and 'long', is only approximate and will be lengthened or shortened in particular cases by exogenous shocks. Even less regular are the intervals between the waves, as these possess the nature of interregnums rather than troughs that are systematically related to the peaks of a 'cyclical' process. The point that needs to be emphasized here is not the regularity of the waves, but the dynamic model that generates them. The dynamic-strategy model incorporates a sequence of strategies that are employed to achieve the objectives of society's decision-makers.

Also of interest are the fluctuations in the growth rates of GDP per capita over the longrun. Rather than the given growth rate of the neoclassical steady state (Figure 10.1), the dynamic-strategy model generates fluctuations around a roughly horizontal trend. This reflects the impact of a sequence of dynamic strategies on the growth of the economy. The higher rates are associated with the expansion of a number of dynamic strategies, and the lower rates are associated with the transitional phases between each strategy. Similar fluctuations, that are not shown in Figure 10.2, are associated with the rise and fall of a number of substrategies within each of these wider dynamic strategies.

A specific dynamic form: England 1000–2000

To bring this discussion closer to reality, the strategic pathway for England from 1000 to 2000 is presented in Figure 10.3. We will deal separately with the dynamic strategies and their constituent substrategies.

The dynamic strategies

Figure 10.3 *illustrates* the historical nature of the three great waves of economic change that have swept across Western Europe over the past

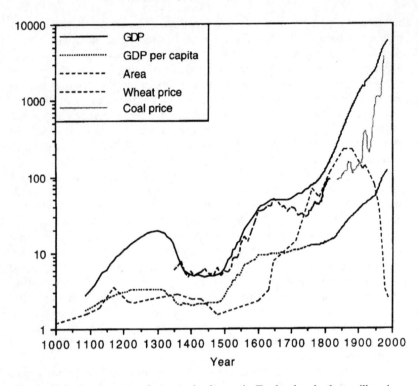

Figure 10.3 Great waves of economic change in England – the last millennium
Source: Snooks (1997:276).

1000 years. It is immediately obvious that the second of these great waves
was foreshortened, an outcome of the Black Death which raged intermittently in England from 1348 to the mid-fifteenth century. Each of these great
waves was driven by a different dynamic strategy. The first wave, from 1000
to 1300 was the outcome of the **conquest strategy**; the second, from 1490 to
1650, of the **commerce strategy**; and the third, since the 1780s, of the
technological strategy. Each of these strategies was pursued through investment in the specialized infrastructure, human skills, and institutions required
to exploit their changing potential. In each case these dynamic strategies
were adopted, developed, and exhausted, thereafter to be replaced, but not
inevitably, by new strategies. Economic growth, therefore, can be and, for the
major part of human civilization, has been generated by strategies other than
technological change.

Throughout the ebbing and flowing of these great waves of economic
change, prices echoed the longrun fluctuations in strategic demand that
can be measured by real GDP (as aggregate demand is the static outcome

of strategic demand). The most representative prices before the Industrial Revolution are wheat prices, and thereafter coal prices, both of which are presented in Figure 10.3. Even the so-called 'price revolution' of the sixteenth century was merely part of this overall pattern, which is driven by demand rather than supply (usually identified with the amount of gold and silver brought back from the New World). Our evidence shows that prices had been rising rapidly for about two generations before the flow of Spanish silver reached 'full flood' in the 1560s and that the supply of silver was not sufficient to satisfy demand, thereby requiring the use of gold (not previously used as currency) as well (Snooks 1997a: ch. 10). The dynamic-strategy model, therefore, treats longrun price increases as a response to changes in aggregate demand (real GDP) that in turn are driven by strategic demand arising from an unfolding dynamic strategy. In the shorter term it is possible that a sudden increase in bullion – the pursuit of which is driven by the unfolding dynamic strategy – might lead to an increase in prices, but in the longer term the money supply will adjust to the requirements of strategic demand. Money is merely a facilitating institution. It is significant that longrun price increases are a natural outcome of the dynamic process, and that longrun price stability or decline is associated with zero or negative longrun growth. We shall return to this relationship when specifying a growth–inflation curve in Chapter 11, and when considering policy for a dynamic society in Chapter 17.

As suggested in the general model, the intervals between these great waves were not part of a cyclical process but the outcome of a hiatus between strategies – an interval sometimes aggravated by exogenous shocks. This strategic sequence of conquest→commerce→technological change cannot be regarded as inevitable or automatic. Had the final exhaustion of the commerce strategy in the mid-eighteenth century not coincided with the exhaustion of the wider neolithic technological paradigm (discussed later in the chapter) and the subsequent transition via the Industrial Revolution to the industrial technological paradigm, then the strategic sequence would have been conquest→commerce→conquest, as it often was in ancient history. And this would have reversed the development of the facilitating institutions such as the political system (with a backward shift from limited democracy to autocratic rule by a new military elite), the economic system (with a backward shift from mercantile capitalism to a command system of some sort), and the social system (with a return to a more hierarchical structure). The strategy chosen depends on the physical and social environment communicated to decision-makers through changing relative factor prices. Clearly this is not an evolutionary system. These matters have been analysed at length in *The Dynamic Society* (1996) and *The Ephemeral Civilization* (1997a) and the underlying forces have been described by what I call the 'secondary laws of history' (Snooks 1998: ch. 9).

A brief digression is required concerning the nature of economic growth generated by the different dynamic strategies. In *The Dynamic Society* I distinguish between three different forms of economic change: **environmental dynamic change (EDC)**; **zero-sum dynamic change (ZDC)**; and the more familiar **technological dynamic change (TDC)**. Environmental dynamic change is achieved through the dynamic strategy of family multiplication. This involves an increase in the number of family units for the purpose of gaining greater control over unused natural resources with a given state of technology (Snooks 1994a: 127). It leads to population increase and migration and is the basis of the 'primitive dynamic' that I have called the great dispersion, which in palaeolithic times led to the occupation by modern man of all continents except Antarctica. It involves economic expansion (increase in family units) without economic growth (increase in total income per household). Zero-sum dynamic change benefits the dynamic society that employs the conquest and commerce (in contrast to trade) strategies, at the expense of their neighbours. This was the basis of the 'ancient dynamic', which saw the rise and fall of pre-modern societies. And the technological strategy is the dominant dynamic of modern society and, in the past, was employed by strategic pioneers and their followers to transcend exhausted technological paradigms. It was at the very centre of the Palaeolithic (hunting), Neolithic (agricultural), and Industrial (modern) Revolutions or technological paradigm shifts. Unlike the conquest and commerce strategies, it leads to an increase in material standards not only for its host society, but for human society as a whole. The commerce strategy should not be confused with the gains from trade. It involves the aggressive attempt to gain monopoly access to markets and commodities in order to syphon off the gains from trade at the expense of other trading societies. It is a parasitic strategy.

The dynamic substrategies

Within each of these dynamic strategies are a number of substrategies. We will focus here on the substrategies underlying the global technological strategy that has been operating since the late eighteenth century.[2] The global technological strategy has been unfolding for over two centuries since the beginning of the British Industrial Revolution. It is a dynamic process that has been driven by a series of new entrants to the industrial technological paradigm, and that has passed through a number of distinct substrategies.

The pioneering technological substrategy was pursued by Britain between the 1780s and the 1830s. This first-generation substrategy was based on the innovations of practical men and was undertaken through small-scale enterprises that focused on a small range of basic commodities produced in one or two factories under common ownership. These enterprises began as small partnerships and family firms, but gradually gave way to larger public companies. This type of development was well suited to the nation-state that had emerged in Europe in the medieval and pre-modern periods in response to conquest and commerce.

The second technological substrategy was initiated by the other nation-states of Western Europe between the 1830s and 1870s. Earlier experimentation with industrialization on the Continent had been disrupted by a continued fascination with conquest, particularly by France. But in order to compete with Britain in the struggle to survive and prosper, France and Germany – and later Japan – used tariffs to develop the basic industries of the First Industrial Revolution and used the latest capital-intensive technology in engineering and chemicals to develop new industries. These new industries relied to a greater extent than before on scientific ideas and institutional finance. While the enterprises in this second technological phase were more extensive and operated through a wider network of large factories (except in France), they were able to develop within the existing nation-state, or in the newly emerging nation-state in the case of Germany (1871) and Italy (1861). As competition between these nation-states grew more intense during the second half of the nineteenth century, they embarked on a process of empire-building in order to defend their technological strategies. It was an extension of the balance of power concept from Europe to the rest of the world. The important point is that these European empires were not essential economically to the operation of the technological strategy, which is why they were dismantled in the mid-twentieth century when the technological strategy could be defended by the mega-states using nuclear weapons.

The third technological substrategy began in North America in the 1870s and continued for the following century. It was an outcome of a push by industrialists in the USA to drive out the Europeans from their large domestic market and, later, to make inroads into global markets. America was able to do this not by developing a radically different technology but by employing existing technological ideas on a scale that no other nation in the late nineteenth century could emulate. By large-scale investment in mass-production techniques, the USA was able to exploit its large domestic market by supplying goods and services at a price that the Europeans were unable to match. Their secret was the high degree of specialization and division of labour that could be achieved using the assembly-line techniques pioneered by Henry Ford to produce standardized products; and by techniques of mass distribution. Once the local market had been saturated in the 1920s, American entrepreneurs turned their attention, after a hiatus usually known as the Great Depression, to global markets, particularly after the Second World War. This domestic and international success was based on the earlier development of mega-corporations – which could only emerge within a mega-state – producing an extensive range of commodities and services. Some of these corporations had a greater output in their chosen range of commodities than individual European nations. When they established branches in overseas markets these mega-corporations became known as multinational or, more recently, transnational corporations. They are, in effect, agents of the technological strategies of the mega-states, and they play a global role similar to that of the trading joint-stock companies – such as the East India Company – in the age of commerce.

The fourth technological substrategy was developed by innovative nation-states in an effort to undercut the post-Second World War dominance of the USA. It is interesting that those who were most successful were the nation-states that failed in the attempt to meet the American challenge by developing their own mega-states through conquest. Both Germany and Japan found in the 1960s that they could effectively compete against the USA both in its domestic and overseas markets by fully embracing the new microelectronic technology. If they could not transform themselves into mega-states perhaps they could undermine the old basis of the mega-state. Through more efficient production and organization they were able to offer consumers greater variety and choice even though this meant shorter production runs (only one-quarter that of the USA in the production of cars). Japan and Germany were able to combine the old mass-production methods with the new microelectronic technology to make customized consumer products that required greater attention to detail and quality. These products included cars, household appliances, ceramics, textiles, consumer durables, computer software, as well as food and drink. Consumers, tired of standardized products, responded to this greater choice with considerable enthusiasm. The shift of consumers away from standardized products finally forced the USA in the 1980s to compete with these new dynamic strategists on their own ground. But this has not been without its costs, as it is always difficult for a society that has long specialized in a successful substrategy to make a radical change – as in the case of Britain in the interwar years – owing to the heavy investment in the older substrategy.

Finally we come to the fifth technological substrategy that will take human society well into the twenty-first century. With the conclusion of the Second World War it became clear to the nation-states of Western Europe, on both the winning and the losing sides, that no single European nation-state had the economic resources required to wage war successfully, either economic or military, against America. It also became clear that in the future the USSR would become a mega-state as powerful as the USA. Mega-status would be important not only to defend the technological strategy of Western Europe – who had given it to the world – but also to engage in economic bargaining on a global scale, to exercise strategic control over a large market, and to control a large resource base. Clearly the future would be determined by economic giants employing a microelectronic/biotechnological programme. This is the real driving force behind the remarkable attempt to form a mega-state in Europe – remarkable because these nation-states have been competing ferociously against each other for about 1 500 years. By the mid-twentieth century, however, the competition without had finally become more critical than the competition within the struggle to survive and prosper.

English growth rates

Figure 10.4 shows the pattern of growth rates in England during the past millennium. They bear no resemblance to the neoclassical characterization in Figure 10.1. Considerable variation in growth rates occurred over time, ranging from 2.5 per cent per annum in the 1950s and 1960s to minus 0.7 per cent per annum during the first three quarters of the fourteenth century. And there is considerable variation within each great wave, which can be seen most clearly in the case of the last one owing to more abundant statistical data.

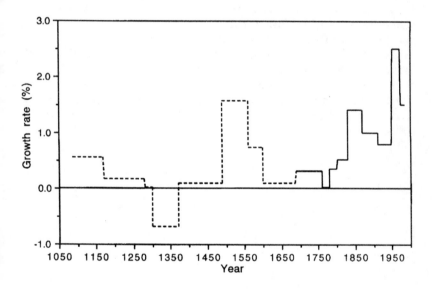

Figure 10.4 Growth rates for England, 1000–2000

Source: Snooks (1993:86).

While this pattern of growth rates reflects the influence of the three dynamic strategies discussed above, some of the extreme highs and lows are a result of exogenous shocks. The Black Death was responsible not only for the negative growth rates in the second half of the fourteenth century, but also for the compressed timescale of the second wave, and for the rapid growth in the sixteenth century owing to the release of pent-up energy once the bubonic plague receded. Similarly the Great Depression and the Second World War were responsible for lower rates of growth in the 1930s and 1940s and, to a large degree, the excessive rates achieved in the 1950s and 1960s, once again due to the release of pent-up energy. In the absence of these exogenous shocks we could have expected a pattern more like, but not necessarily identical with, that in Figure 10.2.

CONCLUSIONS

The strategic pathway, therefore, is an integral part of the process of change resulting from the unfolding of the dominant dynamic strategy. It is not just a set of outcomes. And there is nothing preordained or inevitable about this unfolding process. It involves an interaction of competing strategic pioneers and followers with their physical and social environment as they explore the materialist potential in a dynamic strategy and its various substrategies. This potential is unknown and constantly changing, and must be explored one step at a time. It can be identified, indirectly and approximately, only retrospectively. While the participants in this process do not know how the current dynamic strategy will unfold in its entirety, the more perceptive pioneers will gain a sense of where it could be heading over the next few years, a sense that will influence their expectations of future investment yields.

11 Strategic Demand and the Growth–Inflation Curve

The central concept in this book is strategic demand. It is a force that arises from the unfolding of the dominant dynamic strategy driven by **materialist man** – a force that fluctuates with the changing fortunes of existing strategic opportunities. This is, I argue, an entirely new concept in economics, which promises to redress the balance in a discipline that, since the rejection of 'divine demand' in Adam Smith's system, has adopted a supply-side approach to macroeconomics. And because of this our view of the real world is distorted and our policy advice is inappropriate.

While the orthodox supply-side analysis may not raise debilitating problems in the field of static microeconomic theory – which employs the concept of consumer demand, a static outcome of strategic demand – it cannot cope with real-world dynamics. Difficulties begin to emerge with the supply-side approach when we move to the field of comparative-static macroeconomics. This can be seen in *The General Theory* (1936), where, in the absence of the strategic-demand concept, J.M. Keynes is forced to treat a number of key issues as the outcome of 'psychological laws'. But there are no psychological laws in the social sciences, only economic laws.

A NEW CONCEPT OF DEMAND

What, then, is strategic demand? It is, as we have seen, the effective demand of decision-makers struggling to survive and prosper for a wide range of physical, intellectual, and institutional inputs required to facilitate their strategic pursuit. This is why strategic demand fluctuates in unison with the dominant dynamic strategy and its substrategies. In order to exploit the opportunities provided by the dynamic strategy, the strategic pioneers and their followers need to invest in new infrastructure; purchase intermediate materials; employ labour skills; acquire or construct appropriate buildings, machinery, and equipment; adopt new technologies; gain access to money supplies; and develop new facilitating social rules and organizations. Strategic demand, therefore, is an active and initiating force in society. The supply response will, of course, help determine the extent to which the strategic opportunities can be exploited, but the point to be made here is that strategic demand is the active principle in our model, as it is in reality.

A few examples will illustrate the strategic demand concept. It can be seen most simply and clearly in the early stages of a dynamic strategy, and most starkly for pre-modern dynamic strategies. First, imagine a young entrepreneur struggling to make his way in the world during the early stages of Britain's industrial technological strategy in the late eighteenth century. His aim is to earn extraordinary profits by exploiting an unknown but potentially huge market for cheap cotton cloth. To do so he needs to develop and build machinery embodying a new technology, construct a factory, develop an organizational structure, hire semi-skilled workers, establish workplace discipline, borrow funds, and arrange for warehousing and distribution. These and other developments are an outcome of our entrepreneur's competitive exploration of the new strategic potential — an outcome of the generation of strategic demand rather than a change in consumer demand responding as it does to changes in tastes and income. The same is true of the technological strategy today. Secondly, take the less familiar example of a young farmer–warrior without inherited resources during the early stages of Rome's conquest strategy about 500 BC. To gain land, wives, slaves, and plunder, our young warrior must organize a number of family members and friends to raid a neighbouring settlement. They need weapons, body protection, provisions, means of transporting booty, rudimentary military organization, and rules about conduct and distribution of the spoils. This type of enterprise led five centuries later to an empire that embraced the entire Mediterranean world. Once again this had nothing to do with changing consumer (or aggregate) demand. It was the outcome of strategic demand generated by the unfolding conquest strategy driven by many young ambitious Romans.

Strategic demand is an encompassing concept. Other forms of demand usually dealt with in orthodox economics – such as consumer demand, final demand, and aggregate demand are merely static outcomes of a dynamic system driven by strategic demand. Hence, while strategic demand is an active force in our dynamic model, consumer demand and aggregate demand are merely passive outcomes of this system. In the wider dynamic concept, it is not correct to say that the state of long-term expectations, the propensity to consume, and the liquidity preference are independent explanators of investment, consumption, and the rate of interest. In a dynamic context, investment, consumption/saving, real GDP, and employment are all jointly determined by the interaction of a constantly changing strategic demand and supply-side variables in response to the unfolding dynamic strategy. Consumer demand and aggregate demand (even when correctly measured as a product of market and household requirements) are but distant echoes of strategic demand. They have their place in static macroeconomics – although only in the shortrun when the dynamic strategy cannot be changed – but not in longrun dynamics.

How does strategic demand influence investment and consumption/saving? This question can be answered by comparing the operation of J.M. Keynes' comparative–static model in *The General Theory* (1936) with the dynamic model in this book. While Keynes focused on 'effective demand' (or aggregate demand) in a static world with imperfect markets and institutions, I focus on strategic demand (or dynamic demand) in a dynamic world with changing markets and institutions. Keynes' theory of employment involves three different types of variables: those that are regarded as 'given'; those seen as 'independent'; and those regarded as 'dependent'.[1] The given variables include the quantity and quality of labour and capital equipment, existing technology, degree of competition, consumer tastes, and the social structure. Keynes realized that these variables would change in the longrun, but he thought that in the shortrun they could be safely ignored. The independent variables are the psychological propensities, or societal behaviour patterns, and include the propensity to consume, the schedule of the marginal efficiency of capital, the liquidity preference schedule, and the institutional lender of last resort. And the dependent variables are national income, employment, and the rate of interest, that are determined by the independent variables through the medium of investment and consumption that form the basis for aggregate demand.

Investment in *The General Theory* is determined by the marginal efficiency of capital (or the investment-demand schedule) and the rate of interest. In turn, the marginal efficiency of capital 'depends on the relation between the supply price of a capital asset and its prospective yield' (Keynes 1936: 147). And the rate of interest depends on the state of liquidity-preference (or the demand for liquidity function) and on the quantity of money. These relationships will be discussed more formally in Chapter 13.

Let us first consider the investment-demand schedule. In *The General Theory*'s famous Chapter 12, Keynes argues that prospective yields are determined partly by 'consumers' demand for goods which require for their efficient production a relatively larger assistance from capital', and partly by the 'state of long-term expectation', which is a function of the 'state of confidence' in the future of decision-makers (ibid.: 147–8). But, owing to the comparative–static deductive approach employed by Keynes, he was unable to explain either the determinants of business confidence – referring instead to the role of 'animal spirits' as the outcome of a psychological propensity – or the ultimate nature of the demand for capital.

By adopting a realist dynamic approach, it is possible to explain the ultimate sources of both these givens in Keynes' analysis. First, the demand for new capital goods in a dynamic society is to be found ultimately, not in consumer demand, but in strategic demand, which changes as the dominant dynamic strategy, or substrategy, unfolds. Consumer demand is merely an outcome of the wider dynamic system. Secondly, as suggested in Chapter 9, both investor and lender confidence are outcomes of strategic confidence which also has its source and variations in the unfolding dynamic strategy. By using the dynamic-strategy model, it is possible to explain in economic terms what Keynes had left to the mercy of 'psychological laws'.

In his analysis of the rate of interest, Keynes introduces the second of his three psychological laws regarding the state of liquidity. His liquidity function is the demand for money schedule – reflecting motives concerning transactions, precautions, and speculations motives – which is determined by human psychology. On the other hand, the supply of money is determined by 'the monetary authority', an institutional arrangement beyond the explanatory power of Keynes' 'general' theory. Once again, therefore, Keynes' comparative–static approach leaves the ultimate determinants unknown. Human psychology and institutions are left unmodelled.

In the dynamic-strategy model, the demand for money depends upon the nature of strategic demand via its effects upon the state of the economy. And the quantity of money is an institutional response to the requirements of the dynamic strategy in the light of strategic confidence. Both the demand for and the supply of money changes as individual decision-makers and institutional lenders respond differentially to the expansion, stagnation, exhaustion, and substitution of the dynamic strategy and its substrategies.

Finally, in *The General Theory*, consumption (and, hence, saving) is a function of income and the 'propensity to consume' – the last of Keynes' three psychological propensities or laws. In the short term, Keynes regards as given 'those psychological characteristics of human nature and those social practices and institutions' of human society (Keynes 1936: 91). Once again this is an outcome of failing to model these forces. Keynes argued that, on average, individuals and families will consume only a proportion of any increase in income, owing to the operation of a number of conservative 'subjective factors' that include the desire to guard against unforeseen contingencies; to enable future expenditures concerning old age, family education, and so on; to enable greater independence; to finance investment or speculation; to bequeath a fortune; or to satisfy 'pure miserliness'. Similarly private and public institutions save a proportion of any increase in income. While Keynes regarded these subjective factors as relatively fixed in the shortrun – and hence consumption is a stable function of income – he acknowledged the possibility that they might change in the longrun. But he did not explain or attempt to model this change.

In the dynamic-strategy model, the consumption function is not a stable, psychological propensity, but rather a dynamic relationship that varies according to shifts in strategic demand and strategic confidence as individuals, families, firms, and public organizations attempt to maximize the probability of survival and prosperity over their biological and organizational life-times. Hence, the longrun consumption/saving function depends on changing expectations of life-time incomes and survival circumstances. And, of course, per capita income is an outcome of the unfolding dynamic strategy.

Strategic demand, therefore, plays the dominant shaping role in society. The nature and role of firms and households is largely determined by the unfolding dynamic strategy. Hence, to understand microeconomic structures and processes, we need to work down from the macroeconomic level. This reverses the preoccupation of orthodox economics – of attempting to build up macroeconomic and growth theory from the existing body of microeconomics – over the past two or three centuries. This is brought home most clearly when it is realized that neoclassical microeconomics has little or no relevance to the dynamic strategies of the pre-modern era – an era that encompasses 98 per cent of the span of human civilization and 99.99 per cent of the time since the emergence of modern man. Microeconomics should be the servant not the master.

STRATEGIC DEMAND AND STRATEGIC RESPONSE

The above comparative–static approach can be extended by considering the dynamic interaction between strategic demand and the **strategic response** of supply-side variables – an interaction that gives rise to the strategic pathway. Clearly, the response to strategic demand depends upon conditions concerning the supply of factors of production and of technological and institutional ideas. While the institutional response has been discussed in Chapter 7, the productive response will be dealt with here. As supply-side analysis is the core of orthodox economics, this task can be undertaken quite briefly. What is lacking in orthodox theory is the recognition that the economics of production is part of the strategic response to the unfolding dynamic strategy. In neoclassical economics the supply side is treated as the active force in society – supply creates its own demand – and in Keynesian economics the supply-side variables are merely treated as given.

Central to the strategic demand–response interaction is the role of prices. In the dynamic-strategy model, systematic inflation is an outcome of the growth of strategic demand and of the strategic response of existing resources. Generally, the more rapid the unfolding of the dynamic strategy – and, hence, the more rapid the growth of strategic demand – the higher the rate of inflation. Prices (including wage rates) rise and relative prices change as the dynamic strategy unfolds because of the pressure placed by strategic demand on existing resources and technology. And the rising level of prices, which creates opportunities for extraordinary profits, provides the incentive for the resulting strategic response. The answer to the rhetorical question asked recently by Robert King (1993: 70): 'why are prices sticky in certain historical episodes and rapidly adjusting in others?' is not 'changes in expectations' as he proposes, but changes in strategic demand. It will be recalled that the artificial complications of rational expectations have been swept away by the strategic-imitation model of individual decision-making introduced in Chapter 9. In any case rational expectations would not significantly modify changes in strategic demand, which are driven by biologically determined desires.

Inflation in the dynamic-strategy model, therefore, is both a natural outcome and an essential component of the dynamic process. The model predicts that inflation in the developed world will be a stable, nonaccelerating function of economic growth. Yet, inflation is treated by orthodox economists and policy-makers as an undesirable occurrence that must be rooted out from modern society. We now turn to the strategic response – of population increase, capital formation, and technological change.

Population and labour supply

As demonstrated in Chapter 3, orthodox growth models make a number of rather arbitrary assumptions about the role of population. The classical (Ricardian) model assumes that population is a function of real wage levels, the Keynesian and neoclassical models deal with it as an exogenous shock, and the endogenous growth model usually treats it as an outcome of family income and education. In each case this arbitrary procedure is a supply-side alternative to modelling dynamic demand. And, to make matters worse, it is well known that real wages or real GDP per capita only influence population around subsistence levels, and then largely through mortality rather than fertility. This approach, therefore, has little relevance to developed societies.

In the dynamic-strategy model, changes in both population and labour-force participation rates are a function largely of changes in strategic opportunities. Effective decisions about fertility and participation in the market sector are made by families in response to changing strategic demand (Snooks 1994a: 85–8). The requirement for additional workers depends on the nature of the dominant dynamic strategy and the stage reached in its exploitation.

In the modern era, the two main dynamic strategies have been technological change for 'old' societies and family multiplication for 'new' societies. North America and Australasia in the eighteenth and early nineteenth centuries are good examples of new societies, which were characterized by abundant natural resources and less abundant labour and capital. Because of these factor endowments, and the resulting relative factor prices, new societies initially adopt the family-multiplication strategy, involving reproduction and migration, to exercise control over the abundant supply of natural resources. This takes the form of networks of family farms and associated businesses. It is for this reason that average family size achieved relatively high levels in the USA (8 to 9 members) and Australia (10 members) in the early nineteenth century as the land frontier expanded (Henretta *et al.* 1987: 92, 292; Snooks 1994a: 66). Because the family-multiplication strategy unfolded more rapidly than the rate at which existing families could supply the required labour, the difference was made up by immigrants from Europe. Hence, the strategic demand generated by new societies was largely respons-ible for the massive movement of people from the Old to the New World in the nineteenth century. Once the best land in the New World had been exploited, by the mid-nineteenth century, and these societies had gradually adopted the technological strategy employed by the Old World, the average size of families fell to more traditional levels (of about 5 members).

A notable feature of the technological strategy is that population increase is not essential for generating higher material standards of living. It is for this reason that the size of Western families fell from about 5 to less than 3 members during the middle decades of the twentieth century (Snooks 1994a: 68). This will be important to the future of human society as population densities rise to relatively high levels. But this is not to say that the techno-logical strategy has generated a stationary or even a steadily growing popula-tion. When technological substrategies are unfolding rapidly, the demand for population is greater than when they are approaching exhaustion. During the 1930s, for example, strategic demand for population actually declined owing to the exhaustion of the prevailing American technological substrategy (Snooks 1997a: ch. 11). Population and labour-force fluctuations, therefore, are a response to fluctuations in strategic demand.

This was also true of the more distant past. As the commerce and con-quest strategies unfolded, the demand for labour increased substantially in order to create armies, to settle conquered lands, and to establish trading colonies. The incentive for families to multiply took the form of growing opportunities to bring back plunder or profits and to acquire land cheaply. When the expansion of strategic opportunities took place at a greater rate than the demographic capacity of the conquest or commerce society, slave labour from conquered lands was also used (Snooks 1997a: chs 6–9). And when these dynamic strategies experienced fluctuating fortunes or were, finally, exhausted, population growth slowed, stagnated, and even declined. Of course, the conquest strategy has not been limited to the distant past. In the 1930s the 'fascist' regimes in Italy, Germany, and Japan embarked on conquest strategies that generated demands for increased populations to fight wars and to settled conquered lands. And as these strategies out-stripped the demographic capacities of domestic populations, slave labour was employed on a massive scale.[2] In the dynamic-strategy model, therefore, population changes are explained endogenously.

Capital formation

The dynamic-strategy model tells us that capital formation, like population increase, responds to changes in strategic demand. With the development of strategic opportunities there is a need for new investment in strategic infrastructure; industrial, commercial, public, and residential structures; plant and equipment; and transport and communications facilities. This strategic demand is communicated to families, which are the ultimate owners of firms as well as households, through the growing opportunities to invest and profit from this investment. If expectations in this respect are satisfied by a subsequent return flow of material goods, strategic confidence increases and investment in strategic opportunities continues.

Community investment can be categorized according to whether it is a direct or indirect response to strategic demand. A direct response includes investment in new technologies and the infrastructure required to support those technologies, whereas an indirect response includes investment required to meet the demands of a growing population enjoying a growing standard of living. As we have seen, population increase is itself a direct response to expanding strategic demand. Direct investment facilitates the unfolding dynamic strategy, whereas indirect investment supports the living standards of the population. We would do well to remember which is which.

The type as well as the amount of investment undertaken depends on the strategy pursued. We are all familiar with the capital formation required to facilitate the modern technological strategy. It mainly involves investment in new technologies and in the urban centres that cradle them. Owing to our lack of familiarity with other strategies, their strategic imprint on capital formation stands out more clearly. In conquest societies, strategic investment takes the form of military plant and equipment, military transport and communication systems, and structures for imperial organization; while in commerce societies it includes mercantile and naval shipping, docks and warehousing, and financial structures. Investment in productive activities such as agriculture and manufactured consumer goods is far less significant in pre-modern societies. Thus, strategic demand determines the nature of capital formation as well as its rate of change. This conclusion contrasts starkly with the way a faceless investment is treated as a response to either exogenous shocks or endogenous supply-side forces (really assumptions) in orthodox growth models.

Technological change

In modern industrial societies, technological change lies at the very centre of social dynamics. It is the strategy by which modern economic growth is achieved. In the pre-modern world, however, technological change was merely a subsidiary strategy employed in support of the dominant strategy of either commerce or conquest. Indeed, in the ancient world there was little technological improvement in agriculture or industry, but considerable technological improvement in military equipment and machinery, military roads, naval vessels, military tactics and organization, imperial administration, and urban structures and facilities; or, alternatively, in merchant shipping, facilities for distribution, communication, finance, and commercial organization and accounting practices.

Prior to the development of the dynamic-strategy model this selective technological capability appeared paradoxical: Why were the ancients good at military technology, but not at production technology? For those who are interested, the answer is to be found in *The Dynamic Society* (1996): in the past the universal objective was to generate extraordinary profits through the exercise of control (either through conquest or commerce) over *external* resources, whereas in the modern era it is to generate extraordinary profits through the more intensive use of *internal* resources.

The present and future role of technological change can be understood only if we place it within the context of the past. I will be brief, because it has been the subject of the above book. We need to be aware of the great technological paradigm shifts that have transformed human society in the

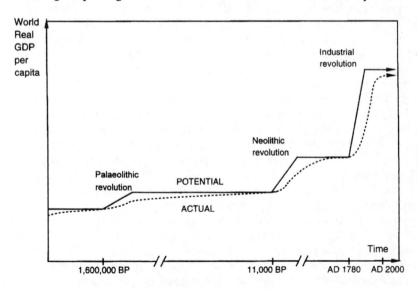

Figure 11.1 Great technological paradigm shifts, last 2 million years

Source: Snooks (1996:403).

past and will transform it in the future. As can be seen from Figure 11.1, there have been three technological paradigm shifts, or technological revolutions, in human history – the Palaeolithic Revolution about 1.6 million years ago, the Neolithic Revolution about 11 000 years ago, and the Industrial Revolution about 200 years ago. Despite the few observations, it would seem that the process by which technological paradigm shifts emerge is accelerating. The interval between the Palaeolithic and Neolithic Revolutions was about 1.5 million years, and that between the Neolithic and Industrial Revolutions was about 10 000 years; the time taken for the technological shifts to occur involved hundreds of thousands of years for the Palaeolithic, 4 000 years for the Neolithic, and 100 years for the Industrial Revolutions; and the time taken to transmit each of these new paradigms around the known world was about 1.2 million years for the Palaeolithic, 3 000 (plus) years for the Neolithic (in the Old World), and 200 (plus) years for the Industrial Revolutions. The pace of change is accelerating.

The development path implied by the great technological paradigm shifts is shown in Figure 11.1. It has been designed to show two things: the stepped profile of *potential* real GDP per capita at the global level made possible by the three technological revolutions (heavy line); and the more gradual expansion in *actual* real GDP per capita (broken line). The *potential* GDP per capita level increases relatively steeply – becoming more steep as we approach the present – during the revolution, but thereafter becomes stationary for much longer periods of time. It indicates the vast increase in productive potential of natural resources as a result of the new technology. On the other hand, *actual* GDP per capita grows only gradually to the potential ceiling and does so through a wave-like growth path.

This catching-up process by *actual* GDP per capita is driven by a number of dynamic mechanisms that are specific to their eras, yet they all embody the general strategic demand–strategic response mechanism. For example, prior to the Neolithic Revolution it was a process of global dispersion of the families of man (the 'great dispersion'); prior to the Industrial Revolution it was a process of the circular rise and fall (the 'great wheel') of civilizations based on the conquest and commerce strategies; and since the Industrial Revolution it has been a process of longrun linear fluctuations (the 'great waves' of economic change). These dynamic mechanisms gradually exhaust the prevailing technological paradigm by fully exploiting the capacity of the global resource base. Once the technological paradigm has been exhausted the only way forward – to avoid societal collapse – is to invest in a new technological paradigm. And at this stage, and only at this stage, it becomes economically feasible in benefit–cost terms. These technological paradigm shifts, therefore, are responses to changes in strategic demand. Of considerable interest is what the future may bring when the current industrial paradigm has been exhausted, as will inevitably happen, probably in the twenty-first century.[3]

EVIDENCE FOR THE STRATEGIC DEMAND–RESPONSE MECHANISM

In the dynamic-strategy model, the role of prices is central to the interaction between strategic demand and strategic response. As argued above, the unfolding dynamic strategy generates an increase in strategic demand that places pressure on existing resources, technologies, and institutions and leads, thereby, to an increase in prices (including wages) and extraordinary profits. Rising prices, therefore, provide the necessary incentives for the strategic response, which involves an increase in population, capital formation, human capital, and technological and institutional change. Prices will continue to rise until the prevailing dynamic strategy/substrategy has been either exhausted or derailed by exogenous shocks or ill-advised government policies.

While this model is based upon my earlier historical research (Figure 10.3), we need to explore it more formally here. Yet this is not a full-scale empirical study (which will be undertaken in a forthcoming book), rather it is an exercise to see if the growth–inflation predictions of my model are consistent with real-world evidence. As real GDP per capita can be regarded as a measure of the unfolding dynamic strategy, I will postulate a simple empirical model in which the rate of inflation is a stable function of the rate of economic growth. The dynamic-strategy model suggests that in order to launch a new technological substrategy and to achieve any growth at all, it is necessary for an economy to generate a moderate rate of inflation. Without this base level of inflation there will be no strategic response and, hence, no sustained economic growth.

Of course, economic growth is not the only determinant of inflation. For this reason it is necessary to draw a distinction between the systematic element in price increases, which I will call **strategic inflation**, and the more random elements, which I will call **nonstrategic inflation**, that are the outcomes of exogenous shocks (such as wars, epidemics, and resource bonanzas/crises) and institutional problems (such as inappropriate action by central banks, trade unions, and arbitration commissions). I will refer to total price increase as **nominal inflation**. Not surprisingly we face a problem in distinguishing between strategic inflation and nonstrategic inflation in the real world. This problem has increased during the twentieth century, particularly since the Second World War, as a result of the emergence of central banks with greater discretionary powers of intervention. Before the 1940s, the money supply was more directly responsive to market forces. Hence, it is in the historical data that the progress of strategic inflation can be seen most clearly.

The very longrun growth–inflation curve

By observing the parallel growth in prices and real GDP (both total and per capita) over the past millennium for Britain (Figure 10.3), it becomes clear that, in the very longrun, inflation is a positive function of economic growth.[4] This relationship is presented formally as a growth–inflation curve in Figure 11.2. The data underlying this very longrun curve comprise compound growth rates for inflation and real GDP per capita for Britain for each 10-year period over the six centuries from 1370 to 1994. As I am interested in the normal relationship between growth and inflation, only the positive values have been graphed and evaluated.[5] The econometric results confirm the original, visually based conclusion: both the constant and growth coefficients are significant at the 1 per cent level, there is no serial correlation or heteroskedasticity, and the function passes the specification tests.[6]

What does the very longrun growth–inflation curve tell us? In a timeless sense, Britain could expect that the launching of a successful dynamic

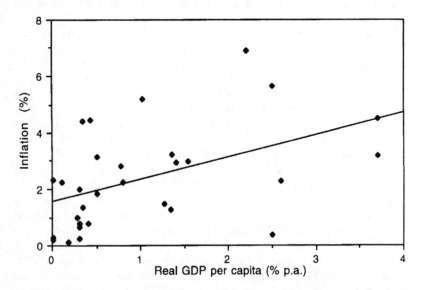

Figure 11.2 The very longrun growth–inflation curve, Britain 1370–1994
Note: Only positive values are used.

Source: Estimated from data in Snooks (1994b: 77–8) and Figure 10.3 above.

strategy or substrategy would require an initial rate of inflation of 1.6 per cent per annum, which would increase by 0.78 percentage points for every unit increase in the rate of economic growth up to at least 4 per cent per annum. In other words, in the very longrun, inflation is a systematic and stable function of the dynamic process. This stability, which contrasts starkly with the situation in some developing countries, is the outcome not of sociopolitical factors but of a successful dynamic strategy. While Britain is pursuing a viable dynamic strategy, as it has done over the past six centuries, there is no danger of inflation raging out of control. This would only occur if the dynamic strategy were permanently derailed as in some Third World countries. Even the rapid acceleration of inflation resulting from massive exogenous shocks (the Korean War and the OPEC oil crisis) was brought rapidly under control. Figure 11.2 also tells us that the very longrun growth–inflation curve is not vertical as neoclassical theory would lead us to expect.

These results are very robust, because between 1370 and 1994 Britain passed through three very different dynamic strategies – conquest, commerce, and technological change – together with a large number of contrasting substrategies. This has particular interest and importance because it suggests that the nature of the dynamic process transcends the type of dynamic strategy or substrategy being pursued. In other words, a similar relationship between growth and inflation existed throughout all these strategies and their many substrategies. This will be confirmed when we examine the longrun and shortrun growth–inflation curves.

The longrun growth–inflation curve

By employing *annual data* for Britain over the period 1870 to 1994, it is possible to estimate the growth–inflation curve for her mature technological strategy. The longrun growth–inflation curve presented in Figure 11.3 (positive values only) is remarkably similar to the very longrun curve. Once again both the constant and growth coefficients are significant (at the 5 and 1 per cent levels respectively), although the goodness of fit statistic is lower, and some of the diagnostic tests are less conclusive.[7]

This longrun growth–inflation curve suggests that the launching of a technological substrategy in Britain at any time during the past century would have required an initial rate of inflation of about 2.2 per cent per annum. Subsequently, this rate of inflation would increase by 0.87 percentage points for each unit increase in the rate of economic growth up to at least 8 per cent per annum. Once again we can conclude that inflation, which is a systematic outcome of the dynamic process, is both stable and nonaccelerating.

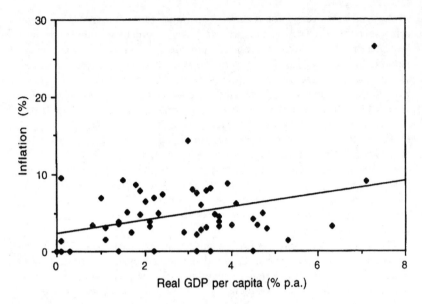

Figure 11.3 The longrun growth–inflation curve, Britain 1870–1994

Note: Only positive values are used.

Source: Estimated from data in Mitchell (1988) and Figure 10.3 above.

The shortrun growth–inflation curve

But do these longrun curves bear any relation to the shortrun curve? This question will be dealt with in two stages. First, I will employ cross-section data for all OECD countries since 1960 and, secondly, I will examine time-series data from 1961 to 1994 for a number of representative OECD countries. As will be seen, the more intrusive role of institutions in the modern economy tends to obscure the underlying systematic relationship between growth and strategic inflation. This is not an issue for the OECD cross-section growth–inflation curve, which possesses statistically significant results and passes the usual diagnostic tests. The individual country time-series curves, however, are more prone to the influence of institutional interference and policy errors that generate nonstrategic inflation. While a number of countries exhibit statistically significant results, there are some that do so only when proxies for institutional bungling in the money and labour markets are included. But even in the latter, the statistical constant – the initial inflation requirement – is always significant.

Figure 11.4 presents the cross-section data, which comprise average compound growth rates of inflation and real GDP per capita for all OECD

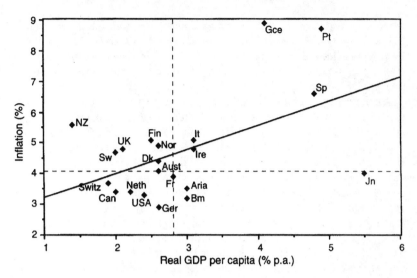

Figure 11.4   The shortrun growth–inflation curve, OECD countries, weighted averages for 1961–73 and 1983–93

Note: The countries include: Australia (Aust), Austria (Aria), Belgium (Bm), Canada (Can), Denmark (Dk), Finland (Fin), France (Fr), Germany (Ger), Italy (It), Japan (Jn), Netherlands (Neth), New Zealand (NZ), Norway (Nor), Sweden (Sw), Switzerland (Switz), United Kingdom (UK), Greece (Gr), Ireland (Ire), Portugal (Pt), Spain (Sp), and USA.

Source: Estimated from data in Maddison (1995).

countries during the combined period 1961 to 1973 and 1983 to 1993 (the OPEC crisis years have been excluded). This procedure can be expected to eliminate the random impact of exogenous shocks and minor institutional difficulties and errors of judgement. What does this modern growth–inflation curve show? First, it demonstrates a remarkably similar relationship to that in the historical data.[8] Once again the relationship is positive and stable, with the same slope coefficient as the longrun and very longrun functions. And as before, the constant and growth coefficients are statistically significant at the 1 per cent level, the goodness of fit (0.22) is relatively high, and the diagnostic tests are satisfactory.[9] The shortrun curve suggests that, on average, the launching of a successful technological substrategy in the modern period will require an initial rate of inflation of 2.5 per cent per annum, but that the growth rate can be increased to at least 6 per cent per annum with only a modest increase in the rate of inflation of about 0.78 percentage points for each additional unit of economic growth. By excluding the outliers of Greece and Portugal, the growth–inflation curve becomes much flatter – like the individual country curves – with an initial rate of inflation of 3.7 per cent per annum, and a slope of 0.2 percentage points for each additional unit of economic growth. It is interesting that not one OECD country over the post-1960 years achieved an average inflationary rate below 3 per cent, nor above 10 per cent – typically it was between 3.5 and 6 per cent. Once again this is the type of outcome my dynamic-strategy model predicts.

Secondly, Figure 11.4 shows the *average* growth–inflation outcomes of more than a score of countries possessing different strategic demand–response interactions. During the second half of the twentieth century, each OECD country (possessing a different set of factor endowments) can be thought of either as pursuing a different technological substrategy or as experiencing a different phase of the same substrategy. Owing to these different demand and supply characteristics, each country will enjoy different rates of economic growth and inflation. If we change the time period the scatter pattern remains much the same, but the countries marginally change their relative positions owing to the different timing of the unfolding and replacement of their respective substrategies.[10] The conclusion to be drawn is that at any point in time any one of these countries can, by employing an appropriate dynamic strategy, expect to increase its rate of economic growth with only a marginal increase in inflation, provided it can avoid excessive institutional intervention in the money and labour markets.

Thirdly, and more speculatively, Figure 11.4 suggests that there is also a pattern in the way OECD countries are grouped around the growth–inflation curve. A pattern that is determined by the nature and phase of individual dynamic substrategies. The diagram has been divided into quadrants so that there are approximately equal numbers of countries in each. As it turns out France, with an average rate of growth of 3.2 per cent per annum and an average inflation rate of 4.6 per cent per annum, is the axis country in the modern period. Countries in each of these quadrants display an interesting uniformity. The north-west quadrant (lower growth/higher inflation) is occupied by what I call 'developed natural-resource strategists', such as Australia, New Zealand, and the Scandinavian countries; the south-west quadrant (lower growth/lower inflation) by the 'old industrial strategists', such as USA, Germany, France, the Netherlands, and Switzerland; the south-east quadrant (higher growth/lower inflation) by the 'new industrial strategists', such as Japan and Austria; and the north-east quadrant (higher growth/ higher inflation) by the 'developing natural-resource strategists', such as Ireland, Spain, Portugal, and Greece.

Two points can be made about this growth–inflation distribution of OECD countries. In the first place, the distribution between quadrants depends largely on the type of substrategy being employed, which includes: the more traditional, large-scale industrial production of the old industrial strategists; the more modern, microelectronic/biotechnological industrial production of the new industrial strategists; the technological catch-up of the developing natural-resource strategists; and the more advanced production of the developed natural-resource strategists. And in the second place, it is important to realize that location in these quadrants is not fixed. As the prevailing individual substrategy unfolds and is replaced, some countries are likely to change quadrants. Except for those countries pursuing catch-up strategies, this is a gradual process ranging over at least two generations. These empirical issues will be explored more fully in a forthcoming book.

Finally, how should we interpret the different growth–inflation outcomes of countries in these quadrants? The dynamic-strategy model suggests that the north/south divide should be regarded as a distinction between the higher/lower incentives required in the dynamic process. Those countries in the northern half of Figure 11.4 require higher incentives to elicit the appropriate response to changes in strategic demand, while those in the southern half require lower incentives. But once the process is underway (as is revealed from an examination of individual countries), those with a lower initial inflation requirement typically experience upward-sloping growth–inflation functions, while those with higher initial inflation requirements typically experience downward-sloping functions.

The east/west divide should be thought of in terms of greater/lesser strategic efficiency. This concerns the ability to use available resources to generate economic growth, which largely depends upon the nature and phase of prevailing technological substrategies for individual countries. In the western half of Figure 11.4 individual countries are employing strategies that are close to exhaustion, while in the eastern half they are employing new strategies or are involved in technological catch-up.

The cross-section data suggest that further interesting insights might be gained from an examination of individual OECD countries using time-series data since 1960, but excluding the OPEC crisis years. While I will generalize from the entire OECD group, only selected material will be presented (in Figure 11.5) to illustrate the points being made.

Individual time-series price data for the modern period are often strongly influenced by institutional interference in the dynamic process. Hence we will not necessarily find a statistically significant relationship between growth and inflation at this level. As it turns out, significant growth–inflation relationships were found for Japan, Spain, and Greece, but not for Britain, USA, France, or Germany. Yet in all cases examined, the constant was significant at the 1 per cent level. This suggests that the growth–inflation curve for these countries is a horizontal band in which the values for individual years are influenced by institutional variables.

To construct a fully specified model to explain nominal (rather than strategic) inflation we need to include proxies on the explanatory side in order to capture the role of institutional intervention. Unfortunately there

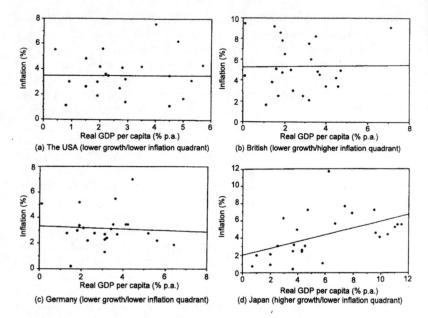

Figure 11.5   The shortrun growth–inflation curves for the USA, Britain, Germany, and Japan, 1961–94 (excluding OPEC crisis years)

Source: Estimated from data in Maddison (1995) and *IFS Yearbook*.

are no really suitable proxies, because variables such as nominal wages and money supply cannot be regarded as independent of the growth process. In large part they are a response to strategic demand. But, for what it is worth, when I used those proxies to explain inflation in the cases of Britain and the USA the significance, goodness of fit (in the range 0.45 to 0.64), and the various diagnostic tests improved quite dramatically. These results suggested that economic growth was the determinant of a process of systematic inflation with relatively high initial inflation requirements typically ranging from 4 to 7 per cent per annum, and that economic growth could be geared up to 12 per cent per annum with only a marginal increase or decrease in the rate of inflation. The reason inflation may rise higher in some countries and in some years is because of excessive and ill-advised institutional intervention by central banks in money markets and by trade unions and arbitration commissions in labour markets, not because of high rates of economic growth. There is a delicious irony here. In the absence of public intervention, the nominal rate of inflation would have been closer to the strategic rate. Finally, it should be noted that these results suggest that, in comparison to the longrun and very longrun, the shortrun growth–inflation curve has a higher initial inflation requirement and for some countries it is much flatter. This is the result of different dynamic mechanisms in different strategies and substrategies pursued over time.

The most important conclusion to emerge from this attempt to quantify the growth–inflation curve is that inflation, which is an essential part of the dynamic process, is a stable function of economic growth. Erratic bouts of nominal inflation are the outcome of institutional mismanagement. Hence inflation has no life of its own in a strategically viable society. Only when the dynamic strategy irretrievably breaks down and political institutions collapse is inflation likely to rage out of control. One way in which this could occur is if policies that are aimed at eliminating inflation are successful. To permanently eliminate inflation would be to permanently eliminate economic growth. A secondary conclusion is that the data refute the rational expectations hypothesis about the relationship between prices and output.

CONCLUSIONS

Strategic demand is the core concept in the dynamic-strategy model. Generated by a systematic exploitation of strategic opportunities, it calls forth a response from the supply variables of population, workforce, capital formation, and technological and institutional change. Orchestrated by inflation, this interactive process is called the strategic demand–response mechanism. This model predicts that, in a society successfully pursuing a viable dynamic strategy, inflation will be a stable and nonaccelerating function of economic growth. The results of the applied work undertaken in this chapter support this prediction in both the shortrun and longrun. They also give rise to the growth–inflation curve, which suggests that the initiation of sustained economic growth requires an initial rate of inflation of between 3 and 7 per cent per annum (depending on the type of technological substrategy chosen), and that it can be geared up to about 6 per cent per annum with only a marginal increase (or even decrease) in the inflation rate provided there is no monetary mismanagement. This has radical implications for economic policy.

12 The Dynamic-Strategy Model Revisited

It is time to revisit the dynamic-strategy model. Since providing a brief overview at the very beginning we have reviewed the various orthodox approaches to economic dynamics, outlined the likely benefits to be gained from the inductive approach, and examined in some detail the main components of the model. Attention has focused on the strategic principle of dynamic order, the role of materialist man, the realist dynamic form of the model, and the operation of the new concepts of strategic confidence and strategic demand. We need to draw the various components of the model together in order to show how it works. This will also form a basis for the discussion of economic fluctuations in Part VI and for an analysis of political change and policy in Part VII.

THE DRIVING FORCE

The endogenous driving force in the Dynamic Society is the competitive struggle by materialist man to survive and prosper. This is the major outcome of our biologically determined desires that have been shaped by genetic change over almost four billion years. In the dynamic-strategy model, as in life, ideas are an effective way of achieving the object of our desires, but they do so in a passive way. Two major implications emerge from this reality: that altruism is not a prime determinant of human behaviour; and that the decision-making process is not dominated by the neoclassical rationality model. Because these implications are borne out by history, it is necessary to develop realist models of both human behaviour and decision-making.

The concentric spheres model of human behaviour, outlined in Chapter 9, is based on the notion of genetically determined desires, but it allows for the exercise of human freedom of action (unlike the sociobiological model). In this model, the way an individual relates to other individuals and groups depends on their potential contribution to maximizing his or her material advantage. This potential contribution is measured in the concentric spheres model by the 'economic distance' between the self and other individuals and groups who occupy positions on a set of concentric spheres that radiate outwards (Figure 9.1). Underlying this model are two balancing sets of forces, one centrifugal and the other centripetal. The centrifugal force is the incessant desire of the self to survive and prosper, which leads the typical

160

individual to consistently pursue his or her own self-interest. This is the energizing force. The centripetal force, which can be thought of as the economic gravity holding society together, is generated by the self's need to co-operate with other individuals and groups in order to achieve its own objectives through the pursuit of a dominant dynamic strategy. It is through this interaction of competition and co-operation that the individual maximizes the probability of his or her survival and prosperity and that the society prospers. But the underlying condition for the trust required for co-operative activity, which should not be confused with altruism, is the generation of strategic confidence.

If ideas do not drive society, but merely facilitate the desires of its members, we need to replace the neoclassical rationality model with a realist model. Through the inductive method it is possible to derive such a model, which I have called the strategic-imitation model. In reality decision-making is based on the need to economize on nature's scarcest resource – intelligence. Rather than collect vast quantities of information on a large range of alternatives for processing through a mental model of the way the world works, the great majority of decision-makers – whom I have called strategic followers – merely imitate those people and those projects that are conspicuously successful. The only information they require is that necessary to answer the question: who and what is materially successful and why? Hence the important information required by decision-makers is imitative information, not benefit–cost information. Even the strategic pioneers do not employ rationalist techniques when seeking new ways of exploiting strategic opportunities. Rather than exhaustively seeking out the best investment projects, they believe that their investment projects are the best. It is the market that adjudicates.

THE DYNAMIC MECHANISM

The endogenous driving force, as we have seen, is provided by the dynamic concept of materialist man. It is a self-starting and self-sustaining force that drives a dynamic mechanism that has at its centre the pursuit of a dominant dynamic strategy and its component substrategies. This begins as an individual or family activity but, if successful, it is adopted by wider social groupings, at first local, then regional and, finally, national. And it is through the strategic-imitation mechanism, by which successful pioneering initiatives are imitated by a growing number of individuals and groups, that this aggregation process takes place. In this way a successful dynamic strategy becomes the object of political policies controlled by the ruling strategists.

The choice of strategy – from four possibilities including family multiplication, conquest, commerce, and technological change – depends on the underlying economic conditions, such as factor endowments and the nature of external competition. The important point to realize is that investment in these various dynamic strategies is undertaken for the same objective and involves a broadly similar process. The main difference is that investment in family multiplication, conquest, and commerce is undertaken to achieve growth through gaining control of new *external* resources while technological change is used to achieve growth through greater efficiency in the use of existing *internal* resources. As far as the strategist is concerned there is nothing special about technological change. Similarly, within the context of a particular dynamic strategy, entrepreneurs attempt to gain a competitive advantage through the adoption of new substrategies which, where successful, generate new technological styles.

As individuals and governments seek to exploit their physical and social environment, setting in train a mass movement orchestrated through strategic imitation, the dominant dynamic strategy unfolds in the sense that its opportunities are progressively exploited and, finally, exhausted. And it is this unfolding dynamic strategy that shapes the expectations of decision-makers. The eventual exhaustion of a dynamic strategy, as we have seen, is the outcome of the 'law of diminishing *strategic* returns'. The rise and fall of dynamic strategies and their substrategies traces out a distinctive strategic pathway, which provides the dynamic form for my model. This supersedes the arbitrary dynamic forms – the equilibrium growth path and path-dependence – adopted by supply-side neoclassical and evolutionary growth theorists. A dynamic form cannot be deduced logically from a set of assumptions about the production function, particularly when production is only relevant to one type of dynamic strategy. A general dynamic form can only be arrived at empirically.

From historical observation we can derive a general dynamic form that encompasses a series of wave-like surges in economic growth that are separated by intervals of stability or retreat. This sequence consists of 'great waves' of about 300 years and within each of these, 'long waves' of about 40 years. As we have seen, the great waves are generated by dynamic strategies and the long waves by a series of substrategies. The sequence of great waves reflects the sequence of dynamic strategies, each of which passes through a wave-like surge of exploitation and exhaustion. It should be realized that these wave-like surges are *not* part of a dynamic 'cycle', because the intervals between them are not systematically related to the surges before and after. Each of these intervals is a hiatus following the exhaustion of a dynamic strategy during which the strategic pioneers search desperately for a replacement strategy. If they are successful the sequence will continue (often by reverting to an earlier strategy) but, if they are not, the sequence comes to an end and the society collapses. This happened in the case of all ancient societies. Unlike the neoclassical equilibrium growth path, the strategic pathway is not an optimizing concept. It can only be identified retrospectively.

STRATEGIC DEMAND AND STRATEGIC CONFIDENCE

The unfolding dynamic strategy, driven by the competitive energy of materialist man, plays a central role in the dynamic-strategy model. Not only does it provide the model with a realist dynamic form, but it gives rise to two important new concepts in economics that I have called strategic confidence and strategic demand. These concepts explain not only the dynamics of longrun investment and saving that are left hanging in orthodox, comparative-static macroeconomics, but also how dynamic order is generated.

Strategic confidence, which rises and falls with the dominant dynamic strategy and its various substrategies, explains the changing investment climate in the Dynamic Society. It provides a dynamic explanation for Keynes' 'state of long-term expectation'. Accordingly, it plays a central role in determining the willingness of strategic pioneers and their followers to invest, because of its influence on the longrun expected rate of return and in the creation of dynamic order (through encouraging co-operation and an orderly institutional structure). Confidence and expectations rise as the dynamic strategy unfolds, and they decline, stagnate, and possibly collapse as it is progressively exhausted. Strategic confidence also binds society together.

Strategic demand also rises and falls with the dynamic strategy. It is the effective demand exercised by decision-makers for a wide range of physical, intellectual, and institutional inputs required in the strategic pursuit. In exploiting the strategic opportunities, entrepreneurs need to invest in new infrastructure; to purchase intermediate goods; to employ labour skills; to acquire or construct the necessary buildings, machinery, and equipment; and to develop new facilitating social rules and organizations. Strategic demand is, therefore, the central active principle in society. Naturally the supply response of population, capital formation, and technological change, which depends on relative prices, will contribute to the way in which the strategic opportunities are exploited, but they do so passively. Thus we must turn Say's Law – which was accepted explicitly by classical economists and implicitly by neoclassical economists – on its head: in the Dynamic Society, demand creates its own supply.

Strategic demand and strategic confidence together explain the variables that Keynesian macroeconomics either assumes to be given or leaves in the swamplands of 'psychological propensities' and institutional arrangements. The 'state of long-term expectation', the propensity to consume, and the liquidity-preference schedule are all left unexplained in Keynes' comparative–static model of employment. By contrast, in the dynamic-strategy model they are treated as economic rather than psychological or institutional issues, and can be readily explained in terms of strategic demand and strategic confidence. The dynamic-strategy model treats investment, saving/consumption, the rate of interest, employment, and real GDP as joint outcomes of these two concepts. Hence, the saving required to finance investment – one of the great problems for neoclassical economics – is generated by the growth process rather than being its precondition.

The dynamic-strategy model, therefore, is able to encompass *The General Theory* as a special case. This possibility, I like to think, would not have surprised Keynes, who was acutely aware that he was painting a static picture at a point in time rather than exploring a moving picture over time. To do so he was forced to invent psychological laws which filled the gap left by a lack of historical observation. Laws should explain what we know, rather than obscure what we do not know.

The claim made in this book is that the dynamic-strategy model resolves the difficulties experienced in employing Keynesian economics during the volatile conditions of the 1970s. These difficulties drove most orthodox economists back into the neoclassical, supply-side camp. And because of this, macroeconomic policy is currently based on the misplaced microeconomic notions about the desirability of balance – of equilibrium – in internal budgets, external trade accounts, and prices. In order to place Keynesian macroeconomics in a wider framework and to sensibly address issues of macroeconomic policy we need to develop a persuasive dynamic model.

STRATEGIC DEMAND AND STRATEGIC RESPONSE

With the dynamic-strategy model, we can shift focus from comparative–static macroeconomics to longrun dynamics by considering the interaction between strategic demand and the strategic response of supply-side variables. It is this interaction that gives rise to the strategic pathway – the dynamic form of our model – and to the dynamic role played by inflation in facilitating the strategic response. These are the major differences between strategic theory and orthodox theory. In neoclassical economics the supply-side is, by default, treated as the active force in society (supply creates its own demand), which has no place for inflation, while in Keynesian economics the supply-side variables are merely assumed to be given. By contrast, in the dynamic-strategy model, strategic demand provides the active force to which the supply-side variables respond. Strategic inflation, which provides the incentive system in this strategic demand–response mechanism, is a stable, non-accelerating function of economic growth. This theoretical relationship can be empirically estimated in the form of the growth–inflation curve. It has radical implications for policy.

Population, labour supply, capital formation, and technological and institutional ideas all respond to the unfolding dynamic strategy. Changes in these supply-side variables, both in terms of composition and growth rates, are a function of changing strategic opportunities. These variables expand

and become more complex as the dominant dynamic strategy is exploited, and they stagnate, decline, and sometimes collapse, as the dynamic strategy is progressively exhausted. Naturally, supply-side costs play a role in shaping the strategic response, but this is a passive rather than an active role. In this way the supply-side variables are treated endogenously in the dynamic-strategy model. Dynamic demand creates its own supply.

CONCLUSIONS

In a nutshell, the Dynamic Society is characterized as being driven by the biologically determined desires – to survive and prosper – of materialist man, who invests in the most efficient dynamic strategy or substrategy. Feedback is provided by the changing material standards of living. This exploration of strategic opportunities drives the unfolding dynamic strategy that provides a dynamic form for our model – the strategic sequence of great and long waves – and gives rise to parallel shifts in strategic demand and strategic confidence. In turn, these two key concepts are responsible for creating dynamic order and generating an increase in investment, saving, population, labour skills, ideas of all sorts, and institutions and organizations. This self-starting and self-maintaining dynamic process continues only until a dynamic strategy/substrategy has been exhausted – when strategic confidence and strategic demand decline – and will only begin again anew when the old strategy/substrategy has been replaced. If this substitution cannot be achieved, the society will stagnate and, eventually, collapse.

Part VI
The Dynamic Outcome

13 The Orthodox Explanation of Fluctuations

During the twentieth century, business cycles, or shortrun economic fluctuations, have attracted the attention of a large number of leading economists. A sample of these includes economists of the stature of J.S. Duesenberry, Irving Fisher, Milton Friedman, Gottfried Haberler, Alvin Hansen, Roy Harrod, R.G. Hawtrey, Friedrich Hayek, John Hicks, N. Kaldor, J.M. Keynes, Simon Kuznets, R.C.O. Matthews, Wesley Mitchell, Arthur Pigou, D.H. Robertson, Arthur Spiethoff, and Joseph Schumpeter. And since the 1970s there has been an upsurge of interest in short-term fluctuations by advocates of 'real business cycle' theory (Stadler 1994). With the exception of Schumpeter (and possibly Harrod), these economists were concerned with shortrun rather than longrun fluctuations, mainly because the identification and analysis of long waves requires more historical knowledge than most economists possess. Most scholars interested in longrun fluctuations, as we shall see in Chapter 14, tend to be unorthodox, mainly Marxist, in economic persuasion.

The striking characteristic of the large literature on business cycles is its diversity. While there are a number of broad categories into which business-cycle theorists can be placed – such as overinvestment theories, underconsumption theories, psychological theories, monetary theories, and fiscal theories – nearly all of the important contributors to this genre have been able to claim a degree of uniqueness for their theorizing.[1] Accordingly the literature contains a plethora of different interpretations of the recessions of the 1980s and 1990s – to say nothing of the Great Depression of the 1930s – and of different policy prescriptions. The reason for this diversity is quite clear. No one has been able to advance a completely convincing theory of economic fluctuations on either logical or empirical grounds. Even at the end of a century of intensive investigation, there is no consensus as to the cause of the depressions and recessions experienced by developed societies over the past one hundred years.

The objective of this chapter is to explore the reasons for the lack of consensus concerning business cycles and to suggest how this problem might be resolved. An effective way of doing this is to approach the many different explanations through the apparatus sometimes used to examine shortrun fluctuations. No attempt will be made to survey all the available models, not least because that has been done excellently elsewhere.[2]

Currently, most applied macroeconomists (unlike academic theoreticians) approach shortrun fluctuations using a modified Keynesian approach, conveniently summarized through the IS–LM model developed by John Hicks (1937). While this approach is usually thought of as Keynesian, it does reintroduce the classical theory of interest into Keynes' monetary theory (Fitzgibbons 1988: 147–9). It was the beginning of the neoclassical synthesis – the reassertion of supply-side dominance. Basically there are two approaches. Those who, like J.M. Keynes, assume that prices are inflexible in the shortrun, and the real business-cycle theorists who, like the neoclassical economists, assume that prices are flexible in all time periods. Both groups, however, divorce their discussion of shortrun fluctuations from longrun growth, an approach that has characterized orthodox economics throughout the second half of the twentieth century.

THE NEW KEYNESIAN ECONOMICS

Aggregate demand and supply

Mainstream macroeconomists draw a distinction between the shortrun and the longrun in terms of the behaviour of prices. While it is agreed that in the longrun prices are flexible and markets clear, it is thought that in the short-run prices are inflexible because of market imperfections. It is this assumption of price inflexibility that underlies the Keynesian IS–LM model.

In *The General Theory*, Keynes saw imperfections in the labour, commodity, and money markets as arising from institutional rigidities (trade union activities) and psychological propensities (the speculative demand for money leading to a liquidity trap). But he did not spend a great deal of time investigating the issue because the central concept in his theory is effective demand. This matter only assumed a high priority when the Keynesian model came under attack by neoclassical macroeconomists after the mid-1970s. Much of the 'new Keynesian economics' has focused on the reasons for market imperfections and, hence, price and wage inflexibility in the shortrun.What is sometimes overlooked is that Keynes did not claim that wages and prices are rigid, just that markets do not instantaneously and continuously clear (Tobin 1993: 46). The resulting hypotheses arising from this research, which need not be detailed here, deal with: the costs (called 'menue costs') involved in adjusting prices frequently; the staggered nature by which prices and wages do change; coordination failure resulting from imperfect information between firms and other organizations attempting to second guess each other; and 'insider' agreements between workers and management to reduce employment and raise wages above market rates at the expense of 'outsiders' (Gordon 1990; Mankiw and Romer 1991). Of course, this supply-side market failure approach downplays J.M. Keynes' demand-side emphasis on long-term expectations and distorts his vision, all

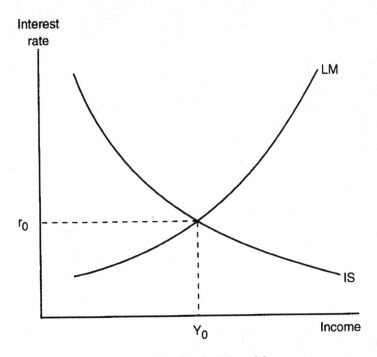

Figure 13.1 The IS–LM model

in the attempt to provide a microeconomic foundation for Keynesian macro-economics.

The IS–LM model is so well known that it now requires little exposition. I will, therefore, be brief. In *The General Theory* there is a complex relationship between investment, the interest rate, and income – more complex than even its author fully realized. This can be sorted out in two stages. First, while investment is determined by the marginal efficiency of capital schedule and the rate of interest (which in turn depends on the demand for and supply of liquidity), and income responds to changes in investment, the marginal efficiency of capital in turn is influenced by changes in income. This can be expressed by the IS (investment/saving) curve in Figure 13.1, which shows the relationship between the interest rate and income.

Secondly, while the rate of interest in Keynes' model is determined by the intersection of the liquidity preference curve and the stock of money (the demand for and supply of money), liquidity preference is also influenced by changes in income, as an increase in income will raise the demand for money. This relationship can be expressed, in real terms, by the LM (liquidity preference/money) curve in Figure 13.1, which describes the various rates

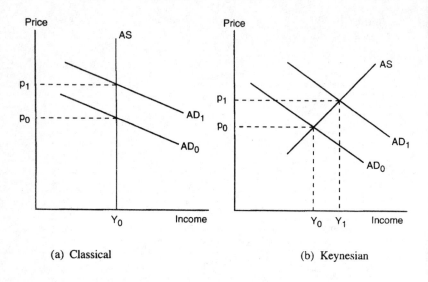

(a) Classical   (b) Keynesian

Figure 13.2 Aggregate demand and supply curves

of interest at different levels of income. The intersection of the IS and LM curves represents simultaneous equilibrium in both the goods market and the money market. It is, in other words, the point at which actual expenditure equals planned expenditure, and where the demand for real money balances equals supply.

The IS–LM model can also be used to derive, in a more sophisticated way than that employed in *The General Theory*, the Keynesian aggregate demand and aggregate supply curves. As there is a separate LM curve for each price level (with a given supply of money), it is possible to derive an aggregate demand curve that summarizes the Keynesian relationship between income and prices (see Figure 13.2, panel (b)). While Keynes does not deal with the aggregate supply curve at length, it is clear from his analysis that his version differs from the classical aggregate supply curve because of a different assumption about price flexibility. In Figure 13.2, panel (a), the neoclassical aggregate supply curve is represented by a vertical line, which implies that output is determined solely by factor supplies and the production function, because the price level always adjusts to equate the quantity of output demanded and the quantity supplied. As shown in this figure, a shift in aggregate demand affects prices but not income. On the other hand, as Keynes regarded prices as inflexible in the shortrun due to market imperfections, the aggregate supply curve slopes upwards to the right. Because of this characteristic, a shift in the aggregate demand curve will lead to a change in income as well as in prices.

The Phillips curve and the natural rate of unemployment

The Phillips curve, which postulates a negative relationship between the rate of unemployment and the rate of inflation (see Figure 13.3, panel (a)) is sometimes justified by its similarity with the aggregate supply curve. During the decade following the observation of this alleged causal relationship by Bill Phillips (1958), inflation was regarded as a stable inverse function of unemployment. In other words if unemployment fell, inflation increased – and *vice versa*. This simple 'model' was thereafter appended to the prevailing Keynesian IS–LM analysis, because it appeared to be able to explain the adjustment of prices that were treated as given in the orthodox analysis.

At the end of the 1960s, the unemployment–inflation relationship was remodelled along more neoclassical lines, when both Milton Friedman (1968) and Edmund Phelps (1968), working from microeconomic principles, introduced an expectations function into the Phillips curve. In this revised model, which was supported by those adopting the neoclassical synthesis, inflation depended on both unemployment and inflationary expectations. But, according to Friedman, the expected rate of inflation can only be used to predict the actual rate of inflation when unemployment is fixed at an equilibrium rate that he called the 'natural rate of unemployment'. This model involves a distinction between the shortrun when fluctuations in

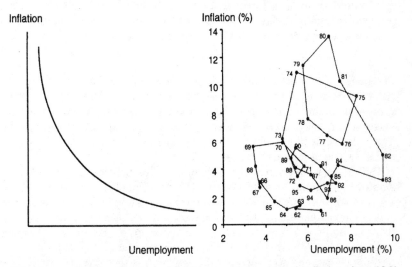

(a) Abstract Phillips Curve   (b) US unemployment and inflation since 1961

Figure 13.3 The Phillips curve and reality

unemployment can affect inflation, and the longrun when actual unemployment gravitates toward the natural or equilibrium rate owing to the adjustment of inflationary expectations. In other words, the trade-off between unemployment and inflation only holds in the shortrun; in the longrun the Phillips curve, like the neoclassical aggregate supply curve, is vertical. This development was an important part of the successful attempt by the prevailing supply-side paradigm in economics to absorb and distort Keynesian demand-side economics. Edmund Phelps (1994) has recently taken this even further by developing a general equilibrium model to explain 'structural slumps' by focusing on aggregate supply rather than aggregate demand. The fact that this model is unable to explain the disparate unemployment experience between the EU on the one hand and the USA and Japan on the other since the early 1980s does not seem to have deterred him.

Friedman's concept of the natural rate of unemployment, more recently called the 'nonaccelerating, inflationary rate of unemployment' (NAIRU), is, therefore, an important example of the gravitational devices employed by a supply-side paradigm unable to model dynamic demand. In this respect it is interesting to read what an observer of the natural rate of unemployment literature has recently written:

> Reading Friedman's (1968) AEA presidential address, I think he is also describing an economy in which at any moment actual unemployment may be either above or below its natural rate, but it is continually gravitating toward its natural rate... Again, it is hard not to see his natural rate concept as the deterministic steady state equilibrium rate of unemployment.   (Rogerson 1997: 90)

The policy implication of this model is that government action designed to reduce the actual rate of employment below the natural rate might appear successful in the shortrun, but the resulting inflation generated over the longer term would force a return to the natural rate of unemployment. This is an interesting example of supply-side determinism, which has had a major distorting influence on economic policy.

The natural rate of unemployment concept faces three major theoretical and empirical problems. First, this concept has no compelling underlying theory. The generalized discussions about labour markets employed to vindicate this concept are rather *ad hoc* and are more descriptive than theoretical. Rather, this concept depends on an empirical relationship that is expected always to hold. This is a problem, because if the empirical relationship fails – if unemployment does not accurately predict inflation – then the natural rate of unemployment concept ceases to be meaningful or useful (Galbraith 1997: 94).

The second major problem facing this concept is that the evidence for the Phillips curve in OECD countries since the 1960s is not very convincing (see

Figure 13.3, panel (b)). Certainly the situation has been complicated by the large increase in oil prices set by OPEC during the 1970s, but even taking supply shocks into account, the story is not as clear cut as many orthodox economists would like (Blanchard and Katz 1997: 66–9). It is difficult to see in the data either the expected shortrun shifts in the Phillips curve as a result of changes in expectations, or the longrun vertical Phillips curve.

Finally, there are considerable difficulties involved in estimating the size of the natural rate of unemployment, an essential step if this concept is to be employed in policy formulation. It is widely acknowledged that the natural rate estimates are imprecise and that the resulting forecasts of inflation are insensitive (Staiger *et al.* 1997: 46–7). Some have even concluded from these results that the natural rate of unemployment does not exist (Galbraith 1997: 99), while others have demonstrated that alternative variables – such as the capacity utilization rate, other labour market variables, interest rates, and some monetary aggregates – are better predictors of inflation than unemployment (Staiger *et al.* 1997: 44–6). The latter suggests that there is nothing unique about the relationship between unemployment and inflation.

These difficulties emerge when attempting not only to predict inflation, but also to explain different relationships between inflation and unemployment in the same economy over time or between different economies at a point in time. A particular worry is the performance of the EU during the first half of the 1990s when stable inflation co-existed with steadily rising unemployment. The usual argument is that these changes/differences can be explained largely by changes/differences in the natural rate of unemployment. But, of course, this merely begs the question of why differences in the natural rate occur. This leads orthodox economists into embarrassing ad hocery; into making lists of variables – such as changes/differences in demographic structure, tax rates, market competition, or productivity – that conceivably might have some impact (Stiglitz 1997: 5–8; Blanchard and Katz 1997: 66–9). It merely demonstrates the poverty of orthodox thinking on this issue. In the next chapter I will employ a single robust model to show not only that there is no *causal* relationship between unemployment and inflation, but also why we expect changes/differences in the *nominal* relationship between them.

EVALUATING BUSINESS-CYCLE THEORY

The IS–LM model is a simple but convenient way of sorting out the different sources of shortrun fluctuations in income. As my realist model does not recognize the role of rational expectations (owing to an entirely different explanation of individual decision-making), the IS–LM diagram can, despite the contrary argument by King (1993), be used for this purpose. These sources, which are the subject of various business-cycle theories, are treated as exogenous shocks to the model. This can be achieved by applying these various theories to the Great Depression, which began in the USA and was quickly transmitted to a fragile world after 1929. Most of the existing theories regarding the onset of the Great Depression can be summarized under five main headings: overinvestment, underconsumption, psychological, monetary, and fiscal.

Overinvestment theories

The most important group of theories about the business cycle concern the issue of overinvestment. These theories can be subdivided according to the main cause of this overinvestment, either monetary forces (Hayek 1933; Robbins 1934), real forces (Cassel 1932; Schumpeter 1939, 1949), or the accelerator principle (Robertson 1915; Harrod 1936; Matthews 1959). This overinvestment leads to growing economic maladjustment that can be either 'vertical' (as between the capital goods sector and the consumer goods sector) or 'horizontal' (as between various productive sectors).

Basically these hypotheses suggest that overinvestment leads to a decline in rates of return, a loss of confidence in future returns and, hence, a sharp fall in investment. This is represented in Figure 13.4, panel (b), showing a contraction in IS, leading to a fall in both GDP and the interest rate. As this accords with the reality of the Great Depression, it becomes a likely contender. Certainly it is one of the most popular 'explanations' of the Great

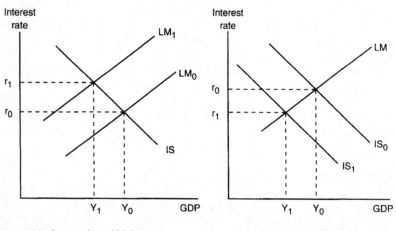

(a) Contraction of LM   (b) Contraction of IS

Figure 13.4 Evaluating business-cycle theory

Depression and it (particularly the horizontal maladjustment or structural disequilibrium version) tends to fit the detailed facts of depression experience (Schumpeter 1939; Butlin 1964; Snooks 1974). The major problem with this hypothesis, which will be taken up in Chapter 14, is that the underlying idea – every boom sows the seeds of its own destruction – is teleological in nature. No persuasive theory has been formulated to explain this idea.

Underconsumption theories

While the theories of underconsumption are generally treated warily, Keynes (1936: 358–71) expressed a degree of empathy with writers such as Bernard Mandeville (1660–1733), Thomas Robert Malthus (1766–1834) and John Atkinson Hobson (1858–1940), although not with the heresies of Major Douglas.[3] This empathy concerned the basic idea in *The General Theory* that, owing to market imperfections, the gap between consumption and the full employment level of GDP will grow as GDP increases, and that it will not inevitably be completely filled by independently determined investment expenditure. While Keynes thought it essential in the midst of recession or depression to expand investment, he also advocated the stimulation of consumption (Keynes 1936: 324–6).

This Keynesian framework appears to provide support for the argument that a major problem in the USA during the 1920s was the stagnation and decline of demand for consumer durables. Could this form of underconsumption have led to the downturn in USA economic activity after 1929? No doubt it could have caused the IS curve in Figure 13.4, panel (b) to shift backwards, leading to a fall in both GDP and the general level of prices. Certainly Keynes' response to such a scenario would have been to expand fiscal policy in order to reduce unemployment and stimulate consumer demand – a reverse shift of the IS curve in Figure 13.4. While this scenario appears to fit the facts of the Great Depression, there is no orthodox model that can explain the saturation of the American market for consumer durables. The dynamic-strategy model discussed in Chapter 14, by contrast, is able to accommodate this scenario.

Psychological theories

Psychological theories, which appealed particularly to British economists in the first half of the twentieth century, are less precise than the above 'objective' theories. The main contributors to this field are Keynes (1936), Pigou (1929), Lavington (1925), and (in the USA) Taussig (1911). Basically these theorists argued that, owing to uncertainty about the future, states of confidence are highly volatile and regularly override the 'objective' forces that are central to alternative theories.

J.M. Keynes in particular based his theory on psychological propensities. In *The General Theory*, as we have seen, Keynes' contribution is based entirely on three psychological propensities – the propensity to consume, the liquidity preference and, most importantly, the 'state of long-term expectation'. It is the state of expectation regarding the future yield of capital goods that, in Keynes' eyes, gives the marginal efficiency of capital such volatility. As he explains: 'a more typical, and often predominant explanation of the crisis is, not primarily a rise in the rate of interest, but a sudden collapse in the marginal efficiency of capital' (Keynes 1936: 315). This collapse in expectations is the result of investor overconfidence during the boom failing to be borne out by subsequent events. It is interesting that Keynes attempts to draw a distinction between his psychological thesis and the overinvestment theories (ibid.: 320–1). Even a large reduction in the interest rate, Keynes thought, would not be sufficient to prevent a dramatic reduction in investment. This psychological impact, as shown in Figure 13.4, panel (b), has a contractionary effect on the IS curve, which leads to a sudden reduction in both GDP and the interest rate.

The problem with Keynes' expectations theory is that it does not contain a model of the cyclical nature of investor confidence. While Keynes puts it down to 'animal spirits', he is unable to explain why investors become excessively overconfident during a boom, why their expectations are subsequently dashed, or why they ultimately recover once more. To explain the apparent regularity of the 'trade cycle', Keynes resorts to non-psychological, or objective, factors such as the length of life of assets and the carrying costs of surplus stocks (ibid.: 317–18). But if we are to make much sense of his expectations hypothesis we need to endogenize Keynes' psychological propensities and, in the process, convert them into economic laws. This is an objective of Chapter 14.

More recently, the psychological argument that seems to appeal to most economists is the 'Wall Street crash hypothesis'. It is usually revived each time there is a serious financial crisis. Interestingly it is expected to operate not through the marginal efficiency of capital schedule, but through the marginal propensity to consume. A stock market crash is seen as the result of overconfidence by investors who become increasingly involved in speculative activities until it is finally realized that the market cannot support the high prices of existing capital assets. When everyone attempts to sell, the stock market collapses. The Wall Street crash hypothesis states that any large stock market crash will reduce the wealth of speculators, which will lead them to reduce their consumption. This will produce a contractionary movement of the IS curve in Figure 13.4 and will lead to a reduction in both GDP and the rate of interest. A surprising number of economists believe that this mechanism was responsible for the Great Depression and that it will generate serious recessions in the future.

While it appears to be compatible with the facts of the Great Depression, there are good reasons for rejecting the Wall Street crash hypothesis. Had more fundamental forces not been operating in the USA during the second half of the 1920s, it is unlikely that the Wall Street crash would have caused more than a ripple on the surface of the economy, because the wealth effect, which is limited to speculators, would have been largely negated by the release of financial capital, previously used for gambling, for more productive purposes. This would negate any contractionary influence on the IS curve. A good test of this argument is the aftermath of the 1987 stock market crash, which many economists (unlike informed economic historians) argued would lead to a severe recession. It did not, not only because of this offsetting mechanism but because in 1987, unlike 1929, the current USA dynamic substrategy was not in the process of exhaustion. This will be discussed further in the next chapter.

Monetary theories

While each author of the monetary hypothesis (Hawtrey 1913; Friedman and Schwartz 1982) provides a different emphasis, the underlying argument is that a downturn in economic activity is the result of a contraction in the money supply. Some monetarists (Hawtrey 1913) even argue that the upswing would go on indefinitely if there was no artificial reduction in the money supply, as a result of the private banking system, the central bank, or some exchange mechanism such as the old gold standard. In other words, the monetary hypothesis is an institutionalist argument: depressions and recessions are the outcome of inadequate institutions and policies rather than of forces that emerge from the dynamic process itself. To support their hypothesis, monetarists draw attention to the fact that the money supply in the USA declined by 25.2 per cent between 1929 and 1933 while the unemployment rate increased from 3.2 to 25.2 per cent. The main reason for this dramatic fall in the money supply was a decline in the reserve-deposit and currency-deposit ratios rather than in the monetary base (currency plus reserves). This appears to have been due to the large number of bank suspensions and closures (some 9000 between 1930 and 1933) rather than central bank restriction (Friedman and Schwartz 1982). And these bank closures had more fundamental economic causes.

The problem here is sorting out cause from effect. It is hardly surprising that the money supply declined by one-quarter during the contractionary phase of the Great Depression as real GDP in the USA over the same period declined by 30.5 per cent. But in order to evaluate what was driving what, we need to refer once again to our IS–LM model. As Figure 13.4, panel (a) shows, an autonomous fall in the money supply would drive the LM curve backwards, increasing the interest rate and reducing GDP. An obvious problem with the monetary argument, however, is that in reality the interest rate fell rather than rose. Indeed in the USA between 1929 and 1933 the nominal interest rate fell by 71.2 per cent (US Census 1960).

Less obviously, the LM curve will only shift backwards if *real* money balances fall which, for the USA, was not the case during the early years of the Great Depression. Between 1929 and 1931 prices fell even more rapidly than the money supply, and only after 1931 did real money balances fall (Temin 1976). At best, money restriction could only have aggravated the decline once it was already well under way. And even then, monetarists need to be able to explain the continuing fall in interest rates. In terms of the standard macroeconomic model, the monetary hypothesis does not appear to be a serious contender for explaining the Great Depression.

Fiscal theories

The final group of hypotheses are also institutional in nature. They are based on the idea of government intervention gone wrong. Prior to the publication of *The General Theory* in 1936, the orthodox view of government responsibility was that it should always attempt to balance its budget. Failure to do so would lead to inflationary pressures that would cause economic difficulties. During the Great Depression, when unemployment was rising rapidly, governments were advised by economists and bankers to balance their budgets. Of course, in terms of the IS–LM model, this would have induced a backward shift of the IS curve that in turn would have led to a reduction in both GDP and the interest rate. This analysis has led Keynesian economists to argue that depression governments must take much of the responsibility for the onset and severity of the Great Depression.

Of course, in theory this makes sense. But detailed studies of the depression (Schedvin 1970; Snooks 1974; Gregory and Butlin 1988) show that contractionary policies were generally forced on governments by their bankers. But, more importantly, it was impossible to actually achieve balanced budgets at a time when revenues, which were collapsing, fell faster than expenditures owing to the inflexibility of government commitments. In fact governments did not achieve balanced budgets until the mid-1930s. Thus, they were not responsible for the downturn and decline – although by pursuing more expansionary policies they could have slowed it down – but they did put a brake on recovery after the mid-1930s. Even the much trumpeted 'new deal' policies were pursued at the expense of government expenditure in more traditional avenues. In effect this involved a shift of full-time workers into part-time jobs. Elsewhere I have called this the policy of 'robbing Peter to pay Paul' (Snooks 1988: 328–34).

There is a strong parallel between orthodox economic thinking in both the 1990s and the 1920s. In many OECD countries, governments and their

advisers have long since rejected Keynesian policy. Many influential orthodox economists have, for no good theoretical or empirical reason, decided
that inflation, the deficit on the current account, and budgetary surpluses are
to be targeted and eliminated. Even if this means increasing the rate of
unemployment in the short term. This action is actually seen as an essential
first step to achieve economic growth and longer term full employment. And
it is just this sort of hair-shirt policy that appeals to governments. Clearly in
the shortrun, such policy will lead to a reduction in GDP and an increase in
unemployment, and in the longrun it will seriously undercut the dynamics of
individual societies and the full employment of their citizens. Old Keynesians, such as J.K. Galbraith (1983) and J. Cornwall (1994), have made this
point forcefully.

Overview

While the IS–LM model can demonstrate the manner in which exogenous
shocks affect GDP, employment, and the interest rate, it cannot explain the
sources of shortrun fluctuations. What we need is a model that can endogenize these sources of change. This is a problem not just for the IS–LM
model, which is a major tool of policy-oriented macroeconomic analysis, but
also for all deductive business-cycle theories dealt with briefly in the above
five categories.

Essentially, existing business-cycle theories have been unable to demonstrate why overinvestment emerges, why the money supply falls, why stock
markets and banks crash, why the level of consumption might be a problem,
why governments feel the need to balance budgets when unemployment is
increasing, or why business expectations collapse suddenly, are slow to
recover but ultimately increase rapidly. We need an encompassing theory
in order to explain these issues endogenously – a model that has eluded
some of the best minds in the economics profession during the twentieth
century. I want to suggest that the reason is neither lack of interest nor lack
of talent, but rather the exclusive adoption of the deductive method that is
incapable of generating an encompassing model. In addition to its deductive
methodology, the economics profession needs to be open to the achievements of the inductive methodology. This objective is pursued in Chapter 14.

A further issue is the well-recognized failure of orthodox economics to integrate the analysis of shortrun fluctuations with longrun growth. In modern
macroeconomics these two fields of enquiry have been completely divorced
from each other. The older classical view (Smith 1776; Malthus 1798; Mill
1848; Marx 1867–94) that the dynamics of human society proceeds in a fluctuating manner has been ignored by modern neoclassical economists. Only that
generation of economists prior to the development of the neoclassical growth

model, and historical economists since then, have been concerned to develop models that deal with both growth and fluctuations. As noted in Chapter 3 above, the neoclassical growth model generates a smooth growth path.

The mid-twentieth century attempts to integrate growth and fluctuations were made by economists working in the Keynesian tradition.[4] Basically their models involve analyses of the growth and fluctuations of effective demand. They treat the growth of effective demand as the outcome of exogenous increases in population and technological change, that in turn define the expansion of 'potential supply' or the 'potential growth rate', which, in Harrodian terms, is the 'natural growth rate'. Shortrun cycles are the outcome of economic fluctuations around this rising 'natural' growth path.

This approach, however, is plagued by a number of limiting problems. First, growth and fluctuations are still treated separately. None of those theorists was able to develop an encompassing model to explain both aspects of the dynamic process. Secondly, the sources of growth – population increase and technological change – remain exogenous and, hence, unexplained. Thirdly, and ironically for a Keynesian framework, the growth of effective demand is really a response to aggregate supply. This approach is merely a dynamic version of Say's Law. And finally, the model, quite unrealistically, is based on the idea of a moving equilibrium.

THE NEW CLASSICAL ECONOMICS

An alternative approach to the analysis of shortrun fluctuations is the real business-cycle theory formulated by neoclassical theorists. This theory is based on the central assumption in neoclassical economics, that prices are completely flexible – indeed perfectly and instantaneously flexible – even in the shortrun. Two important implications arise from this assumption. First, nominal variables such as the money supply and the price level do not influence the real variables of output and employment. Hence the name, 'real' business-cycle theory. This is the slender basis for the neoclassical argument that a deflationary monetary policy will reduce inflation without reducing output or growth. Secondly, real GDP and employment are determined by both the supply of productive factors and the nature of the production function. Consequently we are back in a supply-side world, where demand is merely a response to supply.

While the new classical model builds on Keynesian IS–LM analysis, there are important differences. Because these theorists regard nominal variables as unimportant under a regime of flexible prices in the shortrun, they dispense with the LM curve. Income and interest rates, therefore, are determined by the intersection of the IS (or aggregate demand) curve, and a vertical aggregate supply curve as shown in Figure 13.5, panel (a). In other

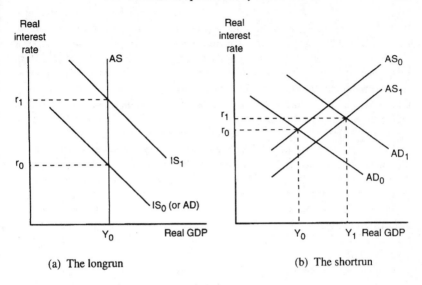

(a) The longrun   (b) The shortrun

Figure 13.5 The new classical model

words, changes in real GDP can only occur as a result of shifts in aggregate
supply, not in aggregate demand.

This new classical model, however, does not accord with some important
aspects of reality. We know that changes in effective demand do influence real
GDP as well as the interest rate. Also, while the model assumes that the supply
of labour is fixed, we know from observation that employment fluctuates during
the course of the business cycle. This has led real-growth theorists to adopt the
Lucas and Rapping (1969) hypothesis, known as 'intertemporal substitution'.
This hypothesis states that workers reallocate hours of work over time in
response to fluctuations in real wage rates and interest rates. The real interest
rate is important in this context because it affects the comparison between wage
rates over time. A rise in the real interest rate will make work today relatively
more attractive than work tomorrow. In other words, the intertemporal wage
rate is calculated by rational workers as $(1+r)w_1/w_2$, where r is the
real interest rate and w is the nominal wage in periods 1 and 2. As a higher
real interest rate makes working additional hours more attractive, the aggregate supply curve will not be vertical, but will rise from left to right, as shown in
Figure 13.5, panel (b). Clearly the new classical AD–AS model is not the same
as the one employed by the new Keynesians, as the vertical axis records the
interest rate (prices flexible) rather than the price level (prices inflexible).

The real business-cycle model, usually in computable general equilibrium
(CGE) form, is activated by exogenous technological shocks that shift

both the aggregate demand and aggregate supply curves, as shown in Figure 13.5 panel (b). An innovation will, on the one hand, increase the supply of goods and services from a given input of factors, thereby shifting the aggregate supply curve outwards; and, on the other hand, this innovation will increase the demand for new products, thereby shifting the aggregate demand curve outwards. The outcome is an increase in real GDP and either an increase or a decrease in the real rate of interest, depending upon the relative impact of the innovation on the aggregate demand and aggregate supply curves. Employment will vary according to the change in the real rate of interest. For the real business cycle theorist, economic fluctuations are a Pareto-efficient response of the society to changes in technology (and, in some instances, tastes). A discussion of the econometrics and ad hocery behind the real business cycle theory is found in Adrian Pagan's Shann Memorial Lecture (1996); and that behind the earlier business cycle literature is found in Mary Morgan's *Econometric Ideas* (1990).

There are a number of severe limitations associated with this theory. Firstly, it is quite implausible that shortrun fluctuations are the result of technological shocks. This is particularly the case regarding the argument that recessions are generated by technological regress. As I have shown elsewhere (Snooks 1993: 258–63), technological regress is possible but only where the exogenous shock is massive, such as the halving of England's population after 1348 owing to the onslaught of the Black Death. Criticism of this nature has led to the introduction of other exogenous shocks, such as shocks to government spending and tastes. Even so these multi-shock models have difficulties in explaining the real world (Stadler 1994: 1778).

Secondly, this model assumes that everyone who wants a job at the market wage rate can get one, and that they can work as many hours as they find attractive at that rate. This reasoning leads to the untenable conclusion that during recessions – even during the Great Depression – the level of unemployment is largely voluntary. Only theorists, and their historian disciples, could come to this type of conclusion, which is denied by the detailed historical evidence.

Thirdly, the argument that, in the shortrun, monetary variables play no role in fluctuations, and that prices and wages are completely flexible, is not supported by a detailed study of reality. Fourthly, like the Keynesian model, real business theory does not endogenize the forces responsible for shortrun fluctuations. Technological change is treated merely as a set of random exogenous shocks, only the ramifications of which can be seen working through this model. Fifthly, most real business cycle models are unable to explain real-world output dynamics. The output simulations generated by their CGE models do not replicate those of the real world without considerable *ad hoc* manipulation. And finally, like the new Keynesian model of shortrun fluctuations, real business cycle theory is totally divorced from neoclassical theories of longrun growth.

CONCLUSIONS

What can we conclude regarding these orthodox models of economic fluctuations? Real business cycle theory is driven not by real-world problems but by the determination to develop a model of shortrun fluctuations based on assumptions that are central to neoclassical theory. The question asked by the new classical theorists is not: How best can we explain shortrun fluctuations observed in reality? but rather: How can we employ existing neoclassical concepts to develop a model that can generate outcomes that might by interpreted analytically as shortrun fluctuations? As we saw in Chapter 3 in regard to growth theory, these are two very different questions that lead to the construction of very different models.

With all its limitations, the new Keynesian model of shortrun fluctuations is at least an attempt to answer the first rather than the second of these questions. The reason that the Keynesian model possesses severe limitations is that its supporters have not been able to develop an encompassing dynamic theory. In the final analysis the Keynesian model, like the neoclassical alternative, acknowledges the primacy of aggregate supply in the longrun. What is needed is a dynamic theory that can model the entire process of economic change by providing a cogent endogenous explanation of dynamic demand as well as of aggregate supply. This is the task in Chapter 14.

14 The Strategic Explanation of Fluctuations

Fluctuations are an integral part of the longrun dynamic process. To understand longrun dynamics it is necessary to build a model that can explain the wave-like trajectory of the strategic pathway, which is composed of a hierarchy of fluctuations ranging from 3 to 300 years. A key argument in this chapter is that it is not valid to dismantle the wider dynamic process to separate the 'cycle' from the secular trend as is often done by trade-cycle theorists.[1] In reality the dynamic process is an indivisible whole, and it must be modelled as such. The longrun 'cycle' does not exist any more than does the shortrun 'cycle' because there is no real-world mechanism responsible for generating a systematic cyclical motion at any level. The same is true of the longrun trend. To think in this fragmented manner is to distort our understanding of longrun dynamics.

The dynamic-strategy approach to fluctuations in both the longrun and shortrun, therefore, is quite straightforward. It is merely a matter of working through some of the implications of the model outlined above. In this way we obtain a better understanding not only of the nature of real-world fluctuations but also of the way in which the dynamic-strategy model works. Accordingly we can integrate the study of both economic growth and economic fluctuations. Light is also cast on existing orthodox theory.

THE MODEL

The fluctuations, or waves, observed in the strategic pathway (Figure 10.2) are produced by the dynamic-strategy model summarized in Chapter 13. This model generates longrun growth through a series of wave-like surges. It does not generate a systematic cycle in which successive booms and troughs are causally related. This, of course, involves a rejection of the central idea in trade-cycle literature. But there are waves within waves. The most prominent of these are the 'great' waves of *about* 300 years and the 'long' waves of *about* 40 years. I say 'about' because the great waves fall in the range of 200 to 400 years and the long waves of 20 to 60 years. There are also shorter waves varying from 3 to 10 years.

Great and long waves

The wave-like surges, as we have seen, are generated by the exploitation of dynamic strategies and substrategies. The largest of these, the great waves, are driven by the dynamic strategies of commerce, conquest, or technological change. The long waves, which should not be confused with the discredited Kondratieff cycles (Solomou 1987), are generated by the various substrategies within each of these dynamic strategies, and the shorter waves are driven by individual projects coordinated through strategic imitation. These waves are measured in terms of real GDP and real GDP per capita. As longrun prices in the dynamic-strategy model (as in reality) are determined by strategic demand, they follow rather than lead changes in real GDP.

The dynamic-strategy model suggests that the rapid expansion and growth of an economy is the outcome of the exploitation of new strategic opportunities. This exploitation generates rapid increases in both strategic demand and strategic confidence, which in turn lead to high levels of investment. Naturally, over long periods of time this strategic unfolding will occur unevenly and there will be times when strategic demand and strategic confidence mark time or even decline temporarily before resuming their upward trajectories. The nature of the response to increasing strategic demand will depend upon factor endowments and the competitive environment. Eventually the prevailing dynamic strategy will be exhausted (when strategic marginal revenues and costs are equated), and strategic demand and strategic confidence will stagnate at a high level. As this occurs there will be a shift of resources from strategic to inflationary activities before the dynamic strategy finally collapses, owing to an inability to service past debts, bringing down with it both strategic demand and strategic confidence. And as strategic confidence shatters so the inflationary bubble bursts. The outcome is a downward spiral into depression which continues until either a new dynamic strategy emerges from the exploration of the strategic pioneers, or, failing this, the society descends into terminal chaos. There is nothing inevitable about the emergence of a new long wave of economic expansion and growth.

It is important to realize that the dynamic strategies and substrategies driving these longrun waves are not one-dimensional. They consist of a package or programme of strategic instruments that are pragmatically designed to achieve the objective of materialist man for survival and prosperity. A dominant dynamic strategy such as commerce will be supported by the subsidiary strategies of conquest (to gain monopolies over trading goods and trading routes) and technological change dedicated to advancing the cause of the dominant strategy of commerce (such as improved shipping, navigation, dock facilities, and so on). Similarly, a technological substrategy will consist of a programme of strategic instruments. While the leading instrument will be innovation, the other instruments will include the penetration and protection of new markets (as undertaken by the USA from the late 1930s); trade negotiations/economic threats; and the threat of large-scale war to control important locations and resources (as undertaken by the USA in Korea,

Vietnam, and the Gulf; and the former USSR in Afghanistan). But it is important to realize that the subsidiary strategies are employed only to support and facilitate the dominant dynamic strategy.

Therefore, while innovation is the leading strategic instrument in the modern world, it cannot be characterized as a simple process involving innovation clusters as argued by Schumpeter (1939; 1949), Rostow (1990), and Freeman *et al.* (1982).[2] The essential feature of the model employed in this book is its strategic nature: if there are no appropriate innovations, then a new long wave of expansion can be launched through the use of an existing technology to penetrate *new* markets – as Britain attempted through its Empire self-sufficiency strategy in the 1920s, and as the USA more successfully achieved by breaking out into the rest of the world from the late 1930s. In extending the scope of the old technological substrategy it is transformed into a new substrategy. Recovery does not necessarily depend on a new outburst of innovation. This is more consistent with the evidence than the simple Schumpeterian innovation hypothesis (Solomou 1987: 100).

Our model tells us that while the wave-like surges are generated by dynamic strategies and substrategies, these waves are not systematically and mechanically related. The only link between them is that they are outcomes of the eternal desire of materialist man to survive and prosper. In other words the trade cycle is a myth. The intervals between the waves are just that – intervals between the exhaustion of one dynamic strategy and the emergence and exploitation of the next. During each of these intervals the strategic pioneers are involved in a desperate attempt to launch a new strategy, owing to the adverse impact of external competition on real living standards. Each interval is a vulnerable time for any society, because strategic replacement is not inevitable. The strategic outcome will depend on the society's resource endowment and the nature of external competition. Failure to generate a new strategy, or substrategy, will lead to stagnation and, possibly, collapse.

Hence, there is no necessary or systematic relationship between one dynamic strategy/substrategy and the next. The driving force, of materialist man, is ever present, but it may fail to generate a further surge in economic growth if there are no further viable strategic opportunities for a society with its particular resource endowment in its particular competitive environment. In these circumstances the driving force may lead instead to rent-seeking activities by the ruling elite, as has been the case at some stage throughout the Third World. Even the existing physical, human, and institutional infrastructure may not be particularly useful because it plays only a passive supply-side role. Say's Law, whereby supply creates its own demand, is the phantom of neoclassical economics. What is needed is the creation of a new source of strategic demand. While this matter is not as potentially disastrous in the case of the exhaustion of a substrategy as it is for a full dynamic strategy, the consequences can involve an extended period of stagnation, of the type experienced by Britain throughout the interwar years or by the USA between the mid-1920s and the Second World War. The more serious case of the future exhaustion of the present industrial technological paradigm may be a problem that Western civilization has to face in the twenty-first century.

In analysing these wave-like fluctuations we need to consider the forces influencing both their shape and duration. The wave-shape of these longrun fluctuations is the outcome of the exploitation and exhaustion of a dynamic strategy or substrategy. It is the exponential nature of the exploitation process that provides the strategic pathway with its upwardly surging nature, as shown in Figures 10.2 and 10.3. And it is the approaching exhaustion of the dynamic strategy that leads to a process of deceleration, stagnation, and downturn, that creates the crest of the wave. Finally, total strategic exhaustion leads, after a brief attempt to defy economic gravity, to the wave's collapse owing to the falling away of both strategic demand and strategic confidence. At this point the energy of the wave is totally dissipated, and further waves can only emerge from the adoption of entirely new strategies and the generation of strategic demand and strategic confidence anew. It is reminiscent of Sisyphus, the Corinthian king of Greek myth, who was condemned in Hades eternally to push a great stone up a steep hill, allow it to roll back again, and to begin again anew.

The precise length of these waves should not concern us greatly, because this will vary within flexible limits as between societies and within societies. This is particularly so if the endogenous dynamic process is subject to exogenous shocks such as unanticipated wars, epidemics, and natural disasters. While recent investigation (Solomou 1987: 12) has concluded that the available evidence for Western Europe and the USA suggests long waves of 20 to 30 years, the evidence for Australasia suggests longer swings in regions of recent settlement of 40 to 50 years (Butlin 1964; Snooks 1994a; Hawke 1985). As we are dealing here with the same strategic phenomena, we should abandon the traditional distinction between Kondratieff and Kuznets long swings and talk only of 'long waves' covering the wider range of 20 to 60 years. But in any case it is far more important to understand the dynamic mechanism underlying the growth process than to be dogmatic about the length of the wave-like surges by which it proceeds. Any predictions we are prepared to make about economic activity in the future, must be based on the dynamic model rather than on fixed (and, hence, inevitably wrong) views about wave length. Much of the recent literature on long waves has focused on the predictive value of the 'cycles' and, as a result, has been largely discredited.[3] This is the old historicist fallacy of the late nineteenth century revisited.

In the dynamic-strategy model, the length of both the great and long wave is determined by two conditions, one general and the other more specific. The general condition concerns the finite economic potential of any dynamic strategy or substrategy. Once a dynamic strategy begins to unfold, a point will always be reached, owing to the law of diminishing strategic returns, when marginal strategic revenue is equal to marginal strategic cost. And at that point the dynamic strategy will be exhausted. The specific condition concerns the nature of the exponential growth process. Why would anyone expect great waves to be *about* 300 years in length and long waves *about* 40 years? The answer is quite straightforward. As this is an exponential growth process (whereby the strategic opportunities are explored as quickly as is possible), and as these opportunities and the means of exploiting them are *both* determined by the prevailing technology, then, in theory, the wavelength should approximate a constant in both categories. This is why we might expect longrun fluctuations of similar length as between societies employing very different technologies. But of course this endogenous process is subject to random exogenous shocks that distort this wave pattern in unpredictable ways.

In other words, the wave-like surges are generated by the nature of the dynamic-strategy mechanism and its underlying forces. They are not an outcome of growing disequilibrium due to overinvestment as many have argued. The observed deterioration in profit rates, increasing structural problems, and growing speculative activity that generally occur towards the end of a long boom are not a cause of downturn, but rather an outcome of approaching strategic exhaustion (Snooks 1997a: ch. 11). The overinvestment hypothesis is a supply-side approach – a long boom sows the seeds of its own destruction – that completely overlooks the existence of strategic demand. And as a result it confuses effect with cause. Also the other conditions normally associated with depressions such as underconsumption, collapse of expectations, reduction in the money supply, and balancing budgets are all a response to the collapse of both strategic demand and strategic confidence. They are not to be regarded as factors initiating the depression. The dynamic-strategy model, therefore, provides an encompassing theory of fluctuations that avoids the mechanistic processes of the accelerator–multiplier type.

The signs of approaching strategic exhaustion may lead many decision-makers to seek better returns in speculative and rent-seeking activities, but they also stimulate strategic pioneers to search for new strategic opportunities. Only when the old strategy collapses are the pioneers joined by the vast army of followers. The degree of success achieved by pioneer and follower alike will determine the length of the interval between the old and new dynamic strategies and, hence, between the old and new waves of economic change.

Shortrun fluctuations

The dynamic-strategy model is also able to explain shortrun fluctuations and, thereby, to integrate them into a holistic analysis of longrun dynamics.

Shortrun fluctuations ranging from 3 to 10 years are also an outcome of the unfolding dynamic strategy with its hierarchy of substrategies within the dominant technological strategy, and of 'strategic projects' within these substrategies.

The strategic projects are not random investment activities undertaken for idiosyncratic reasons, but are related to the requirements of the unfolding dynamic strategies/substrategies. These requirements are expressed through the market incentives generated by strategic demand, and the response of investors is influenced by strategic confidence – both being outcomes of changing strategic opportunities. These investment projects are coordinated through the strategic–imitation mechanism.

Shortrun fluctuations, therefore, reflect the rise and fall of the strategic investment projects. The length of these shortrun waves will depend on the nature of the projects being undertaken. Major infrastructure projects such as transport, communication and power systems, or large urban renewal schemes will generate longer waves of up to 10 years, while new housing projects may generate shorter waves of 3 to 5 years. All these projects, both large and small, are an integral part of the wider technological strategy/substrategy. Naturally, the depth and length of these waves will be influenced by fluctuations in strategic confidence.

The essential point, however, is not the precise depth and length of these shortrun waves of economic activity, but the mechanism by which they are generated. Shortrun fluctuations are the outcome of the exploitation and exhaustion of strategic projects. Like the long and great waves, they arise from the dynamic interaction between strategic demand and strategic response, orchestrated by strategic inflation. These projects are driven by a combination of private small-scale innovations and/or trading ventures, together with public policies of an economic (protection, trade negotiations/hostilities), social (housing, education, and health programmes), and political (war and colonization) kind.

The dynamic-strategy model is able to integrate both shortrun and longrun issues that are dealt with separately in orthodox economic theory. In both the shortrun and the longrun, aggregate demand and aggregate supply are, respectively, an outcome of and a response to changes in strategic demand. In other words, this is a demand-side dynamic model in which the Keynesian variables are static outcomes. The important implication is that Keynes' concepts of propensity to consume, liquidity preference, and state of long-term expectation are transformed from 'psychological laws' into economic variables. As demonstrated in Chapter 10, the state of long-term expectation is a reflection of strategic confidence; the propensity to consume depends on the saving requirements of the dynamic strategy/substrategy, communicated through strategic demand; and liquidity preference is a response to strategic demand and strategic confidence. The dynamic-strategy model, therefore, encompasses the Keynesian comparative–static model.

It also shifts the focus of attention in macroeconomics from the shape of the aggregate supply curve (and hence the degree of market perfection), in both the shortrun and longrun, to the dynamic entities of strategic demand and strategic confidence. Changes in strategic demand continually override these supply-side issues. Price flexibility in neoclassical macroeconomics, like the conditions leading to dynamic equilibrium in neoclassical growth theory, is merely an artificial device to compensate for the absence of any dynamic form in their models that can emerge only from a realistic analysis of dynamic demand.

In the shortrun, the process of depression and recovery is an outcome of the exhaustion of an old technological substrategy and the emergence of a new substrategy communicated through strategic demand, rather than the result of the aggregate supply curve's shape (as in Figure 13.2). And in the longrun, aggregate supply is a response to strategic demand. It is strategic demand that determines the supply response of factor inputs and the nature of the production function. Unlike Topsy it does not just grow as neoclassical economists insist. Hence, there is no such thing as an equilibrium growth path (the 'natural' rate of growth) determined on the supply side by population growth and technological change. By endogenizing the supply-side shocks of orthodox theory, the dynamic-strategy model also dispenses with Say's Law, and banishes the flexible/inflexible prices discussion.

The dynamic-strategy model also undermines the credibility of the natural rate of unemployment concept because, as shown in Chapter 11, inflation and unemployment are independently determined by changes in strategic demand. Inflation is an essential component and a natural outcome of the interaction between strategic demand and the strategic response of existing resources, while the level of output and employment (and, hence, unemployment) is a static outcome of the impact of strategic demand and strategic confidence on investment, government expenditure, and consumption. While there is no *causal* relationship between unemployment and inflation, a *nominal* or statistical relationship does exist as they are outcomes of the same dynamic process. But as this process affects them differentially over time, this purely statistical relationship will also change. Similarly, the pursuit of different technological substrategies, or the adoption of the same substrategy at different times, will lead to different statistical relationships between unemployment and inflation (or a host of other variables) at a given point in history. There is, therefore, no meaningful Phillips curve or natural rate of unemployment. They are merely the artificial constructs of a paradigm unable to model dynamic demand.

This new analysis has major policy implications, as discussed in Chapter 17. Strategic policy goes beyond Keynesian policy in advocating not just repairing deficiencies in aggregate demand but isolating the strategic cause of the downturn and providing the necessary strategic leadership to accelerate the replacement of an exhausted with a new technological substrategy. Strategic analysis also rejects the neoclassical notion of NAIRU, which has led the orthodox consensus to focus on the policy rules of the four zeros – zero inflation, zero budget deficits, zero current account deficits, and zero net borrowings. Instead it advocates an emphasis on economic growth and longrun strategic leadership, all of which will abolish the four zeros.

By now it will be clear that the dynamic-strategy model provides a very different interpretation of the Great Depression in the USA to those discussed in Chapter 13. The Great Depression was an outcome of the exhaustion of a technological substrategy that had been employed by the USA since the 1890s. This substrategy involved the development of large-scale forms of industrial production and distribution in order to exploit the mega-market in North America that had been built up during the nineteenth century (Snooks 1997: ch. 11).

During the 1920s, the gradual exhaustion of the American substrategy generated a number of outcomes that are often regarded as independent causes of the Great Depression. The first of these is the growing saturation of the domestic market for consumer durables. Contrary to orthodox argument, this was due not to 'underconsumption' but to an exhaustion of the domestic market given the state of the existing technological strategy. Secondly, the increasing degree of speculation on Wall Street and elsewhere in the 1920s, which reflected a growing maladjustment on the economy, was the result not of some sort of self-starting and self-sustaining disequilibrium but of an exhaustion of strategic opportunities. In an effort to continue earning extraordinary profits, many former strategists turned to speculative activities where they were joined by swarms of followers. The progressive shift in the balance between strategic activities and speculative ventures during the strategic exhaustion process is fed by the high level of strategic confidence. Only when the dynamic strategy crashes does strategic confidence finally collapse thereby crushing the bubble of speculation. Teleological hypotheses about booms inevitably turning into depressions are here replaced by a demand-side dynamic model.

The downturn and contraction was an outcome of the collapse of the old technological substrategy. This led in quick succession to a sharp reduction in strategic demand for labour, capital, technological ideas, and money balances; a collapse of strategic confidence and, hence, business expectations; and a collapse of speculative activity, most conspicuously and spectacularly on Wall Street. None of these variables, as is usually claimed, were independent causes of the depression. They were merely a passive part of the contractionary process.

The recovery depended on the development of a new substrategy, which ultimately involved the redirection of its existing large-scale production and distribution technology from the domestic to the international market. The Second World War played an important part in this strategic redirection and the recovery, which fluctuated during the 1930s, and cannot be regarded as complete until it was finally accomplished in the second half of the 1940s (Snooks 1997a: ch. 11). A complete recovery and a new phase of expansion after the war could not have been accomplished without the adoption of a new substrategy. This underlines the argument above that there is no 'cycle', only a succession of distantly related waves of economic change. Other measures, such as lower interest rates and the New Deal, merely removed some of the minor obstacles to strategic renewal. The Roosevelt administration failed to provide the strategic leadership that would have made a more proactive contribution to recovery. In this context strategic leadership would have required Roosevelt to understand that the old technological substrategy had exhausted itself and that it was necessary to assist in the redirection of the US economy from the domestic to the international market – to become the financier and the workshop of the world. This is the difference between static Keynesian policies and dynamic strategic policies, even in the shortrun.

In a similar way the dynamic-strategy model can explain changes in the *nominal* relationship between unemployment and inflation in the USA during the last quarter of the twentieth century. The pattern requiring explanation is the rapid and parallel increase in both unemployment and inflation during the 1970s, the subsequent rapid fall of both in the early 1980s, and the changing relationship during the following decade. Throughout this period the alleged inverse relationship is either very weak or not statistically significant (Galbraith 1997: 98). The rise in the average rate of unemployment in the 1970s and 1980s from about 5 per cent to about 7 per cent, was associated with the exhaustion of the technological substrategy that the US had pursued so successfully after the Second World War – the large-scale mass production of consumer and producer durables for the global market (Snooks 1997a: ch. 11). And the fall again to about 5.5 per cent in the 1990s has been due to the adoption of the new microelectronic substrategy pioneered earlier by Japan and Germany. On the other hand, the acceleration of inflation during the 1970s (in two bursts), and its subsequent decline in the early 1980s was, as is well known, an outcome of the OPEC oil crisis – a supply-side shock. Only since the early 1980s have the fluctuations in the inflation rate reflected, once again, the interaction between strategic demand and strategic response. Earlier, the demand effects were overwhelmed by the oil crisis. Finally, it should be noted that the difference between US and EU experience during the first half of the 1990s was due to the shortrun costs associated with the European strategy of territorial expansion into the less prosperous central and south-eastern regions of the continent (Snooks 1997: ch. 12).

In brief, the dynamic-strategy model has a number of significant strengths. It integrates the analysis of economic growth and economic fluctuations into a single dynamic model. It endogenizes the usual sources of shortrun fluctuations. It sorts out the confusion between downturns that are the result of great, long, and short waves. It is able to encompass all other models of shortrun fluctuations, treating the variables they isolate as part of the processes of contraction or of recovery. It provides an alternative explanation of inflation and unemployment to the discredited Phillips curve. And it suggests the need for a radical revision of economic policy in both the shortrun and the longrun.

AN APPLICATION: BRITAIN, 1000–2000

A brief historical discussion of Britain between the years 1000 and 2000 will demonstrate how the dynamic-strategy model works in reality in the very longrun, longrun, and shortrun. The underlying details can be found in my *The Ephemeral Civilization* (1997a: ch. 10). As shown in Figure 10.3 (p. 134), England's strategic pathway traced out three great waves between AD 1000 and 2000, each being up to 300 years in duration. These great waves (which are identified with the upswing only) surged forward during the periods 1000 to 1300, 1480 to 1750, and 1760 to 2000, and were generated by three very different dynamic strategies – conquest, commerce, and technological change. It should be noted that the second great wave was delayed and compressed by the onslaught of the Black Death between 1348 and the mid-fifteenth century. In turn, each of these strategies was composed of a series of substrategies. With the exhaustion of each of these strategies, England was fortunate enough to replace them – after an interval during which extended economic stagnation or decline was experienced – with a new dynamic strategy. English society, therefore, was able to avoid the collapse that had occurred in all ancient societies. Yet this was due more to fortunate timing, coming as it did at the very end of the neolithic technological paradigm, than to superior strategic skills.

These great waves trace out England's strategic pathway generated by the unfolding and replacement of its dynamic strategies throughout the past millennium. The strategic pathway for a conquest or commerce society can be represented by a graph showing the fluctuations in territorial acquisition, because new resources were central to their success. But in the case of a technological society, an index of territorial expansion is totally inadequate.

Instead we need indexes of real GDP and real GDP per capita, because efficiency in the use of existing resources rather than the continual acquisition of new resources is central to the success of the technological strategy. In other words, technological change, broadly conceived, can generate the extraordinary profits relentlessly pursued by materialist man without the need to acquire additional territory. If territory is acquired it is for very different reasons.

The story about the unfolding and replacement of dynamic strategies can be summarized in terms of the real GDP and territorial timescapes in Figure 10.3. While there is a longrun correlation between these two measures of economic change during the first of these great waves, there are shorter periods when a slump in one is compensated for by a boom in the other. Before 1300 the difficulties of pursuing a conquest strategy in a highly competitive environment required the generation of surpluses, to finance England's wars, through increases in productivity and trade. After 1300 the slump in the wool trade led England to focus to a greater degree on territorial acquisition, which brought in plunder and external revenues. But this strategy was to exhaust itself by the beginning of the fifteenth century as the war with France became more costly and unpredictable owing to the growing difficulty of acquiring reliable continental allies. And as the fifteenth century progressed, commercial opportunities became increasingly attractive.

The second great wave from 1450 to 1760, driven by the new commerce strategy, predictably saw a change in the relative importance of our variables in Figure 10.3. Until 1600, commerce-generated increases in real GDP per capita led the increase in territorial acquisition owing to the short-range nature of trade (and, hence, a smaller demand for land bases), whereas thereafter, as Britain gained the ascendancy in its struggle against the Dutch, the roles were reversed as the winner acquired territories that were required to conduct long-distance trade. Only during the third great wave from 1780 to 2000, which was driven by the technological strategy, was it possible to achieve a longrun inverse relationship between these two variables, demonstrating for the first time in history that growing prosperity no longer depended on territorial acquisition. The pursuit of efficiency in the use of existing resources replaced the pursuit of additional external resources. From the mid-nineteenth century, Britain, although continuing to acquire territory in order to defend the technological strategy (an extension of the balance of power concept in Europe to the rest of the world), granted self-government to its Dominions. Despite granting self-government, real GDP per capita continued to increase rapidly, and when Britain completely dismantled its empire after the Second World War (once defence of the technological strategy could be more economically achieved through the threat from nuclear weapons), the growth rate actually accelerated. In a technological age an empire is not required to achieve economic growth and will even act to slow it down.

In order to observe the rise and fall of Britain's dynamic substrategies in the modern era, we need to focus more closely on the third (and current) great wave. A survey of the global technological substrategies was made in Chapter 10. Here we deal with them only as they have affected Britain's growth process.

The third great wave of British growth, beginning in the late eighteenth century, was, as we have seen, driven by the technological strategy. This renewed drive to prosperity came merely a generation after the commerce strategy had exhausted itself. Between the 1750s and the 1780s the British economy stagnated, and the lower strata of society were plunged into poverty, with poor relief increasing from 1 per cent of GDP in 1748 to 2 per cent by 1800 (Lindert 1994: 383). As argued in *The Dynamic Society* (1996), the final burst of commercial expansion brought Britain not only to the limit of the commerce strategy but also to the limit of the neolithic technological paradigm. This can be seen in the well-known slowdown and gradualism of technological change after 1500 (Mokyr 1990: 57–8), the exhaustion of organic materials and fuels from the seventeenth century (Wrigley 1994: 32–8), the shortage of fodder for horses that provided the major source of power and transport, and the scarcity of natural chemicals for a modern urban society (Seaman 1981: 352–5). The response of dynamic strategists in Britain to changing factor endowments and relative resource prices from the seventeenth century was initially to substitute inorganic for organic materials and fuels, and ultimately, from the late eighteenth century, to introduce a new technology to effectively utilize these new resources. The outcome was the modern technological paradigm shift known as the Industrial Revolution.

The subsequent pattern of growth rates (Figure 10.4, p. 139) exhibited by the unfolding of the British technological strategy reflects the impact of a number of substrategies. The initial substrategy, which gave rise to the first Industrial Revolution and its aftermath, focused on the production and export of those goods in which Britain had long had a comparative advantage – textiles, coal, and iron – together with those industrial commodities required to produce and distribute these staples – the steam engine for factories and transport, machinery, simple engineered products, and basic chemicals. But it did so using a new technology. This rough and ready substrategy, which released Britain from a dependence on both depleting organic resources and external territory, turned out to be highly successful in a non-industrialized world, supporting an accelerating growth rate to the mid-nineteenth century. During this pioneering technological substrategy, Britain's growth rate (Table 14.1) exceeded the average for Western Europe by one-third, and matched that achieved by the USA which was reaping the relatively easy gains of westward expansion – of developing its mega-market.

Table 14.1   Global growth rates, 1820–1992 (%pa)

	Britain	USA	Western Europe	Southern Europe	Eastern Europe	Asia	Latin America	Africa
1820–70	1.2	1.3	0.9	na	na	0.1	na	na
1870–1913	1.0	1.8	1.3	0.9	1.2	0.7	1.5	na
1913–50	0.8	1.6	1.2	0.7	1.0	−0.2	1.9	1.0
1950–73	2.5	2.4	3.8	4.8	4.0	3.1	2.4	1.8
1973–92	1.4	1.4	1.8	2.2	−0.8	3.5	0.4	−0.4

Source: Maddison 1995: 62–3.

As other European nations initiated and improved upon Britain's technological and marketing success, generally behind tariff barriers, this first--
generation substrategy became progressively less effective. In the second
half of the nineteenth century Britain was forced by growing international
competition to modify its pioneering substrategy by imitating the new engineering and chemical technology developed in Europe and by achieving
greater scale economies through new forms of industrial and financial organization. Even so, this modified substrategy, which saw growth rates increasing to 1870, became progressively less effective as Western Europe and
North America adopted new technological substrategies. Accordingly, from
1870 to 1913, Britain's growth rate fell to three-quarters of the average for
Western Europe and just over half that of the USA – a set of relativities that
persisted until 1950. By the First World War this late nineteenth-century
substrategy had exhausted itself and could only be continued into the interwar period through its Empire self-sufficiency scheme, by which Britain
exported its unemployed (and some capital) to the Dominions, which, in
return, were meant to provide cheap raw materials and preferentially pro-
tected markets for its manufactured goods. Yet even this failed. The exhaustion of Britain's substrategy, therefore, led to high rates of unemployment –
up to 11 per cent – in the 1920s. And this was exacerbated in the early 1930s
when the Great Depression, originating in the USA owing to the exhaustion
of its own substrategy in the second half of the 1920s, spread to Europe and
the rest of the world.

But the low rates of economic growth in the interwar years motivated a
new generation of strategic pioneers who began to adopt the latest technology and organizational practices from overseas. This included the new-
generation industries of electrical engineering, industrial chemicals,
consumer durables (radio, motor car), and modern electrical household
appliances, together with new large-scale organizational techniques and scientific management practices that had been pioneered in the USA. It was this
transition from the old exhausted substrategy to the new one imported from

overseas that made it possible for Britain to participate fully in the boom of the 'golden age' following the Second World War. The golden age, when British growth rates rose to unprecedented historical levels and finally achieved parity with the USA, was in part due to its participation in a new strategy and in part a reaction to the sudden release from decades of restriction in the form of two world wars and a major depression. The mechanism was similar to that in the sixteenth century when the vice-like grip of a century of pestilence was suddenly released. In both periods the effect, extending from one to two generations, was to double the normal growth rate.

Since 1973 Britain's growth rate has declined once more. Yet this experience is not unique. With the exception of the newly industrializing Asian nations, all other groups – Western Europe, Southern Europe, Eastern Europe, the regions of recent settlement, Latin America, and Africa – experienced a marked slowdown in growth rates (Table 14.1). In my judgement the growth rates achieved since 1973 in the advanced nations approximate the normal longrun rate that can be generated from the competitive pursuit of the technological strategy. Certainly in the case of Britain they compare more closely with growth rates achieved in the heady days of the nineteenth century. The point is that, for a generation after 1950, growth rates were abnormally high as a result of unusual exogenous forces. Nonetheless, in the future Britain can expect to experience a further decline in growth rates when the current technological substrategy exhausts itself, although it will be unlikely to last as long as the last 'exhaustion interval' following the First World War.

CONCLUSIONS

A number of conclusions that possess analytical and policy implications can be drawn from the dynamic-strategy approach to fluctuations in both the longrun and shortrun. The first of these is that there is no such thing as a longrun economic 'cycle', only a strategic pathway composed of a sequence of wave-like surges. Hence, in order to explain longrun fluctuations we must be able to model the entire real-world growth process. The neoclassical growth model is unable to meet this criteria of realism and relevance.

Secondly, a strategic pathway is only meaningful when it is seen as the outcome of individual societies that are pursuing their own strategic objectives. In analytical terms there is no such thing as a 'global cycle', precisely because there is no global society and, hence, no global strategy.[4] The global network of communications between individual societies should not be confused with the existence of a 'world system' that possesses its own dynamic process.

Thirdly, we need to draw a distinction between the way Keynes interpreted unemployment in the interwar period and the way it is seen through the dynamic-strategy model. Keynes and his followers interpreted unemployment in the 1920s and 1930s as the outcome of shortrun problems experienced in factor markets that prevented the achievement of longrun equilibrium, whereas the dynamic-strategy model views it as the outcome of strategic exhaustion in Britain from the 1910s and in the USA from the mid-1920s. The high levels of unemployment are due not to a deficiency of aggregate demand (as such), but to a decline in strategic demand. As we shall see in Chapter 17, the policy implications of these contrasting interpretations are very different.

Finally, we reject the neoclassical notion that GDP in the longrun is determined by aggregate supply, with aggregate demand merely adjusting to it through price flexibility. The dynamic-strategy model suggests that aggregate demand is an outcome of, and aggregate supply is a response to, changes in strategic demand generated by an unfolding dynamic strategy. Say's Law is banished from the longrun as well as the shortrun. This too provides the grounds for a new approach to development policy.

Part VII
Politics and Policy

15 The New Political Economy

As the institutional structure of society provides the vehicle for a growing economy, any satisfactory dynamic theory must be able to explain political as well as economic change. While this is important in the case of developed societies, it is absolutely essential for lesser developed societies.[1] The fact that orthodox economics has not been able to develop a dynamic theory to explain both economic and political change is a major limitation, not only in understanding the real world, but also in providing a basis for policy. The new political economy, true to its neoclassical foundations, provides only a comparative–static analysis of the interaction between special-interest groups and governments on distributional issues.

AN OVERVIEW

Neoclassical general equilibrium theory has nothing to say about political change, about the process of policy formulation, or about the relationship of both to economic growth. The underlying assumption in welfare theory is that governments, which exist to facilitate private enterprise, pursue benevolent economic and social policies that minimize the amount of distortion created by their presence. To redress the balance between neoclassical theory and a reality in which governments intervene in markets on a major scale, some economists have attempted to formally analyse political processes. This literature, which has become known as the 'new political economy', deals, in a comparative–static manner, with the interaction between the state and special-interest groups in an exchange of economic rents for political power.

There are three main strands in the 'new political economy' literature. First, there is the 'public-choice' theory, and the constitutional economics that rises from it, of James Buchanan, Gordon Tullock, and their many followers. Departing from the assumptions of welfare economics, the public-choice theorists recognize that both the public and private sectors are involved in rent-seeking activities, mainly as a result of government intervention. As this wastage cannot be eliminated either by economic competition or electoral processes, they argue the need for constitutional rules which, they insist, should reflect the preferences of all citizens.

Secondly, there is the 'collective action' theory that has its origins in the works of Mancur Olson (1965; 1982). Owing to the 'free-rider' problem, special-interest or lobby groups emerge to pursue distributional rather than growth objectives. While there are initial difficulties in forming these groups, they will gradually multiply and impact adversely on the level of efficiency and the rate of economic growth. This theory has been extended recently to show how these lobby groups interact with government to produce policies that deviate from the Pareto optimum.

Thirdly, there is the new institutional economics of Douglass North and his followers, who emphasize a broader exchange between governments attempting to maximize revenue, and individuals and groups wanting to maximize their wealth through the minimization of transaction costs. The weaker the constraints on government power, the greater the deviation from some measure (they reject Pareto optimality) of institutional efficiency. This approach sees a more positive development role for the state.

PUBLIC CHOICE THEORY

The basic belief of James Buchanan and his followers is that the role of government should be restricted to protecting individuals and property rights and to enforcing private contracts. The underlying presumptions are that individual choice is the basic unit of analysis and that the individual is the ultimate source of 'value' (Buchanan 1987: 586). This is also partly an outcome of the shortrun static outlook of neoclassical theory. If a government exceeds this role, it will create wasteful social activity in the form of public and private rent-seeking. Governments will grow out of control by seeking to maximize revenue in a manner unconstrained by 'moral rules', while lobby groups will invest time and resources in attempting to persuade politicians in power to redistribute income in their favour through tariffs, subsidies, tax concessions, and export bounties. The end result is to divert resources from their most efficient use.

The argument in Buchanan *et al.* (1980) is that lobbying, which is privately rational but socially wasteful, is largely an outcome of government intervention in the market. If the role of government is restricted to providing institutions and organizations required to facilitate private activity, this problem will be minimized because any economic rents that arise will be largely dissipated by competitive forces. This they see as central to the dynamics of the market economy. But, if government is involved on a significant scale in market intervention, rent-seeking will become endemic, resources will be diverted permanently to less productive activities, and economic growth will not be maximized. To prevent these socially undesirable consequences, constitutional rules that reflect the electorate's preferences will be required to constrain government intervention. This is not something that can be left to either the market or the electoral process.

The role played by the state is investigated further by G. Brennan and J. Buchanan (1980). They argue that the role of government is essentially predatory, in that its objective is to maximize revenue. Government is characterized as a leviathan that pursues its own self-interest rather than the overall interests of the community as assumed in welfare and Keynesian economics. In the absence of 'moral constraints' in contemporary government of the type claimed by J.M. Keynes (Fitzgibbons 1988: 179), the only way to constrain the revenue-seeking desires of the ruling elite is through generally accepted constitutional rules.

Brennan and Buchanan contrast their model of leviathan with the 'conventional wisdom' in neoclassical economics, which is based on the assumption that the government will raise 'a fixed and exogenously determined amount of revenue'. The orthodox question then is: How should these taxes be levied in order to minimize welfare loss? Buchanan has always rejected this welfare approach on the grounds that Pareto optimality has no empirical grounding, and has maintained that it is better to define good decision rules than to establish optimal solutions (Sandmo 1990). Buchanan (1987: 587) rejects the 'Paretian test' of productive and distributive efficiency for the 'Wicksellian test' of 'unanimity or consensus' on the grounds that the ultimate source of value is the individual. Accordingly, on the issue of taxation Brennan and Buchanan substitute the question: How can constitutional rules be framed regarding taxes that will constrain government revenue-seeking? They suggest that 'Leviathan's revenue-raising proclivities might be efficiently constrained by some appropriate selection of tax bases and tax rates' (ibid.: 107). In particular they are concerned to prevent governments gaining access to 'capital levies' and 'public debt', because of implications for 'future revenue potential'. They claim that their conclusions and recommendations are significantly different to those arrived at by conventional neoclassical analysis. Nevertheless, they embrace the supply-side approach of orthodox economics.

COLLECTIVE-ACTION THEORY

Like the public choice theorists, Mancur Olson (1965; 1982) believes that the degree of efficiency and the rate of economic growth will only be maximized if markets are allowed to operate with minimal intervention from special-interest groups. But, unlike Buchanan, Olson believes that the most dangerous form of intervention is from 'special-interest organizations' rather than the state. He sees the accumulation of these organizations in a 'stable' society leading to a decline in both the level of efficiency and the rate of economic growth. Olson even argues that in some countries, totalitarian governments swept away many of the special-interest organizations, which in turn led to improvements in both efficiency and rates of economic growth. What he has in mind is Germany and Japan in the 1930s and 1940s in which right-wing governments that eliminated left-wing labour organizations were followed by governments imposed by the Allied Powers that eliminated right-wing organizations.

In *The Logic of Collective Action* (1965), Olson argues that the emergence of special-interest organizations in a market economy is not as easy as many suppose. The reason is that individuals pursuing 'rational, self-interested behavior' will have little incentive to invest time and resources in lobbying government to achieve 'collective goods' that have to be shared by all its members. He argues that this 'free-rider' problem, although he does not employ the term, is greater for large organizations than for small organizations, because the potential benefit is shared equally between the membership.

Yet, Olson admits, market societies possess many special-interest organizations both large and small. His explanation is that their prime-movers, the 'political entrepreneurs', employ a range of 'selective incentives' to coerce/encourage the active participation (in terms of time and/or membership dues) of potential beneficiaries. These sticks and carrots, which are necessary in a supply-side world, include economic and social penalties and rewards. Small lobby groups have an advantage over their larger brethren in that they tend to be more homogeneous and can reach agreement more effectively and efficiently. Also they have fewer members to share the rewards. This is why special-interest organizations are producers rather than consumers. Olson (1982: 31) explains:

> the larger the number of individuals or firms that would benefit from a collective good, the smaller the share of the gains from action in the group interest that will accrue to the individual or firm that undertakes the action. Thus, in the absence of selective incentives, the incentive for group action diminishes as group size increases, so that large groups are less able to act in their common interest than small ones.

In *The Rise and Decline of Nations* (1982), Olson attempts to extend the collective-action model to explain the different economic performance between 'developed democracies' since the Second World War. To do so he draws nine 'implications' from his earlier model that he considers relevant to modern economic growth. The main thrust of these implications are: that 'stable societies' (in the absence of exogenous shocks) will accumulate more 'collusions and organizations for collective action over time'; that these organizations will be more concerned with distributional rather than growth objectives; that this will 'reduce efficiency and aggregate income ... and make political life more divisive'; that these 'distributional coalitions' will be less efficient than their constituent parts, will 'slow down on society's capacity to adopt new technologies and to reallocate resources' and, hence, will reduce the rate of economic growth; and, finally, that the accumulation of distributional coalitions will increase the complexity of government regulation and, hence, change the 'direction of social evolution' (Olson 1982: 74). Only when subjected to exogenous shocks, such as wars and economic and political crises, will these distributional coalitions be disrupted and will the economy surge forward.

Using these deductive 'implications' derived from his original collective-action model, Olson attempts to explain differential economic performance. Basically the network of special-interest organizations is seen as growing upon the body of a dynamic society like barnacles on the hull of a sailing ship – the driving force of which is left unmodelled – thereby regulating its efficiency and growth rate. With the passage of time these organizations become more powerful and intrusive and act to slow down the rate of economic expansion and growth. Only when these distorting growths are swept away by some random upheaval will the society surge forward economically once more. While Olson emphasizes that history is complex and that his theory should not be used as a 'monocausal explanation', he clearly regards it as possessing considerable explanatory power. Even the title suggests this.

More recently the collective action approach has been developed to model the interaction between lobby groups and the government when each is pursuing its own self-interest. Olson failed to model either the role of the state or the state–lobby interaction. Trade policy is one of the main applications of these models.[2] They begin with the neoclassical puzzle: If free trade is Pareto optimal, why is trade protection so widespread? Why not pursue free trade with 'side payments for the winners to compensate the losers'? (Krueger 1992: 109). The new collective-action answer is that protection is an outcome of the interaction between politicians and lobbyists (Magee *et al.* 1989). In effect, trade policy has been hijacked from self-seeking governments by special-interest groups. According to this view, governments have no strategic vision and do not provide strategic leadership.

The model can be briefly summarized. Lobby groups provide campaign funds to political candidates who are willing to grant appropriate levels of protection in their industries (Hillman 1989; Grossman and Helpman 1994) or, alternatively, an incumbent government will set trade policies in order to maximize its political support (Hillman 1982). In these models an explicit demand–supply framework is used, wherein the lobbyists, with preferences set by factor endowments, are the demanders of policy outcomes, and the government is the willing supplier. Studies based on this model are concerned with the structure of protection that emerges from the political equilibrium together with the contribution made by the different lobby groups that support the policy outcome. Even though there is an attempt to model the role of the state, it is unlike the predatory leviathan of public-choice theory or the controlling force for good or ill in the new institutional economics model.

THE NEW INSTITUTIONAL THEORY

Douglass North (1981; 1990), like the public-choice theorists, focuses on the central role of the state, but unlike them he views government as having the potential to play a positive as well as a negative role. The outcome in North's model depends on the strength of competitive forces. Also, unlike the collective-action model, North does not highlight the role of special-action organizations, rather he focuses on the way organizations in general react to institutions established by the state. In North's model it is the state that is responsible for rent-seeking as individuals merely respond passively to the institutions established by government.

North's theory of the state is based on the central idea that it trades revenue for 'protection and justice' (which includes establishing and super-vising property rights and contracts) with a population of individuals pursu-ing wealth maximization (North 1981: 33–6). This exchange arises because of the economies of scale involved in the provision of these services. The state's objective is to maximize revenue, which it pursues by 'acting like a discrim-inating monopolist, separating each group of constituents and devising prop-erty rights for each'. Like Brennan and Buchanan, North provides the state with a revenue-seeking objective but, unlike them, he argues that market constraints are binding. North (ibid.: 35–6) explains that 'the state is con-strained by the opportunity cost of its constituents, since there always exist potential rivals to provide the same set of services', because revenue-seeking leads to market inefficiency. The rivals waiting in the wings for a takeover bid, include potential leaders within society and aggressive states without. North, as an economic historian, has a much better feel for reality than Brennan and Buchanan.

In North's model, a tension exists between the revenue-maximizing object-ives of the state and the wealth-maximizing motives of its citizens. On the one hand, the state needs to establish a set of property rights specifying the ownership structure of both the factor and commodity markets to maximize the rents that it can extract; and on the other, it will need to reduce transactions costs both to satisfy its clients and to increase output so as to enjoy growing revenues. But as the property rights structure that will allow the ruler to maximize rents conflicts with the most efficient structure that will maximize economic growth, the political and economic outcome is potentially unstable. A takeover from within or without is always a possibility.

An important variable in North's model of political institutions is ideology. To achieve their objectives, individuals need to accept constraints on their behaviour. This is achieved not only through contracts and institutions but also by ideology. We are told that ideology, in addition to rationalizing the world around us, economizes on the amount of information that is required to supervise contracts, and it helps to overcome the free-rider problem explored so painstakingly by Olson. North even believes that ideology underpins the stability of institutions.

EVALUATING THE NEW POLITICAL ECONOMY

By briefly evaluating three major strands of the new political economy, I can also introduce, as a basis for contrast, the strategic model of political change and policy formulation to be analysed in Chapter 16. Public-choice theory has an unrealistic quality in terms of both the perceived role of government – ideally as well as in reality – and the recommended solution to state intervention. In the first place, public-choice theory fails to recognize an independent and positive role for government. It is, in their view, an institution out of control and arrayed against individuals. North's perception of the market constraints on the actions of the state is far more realistic. As demonstrated in Chapter 16 it is the strategic struggle between the strategists and their rulers that constrains the activities of government. In reality governments only lurch out of control when they are hijacked by professional revolutionaries (in my terms, antistrategists). Yet even North fails to see the role of strategic leadership that all governments are compelled to adopt if they expect to survive. The reason for this neglect by the new political economy is the exclusive focus of neoclassical economics on supply-side forces. Strategic demand has been totally overlooked.

What the public-choice theorists want to achieve is an emasculated state that is concerned only with the provision of public goods such as the protection of individuals and property rights and the enforcement of private contracts. Such a state would be incapable of providing strategic leadership as states have always done by spearheading the conquest, commerce, and technological strategies. It could not possibly play any dynamic role. This libertarian belief is consistent, of course, with the passive role expected of governments in neoclassical general equilibrium theory. Consider, for example, the antihistorical assertion by an orthodox trade theorist to the effect that countries do not compete with each other, and that 'countries [in contrast to corporations] ... do not go out of business' (Krugman 1996: 6).

To the contrary, the history of civilization is the history of the rise and fall of societies – of countries 'going out of business'.

Public-choice theory also has a totally unrealistic view of the way in which their ahistorical role for the state could be achieved. They see a special role for intellectuals in establishing constitutional rules that will strip the state of the ability to provide strategic leadership. Brennan and Buchanan (1980: 207) in their concluding paragraph assert that:

> Modern man did change his sociopolitical rules; he did once emerge from the Dark Ages. In doing so, he was guided, not solely by science and not primarily by blind evolutionary change, but by the reasoned speculation of persons who dared to think in terms of rules other than those under which they lived. They dreamed of possible futures, and some of their dreams were realised.

This is, in my view, based not only on an inflated perception of the role of ideas in driving society but on a completely incorrect reading of history. Changes in rules have been driven not by the dreams of modern man but by the desires of universal man. Ideas are the facilitator of desires (Snooks 1996; 1997a).[3] Modern intellectuals who, like Plato in ancient Athens, attempt to reshape society's institutions contrary to human desires (and why else attempt to reshape them?) are doomed to failure.

There are a number of major problems with the collective-action model both old and new. Olson's model has at least three important limitations. The first is his failure to distinguish between different kinds of special-interest organizations. While he mentions the wider aspirations of 'encompassing' organizations, he focuses on 'distributional coalitions'. What he totally omits are those strategic organizations (discussed in Chapter 16) that are pursuing new dynamic substrategies. This is a critical omission because these are the organizations driving society. They have a number of characteristics that are relevant to the issues raised in this chapter:

- The new substrategy promises unlimited returns. Because of this the size of the group is irrelevant. This is the outcome of modelling the demand side, rather than just the supply side, of societal dynamics.
- Members of the strategic organization are held together by a faith in the potential rewards of the new dynamic substrategy. This is the outcome of strategic confidence. There is no need for sticks and carrots, wielded by 'political entrepreneurs'.
- The strategic lobbyists play a positive and productive role as the driving force in human society.

It is essential, therefore, that we distinguish between strategic and antistrategic organizations.

Secondly, there are very real dangers in using a partial comparative–static model – particularly of a deductive nature – to explain the 'rise and decline of nations'. It is just not possible to explain the dynamics of real-world societies in this way, and there is a great danger that it will distort our understanding of the growth process by highlighting the wrong variables, thereby confusing effect with cause. Indeed, the emergence of larger numbers of 'distributional coalitions' is not the cause of declining economic performance, rather it is an outcome of the progressive exhaustion of the old dynamic substrategy. As strategic opportunities decline, entrepreneurs look for other ways of earning large surpluses, including the direction of available resources increasingly to speculative activities and to lobbying. These are all antistrategic activities. Conversely, the reduction in antistrategic activities occurs not as a result of exogenous shocks but as an outcome of the emergence of a more profitable new dynamic substrategy. In a society pursuing a successful dynamic strategy, therefore, the higher strategic returns keep unproductive activities under control.

Finally, collective-action theorists fail to model the role of the state very effectively. Olson does not model it at all, and even the more recent models treat the state as a compliant, self-interested party to rent-seeking. Needless to say this is sometimes true, but they totally overlook the main reason for the emergence of the state – to supply strategic leadership. Those governments that fail to fulfil this role fail to survive.

Douglass North, by virtue of his better understanding of history, provides a more realistic interpretation of the role of the state. But even so there are a number of major limitations with his institutionalist model, which arise from his commitment to basic neoclassical theory. First, North, like all the contributors to the new political economy, overlooks the role of strategic leadership. Secondly, like the rest, he adopts a neoclassical supply-side approach, thereby overlooking strategic demand which is responsible for bringing institutions into being and for shaping them. Rather, North sees the emergence of institutions as a response to transaction costs, mainly the costs of information. This supply-side approach is an outcome of adopting the flawed neoclassical decision-making model.

Finally, in my view, North overplays the role of ideology. While I agree that ideology assists in the achievement of social objectives, I disagree with North about the reason it is employed and about its wider role in society. North argues that ideology is important because of the costs involved in enforcing contracts, whereas I see it as a trigger for the strategic imitation mechanism which economizes on intelligence in both decision-making and in contract-enforcement. Ideology is employed by the state and by dissidents to provide an example of imitation for their respective constituents. It is part of the dynamic tactics of order and of chaos. Also we differ over the wider role of ideology in society. North claims that it underlies the stability of institutions, whereas in the dynamic-strategy model that role is played by strategic confidence, which arises from the demand rather than the supply side. And it is strategic confidence that determines the relative success of the dynamic tactics of order and of chaos.

CONCLUSIONS

The new political economy has yet to provide a satisfactory model of political change, and its model of policy formulation is indeterminant. While the former is self-evident, the latter requires further comment. Within the 'demand–supply' framework of policy formulation, a range of models have emerged. Some of these models focus on the 'demand' side (lobbying organizations), while others focus on the supply side (the state). On the supply side, the perception of the state varies dramatically, ranging from benevolent welfare agency, to self-interested instrument of change, to predatory Leviathan. Similarly, on the 'demand' side, the view of organizations ranges from profit-seeking to rent-seeking bodies. On purely logical grounds these models are equally valid. And this framework could accommodate an even greater variety of deductive models. Only through the inductive approach is it possible to determine the structure of the real model.

In the following chapter a realist model of both political change and policy formulation is developed. It shows how an integrated analysis of economic and political change can be constructed. This is achieved by placing the supply-side approach of neoclassical economics within a wider framework orchestrated by strategic demand.

16 The Strategic Model of Politics and Policy

A major limitation of neoclassical economic theory, which dates back to the late nineteenth century, is an inability to model both economic and political change. Chapter 3 made it clear that the neoclassical growth model has nothing to say about the political process. Even the new political economy, which emerged in the 1970s and 1980s, involves only the application of static neoclassical theory to an analysis of policy formulation. It is also theoretically indeterminate in the sense that it contains no criteria for discriminating between a large number of possible theoretical forms. And it is totally divorced from the economic growth literature. An attempt will be made in this chapter to show how economic and political change can be related, by employing the dynamic-strategy model.

THE MODEL

Political change and the strategic struggle

Strategic demand is the cornerstone of my model of political change and policy formation. Political institutions and organizations change as strategic demand changes in response to the unfolding dynamic strategy. Political change, therefore, is part of a secondary dynamic mechanism. This process of political transformation is dominated by the struggle between various societal groups for control of the dynamic strategy. By controlling the dynamic strategy they control the sources of their income and wealth. Hence the **strategic struggle**, which involves the use of political instruments of order and chaos, is fundamentally an economic struggle – a struggle for survival and prosperity. It is one of the 'primary laws of history' (Snooks 1998: ch. 8).

The political instruments of order and chaos, as argued in *The Dynamic Society* (Snooks 1996: 184–7), are the tactics employed by materialist man to maintain or to gain strategic control. The tactics of order include the establishment of laws, regulations, and ideology aimed at achieving compliance; and the tactics of chaos include the use of protest, rebellion, and revolution to break down the excluding order. Those groups involved in the strategic struggle can be classified as follows:

- the strategists (or profit-seekers)
  — old strategists – supporters of the traditional strategy
  — new strategists – supporters of the emerging strategy
- the nonstrategists (coerced workers and dependants)
- the antistrategists (or rent-seekers)
  — conservative antistrategists
  — revolutionary antistrategists.

All societies at any given time contain representatives of these strategic groups, which are involved in a continuous struggle against each other for influence and control over the sources of income and wealth, and against governments that either do not provide effective strategic leadership or do not give good strategic value for money. The relative importance in society of these groups changes considerably over time, not as a simple progression but as a complex yet predictable function of the unfolding dynamic strategy.

We need to define these strategic categories. The **strategists** are the driving force in society who invest time and resources in pursuing and profiting from the available dynamic strategies and substrategies. I call them profit-seekers because the returns they seek are from investment in activities that generate growth rather than a redistribution of a given GDP per capita in their favour. Strategic investment includes both physical and human capital. Failure to realize this defining characteristic led Marx to misunderstand the nature of capitalism. As the largest profits are obtained from exploring the dominant dynamic strategy, it attracts the attention of the most ambitious, risk-taking entrepreneurs. The less ambitious and more risk-averse, however, will find material comfort in the supporting or secondary strategies. This is not a homogeneous group, as it consists of old strategists who support the traditional strategy/substrategy and new strategists who explore the emerging strategy/substrategy. As the old strategy shows signs of exhaustion, these two groups struggle for power. The strategic struggle, therefore, is not central to the fundamental dynamic process but a response to it. It is part of the secondary dynamic mechanism.

The **nonstrategists** are unable to invest in the prevailing dynamic strategy, largely because they are controlled and exploited by the strategists. While this is not a very large group in our modern technological society – being restricted to minors and social deviants – there have been times in the past when it included the great majority of the population. Yet rather than declining over time in a linear fashion, the role of the nonstrategist has passed through a great circle from early hunter-gatherer societies, when the family controlled economic activities and the participation rate was high, to ancient and medieval societies, when small ruling elites forcibly employed large numbers of dependent labourers and slaves; to today, when the great majority actively participate in the prevailing strategy. The circle is complete, but not necessarily fixed.

The **antistrategists** pursue the objective of income redistribution rather than economic growth. They consist of two different types, the conservative antistrategists who pursue their objectives peacefully, and the revolutionary antistrategists who attempt to hijack the dynamic strategy. The conservative antistrategists establish legal organizations to lobby the government to exchange a degree of monopoly power over production or trade in specified commodities for campaign funds. In a viable society that is successfully pursuing a dynamic strategy, the success of these antistrategic organizations will be limited because the rate of return on investment will be higher in strategic activities. Only when the old dynamic strategy/substrategy is exhausted and a new substrategy is slow to emerge will the network of antistrategic organizations increase significantly.

There are some conservative antistrategists who, while not wanting to destroy the prevailing dynamic strategy, attempt to exploit it through illegal means. This is the case with the Mafia and similar organizations in other societies. While such predatory activity is tolerated when it amounts to only an insignificant part of total strategic activity owing to the costs of eradication, it will be attacked seriously by strategic leaders when it threatens to endanger the prevailing dynamic strategy.

The revolutionary antistrategists comprise that small, but extreme and ruthless minority dedicated to overthrowing the dynamic strategy for their own rent-seeking purposes. While this group is always present in society, it comes to prominence during times of crisis. If successful in capturing the reigns of power – such as the Bolsheviks in Russia, the Nazis in Germany, the militarists in Japan, and the Marxists in China – they establish repressive economic and political systems. These command systems are designed to eliminate existing strategists, to prevent the reemergence of potential strategists, and to facilitate the pursuit of rent-seeking. The most successful revolutionary antistrategists are those who are able to involve potential strategists in the rent-seeking command system – as in the USSR – because it widens the network of people who have a vested interest in its survival. But this is only relative, as survival of an antistrategic society is limited to two or three generations in a competitive world (Snooks 1997a: ch. 12).

The nature of the struggle between these strategic groups depends on the type of dynamic strategy being pursued and the stage of strategic development that has been reached. At the beginning of a new dynamic strategy, the new strategists will be in the ascendancy as the successful pioneers are followed by swarms of imitators who generate an effective demand for a wide range of new institutions. By the middle development phase there will be a healthy balance between strategic groups and an increasing exercise of the political instruments of order, resulting in a slow-down, even stagnation, of institutional change. Periods of rapid institutional change, therefore, will be followed by periods of stability. But this should not be regarded as the equivalent of the biological concept of 'punctuated equilibria' as some have claimed (Hodgson 1993). It is the outcome of forces on the side of strategic demand rather than on the evolutionary supply side.

As our society approaches strategic exhaustion, the conflict between the old and new strategists will increase, with each resorting to the tactics of order (repression) and chaos (dissent) respectively. Also antistrategic activity will become more noticeable. Eventually a transfer of political control from the old to the new strategists will occur, either peacefully or through revolution. If the revolution erupts at a time when the new strategists do not possess sufficient economic power to quickly overwhelm the old strategists, there is the possibility that a determined and ruthless group of antistrategists might exploit the resulting chaos and hijack the revolution, as in the USSR in late 1917. Seizing their opportunities the antistrategists, initially with the support of the nonstrategists and some conservative antistrategists, ruthlessly eliminate all existing strategists, both old and new, and construct a command system that not only enslaves the nonstrategists and prevents them giving rise to new strategists, but maximizes the extraction of rents from all the people.

It needs to be emphasized that this political transformation is not an evolutionary process. An example will clarify the issue. Despite the apparent evolutionary progression in English political institutions over the past millennium, **strategic reversals** are possible. While England experienced a conquest→commerce→technological sequence, there was nothing inevitable about this. It was, as we have seen, the outcome of a particularly fortuitous and happy coincidence: the exhaustion of the commerce strategy in the mid-eighteenth century coincided with the exhaustion of the neolithic technological paradigm. Had the commerce strategy been exhausted at the middle rather than the end of the neolithic technological paradigm, then the strategic sequence would have been conquest→commerce→conquest, as it was for ancient Greece. Such a strategic reversal would have led to a reversal of political forms, although they would not have been identical to those in earlier times because of changes in relative institutional prices. Old commerce strategists would be overwhelmed by a new military elite that would require different political, social, and economic institutions. In particular, democratic institutions would be dismantled and replaced by more repressive institutions controlled by the new men of conquest. The strategic reversal, therefore, leads to a reversal of strategic demand and, hence, of institutions. This is why institutional change is not an evolutionary process.

When focusing more closely on the modern era, we need to ask whether the sequence of technological substrategies also has a determining influence on political change. While they do, their influence is of a more subtle but nevertheless significant kind. As each technological substrategy has become increasingly sophisticated, the demands on the wider community for the acquisition of human capital have increased. To meet these demands the entire population has been required to invest in higher levels of education, and this investment has led to greater strategic participation and the need to protect these investments and the correspondingly higher incomes. In other words, within a potentially democratic political framework established by the dynamic strategy of technological change, the degree of strategic and, hence, political participation has increased in response to the emergence of new and more technologically sophisticated substrategies.

Once again we should realize that there is nothing inevitable about this process. If technological regress occurred, as it would in the face of severe exogenous shocks such as an epidemic on the scale of the Black Death, a massive asteroid collision, or a major nuclear incident, then there would be a reversal of the technological substrategy that would halt, and even reverse, the democratization process. And if, during such a crisis, an extreme group of ecological antistrategists hijacked the political process and brought the technological strategy to an end, the old conquest strategy would emerge once more. These scenarios may be extreme and unrealistic (yet we should not forget the equally unlikely assumption of power by Hitler in Germany), but they make my point about the reversibility of political change.

While the changing political process is similar at both the strategic and substrategic level – as it is the outcome of the strategic struggle – there is a major difference. At the strategic level the struggle is between supporters of entirely different strategies (such as conquest and commerce or commerce and technological change), whereas at the substrategic level it takes place between factions within a single strategy. In other words, at the substrategy level, all participants accept and support the existing economic/social/political system. And the strategic struggle involves the pursuit of more advantageous positions within that system. Accordingly, neither the new or old **strategic factions** wish to pursue their struggle to the point where the existing system breaks down. Instead, they pursue their differences through existing democratic structures – although they will need to modify them in the process – to achieve a redistribution of income from the old to the new strategic faction.

An important mechanism in the transfer of support from the old to the new strategy/substrategy is what I have called **strategic imitation**. It is the mechanism by which strategic pioneers who earn extraordinary profits are followed by a growing proportion of the population eager to share in the spoils. This response is so regular and so strong that it has been included as one of the 'primary laws of history' (Snooks 1998: ch. 8). As argued in Chapter 9, imitation is the basis of economic decision-making. Individuals, in making decisions, seek information not regarding all the variables required to compute complicated rates of return on alternative investment projects, but only on who is successful and why. Strategic imitation, therefore, eliminates both the need for expensive searches claimed by the new institutionalists, and the need to assume perfect knowledge and processing abilities claimed by neoclassicists. This is the case for both decision-making and the enforcement of contracts.

How does the strategic imitation process work? A new strategy/substrategy begins in a small way as a few pioneering strategists invest in new and very risky ventures. Those who succeed earn extraordinary profits, which attracts the attention of private profit-seekers and public revenue-seekers. Before long they are imitated by a large number of opportunistic strategic followers. As the new strategists become increasingly wealthy, their influence over government policy increases through the creation of strategic lobbying organizations. Eventually, their representatives take control of government and, hence, of society's dominant strategy/substrategy. These representatives are expected to provide active strategic leadership both within and without the society. If they fail to do so they are removed. It is through the strategic-imitation mechanism, therefore, that the new activities of a handful of successful pioneers become the focus of a society's dynamic strategy and supporting policies.

Clearly the dynamic-strategy model is diametrically opposed to Karl Marx's concept of class and class struggle. In the above model, the defining characteristic of a strategist is that he or she invests in either physical or human capital which is required to participate in a society's dynamic strategy. By contrast, Marx's concept of class and class struggle is based on ownership of the means of production; hence, the population of a modern technological society is divided into 'capitalists' and 'workers'. What Marx did not realize is that all 'classes' in the technological society – including 'capitalists' and 'workers' – are part of the strategist group because they invest time and resources in the prevailing substrategy and they benefit from the returns to this strategic investment. Rewards depend not on the type of ownership of the means of production as Marx argued, but on the amount and quality of strategic investment. 'Workers' as well as 'capitalists' have a stake in the technological society. Neither group has any intention of destroying it.

In the dynamic-strategy model, therefore, there is no critical conflict between 'capital' and 'labour', because they all accept, pursue, and benefit from the technological strategy. The objective of the struggle between strategic factions in contemporary society is to marginally influence the distribution of a growing real GDP per capita, not to cripple or destroy the technological strategy. Both 'capital' and 'labour' are on the same side in the more critical struggle against rent-seeking antistrategists. This is why there has been no real proletarian revolution – only antistrategic takeovers, albeit in the name (only) of the proletariat – in any technological society. This is why Marx was wrong. Quite incorrectly he saw all 'capitalists' as rent-seekers (as exploiters of labour) rather than as profit- seekers; and he saw 'class struggle' as the central (rather than the secondary) mechanism in the rise and fall of 'capitalism'.

The key to understanding sociopolitical dynamics is the realization that it is a function of the unfolding dynamic strategy. As strategic demand changes so do society's institutional and organizational structures. Elsewhere I have called this the 'fundamental law of institutional change' (Snooks 1998: ch. 10). And it is on this law that all other laws of institutional change are based. The chief of these involve the growing democratization of institutions and organizations, their growing size and complexity, and their continuing cohesion. These outcomes are usually regarded as the inevitable result of some sort of evolutionary process.

But in reality, institutions and organizations will only become more complex and democratic and maintain functional integrity if a viable dynamic strategy continues to unfold, if an exhausted strategy can be replaced, and if there is no reversal in the strategic sequence. If, however, an exhausted strategy cannot be successfully replaced, existing institutions will eventually be hijacked by antistrategists who will change them into instruments of exploitation. And if the strategic sequence is reversed, then the complexity, size, and degree of democratization of sociopolitical structures will also be reversed. This, as history attests, involves a law-like relationship.

Policy formulation

The dynamic-strategy model of policy formulation provides a framework for considering the new political-economy models. Policy-making should be seen as a response to the unfolding dynamic strategy both by the demanders (the lobby groups) and the suppliers (governments) of policy. While lobbyists and governments have different objectives, they are both conditioned by the prevailing dynamic strategy and substrategy. Both are influenced by the same strategic environment.

As argued earlier, the elected government in any successful technological society will be required to represent and be responsive to its strategists. This is, as we have seen, the outcome of the strategic-imitation mechanism. While elected governments will not always formulate policies that are acceptable to the majority of electors, if the electorate feels sufficiently aggrieved the offending government will be swept away. All elected governments are

expected to provide strategic leadership and to support the objectives of the
strategists. It is in this particular sense that societies (as well as individuals)
can be said to pursue dynamic strategies.

What are the objectives of the demanders and suppliers of economic policies? The demanders of policy have objectives that are directly attuned to the
unfolding dynamic strategy. Strategic demand is generated for a range of
inputs, one of which is support from society for the investment projects of
strategists. This assistance may take the form of provision of strategic infrastructure, active trade negotiations with other societies, defence of trading
routes and overseas trading institutions, military threats and even action against
offending societies, and protection of the dynamic strategy in general. In other
words, the demand for economic policy is an aspect of strategic demand.

The suppliers of policy have objectives that are less directly, but no less
firmly, related to the unfolding dynamic strategy. Clearly individual parliamentarians are, on average, primarily interested in pursuing their own material
interests, which can be measured in terms of their length of stay in parliament
and the heights to which they might rise. Both considerations determine the
nature of their salaries, other benefits, and pensions, together with subsequent
opportunities in society once their days in parliament are over. Parliamentarians, therefore, are responsive to those who are responsive to strategic
demand. Further, this material self-interest is pursued within the prevailing
strategic framework, which conditions the way they see their own future and
that of society as a whole. This provides scope for perceptive and imaginative
government leaders to sketch out a vision for their community and to provide
positive leadership rather than just responding to the strategists.

The dynamic-strategy model, therefore, provides a framework that can
explain the interaction between the demanders and the suppliers of economic policy. For a viable technological society in which politicians are
elected democratically, the government and the strategists react not only to
each other but to the unfolding dynamic strategy. In such a framework
governments are not the predators, the rent-seeking collaborators, or the
compliant welfare agencies they are often assumed to be. It is strategic
demand that shapes the actions and responses of both groups.

What are the implications of the dynamic strategy for the models of the
new political economy discussed in Chapter 15? First, the introduction of
strategic demand provides a determinate dynamic structure for the economic
model of policy formulation. It does this by showing how policy is related to
the wider dynamic process of society. Hence it resolves the difficulty faced by
the new political economy resulting from the infinite number of possible
models that emerge from their supply-side analysis. And it treats the policy
issue in a dynamic rather than a comparative–static manner.

Secondly, it resolves the existing problem of how to treat the supplier of
policy. The new political economy has characterized the role of governments in

a variety of ways, ranging from predator to welfare agency. This indeterminacy is resolved once again only once strategic demand is introduced. Predatory governments emerge only in societies ruled by antistrategists who pursue rent-seeking, rather than by strategists who pursue profit-seeking. The reason behind this is that the activity of governments in strategic societies is con-strained by the strategic struggle. Antistrategic societies are those that have failed to replace old exhausted strategies with viable new strategies, or have been hijacked before these new strategies become effectively established. On the other hand, no society is ruled by governments of the type suggested by neoclassical welfare theory. Governments do not attempt to maximize the welfare of the entire group – only of the strategists. The importance of this becomes clear when we remember that in societies pursuing non-technological strategies, the proportion of strategists is quite small. No government is bene-volent, because all governments pursue their own self-interested objectives within a dynamic strategic framework. The question is not what policy will generate Pareto optimal outcomes, but what policy will most effectively facil-itate the exploration and exploitation of the prevailing dynamic strategy. Suppliers of policy should not be treated as independent entities for good or evil. They are leaders of the dynamic strategy.

AN APPLICATION: ENGLAND 1000–2000

The operation of the dynamic-strategy model of political change can be effectively illustrated by applying it briefly to the case of England over the very long period 1000 to 2000. This will link up with those applications to the same society and time period concerning longrun dynamics (Chapter 10) and economic fluctuations (Chapter 14). A more detailed analysis of political (and socioeconomic) change has been conducted elsewhere (Snooks 1997a: ch. 10). England has been chosen as a case-study because over the past one thousand years it spans the rise and fall of three separate dynamic strategies and because it was the first society to adopt the technological strategy.[1] As before, this analysis is centred around the unfolding of the strategic sequence of conquest→commerce→technological change.

The conquest strategy, 1000–1450

The vehicle of change for the conquest society in Western Europe was the nation-state, strategically directed by a hereditary monarchy. In England the nation-state emerged in the ninth and tenth centuries as the Anglo-Saxons attempted to throw back the invading Scandinavians. The nation-state, therefore, was an outcome of the conquest strategy as well as being its vehicle of change.

The dynamic strategists in this political system were the king and his great magnates, who struggled against each other for control of the conquest strategy. But as they all participated in and benefited from this strategy they had no intention of pushing these conflicts to the point of derailing it. To accommodate this struggle for power in a non-disruptive way, a rudimentary form of parliament was formed in the mid-thirteenth century. Conquest down to the mid-thirteenth century was financed in part by the imposition of taxes on the growing surpluses generated by agriculture and, increasingly, on the profits of commerce. As we shall see it was the strategic struggle between the ruler and the strategists that constrained the revenue-seeking objectives of government and ensured that they provided strategic leadership.

While the ruling warrior elite controlled the profits on agriculture, the new middle classes held a monopoly over commerce. And in order to tax these growing commercial interests, the king found it necessary to gain their formal approval by inviting their representatives (in the late fourteenth and early fifteenth centuries) to attend parliament at Westminster. From this time parliament became the stage for a series of desperate struggles between the aristocratic supporters of the old conquest strategy and the middle-class supporters of the new commerce strategy. These struggles were not finally resolved in favour of commerce until the civil wars of the mid-seventeenth century. Political change in England, therefore, was the outcome of both the struggle for control of the prevailing dynamic strategy and the struggle between alternative dynamic strategies.

The Anglo-Saxon (to 1066), Norman (1066–1135), and Angevin (1135–1227) kings were unable to rule without the active support of their nobles. Together they planned, executed, and shared in the rewards and losses of the unfolding conquest strategy. The greater among the nobles – the ealdormen/barons – not only advised the king through his council and stood beside him in battle, they also presided over the shire courts that administered the king's laws and raised his taxes. The lesser nobles – the thegns/knights – led their peasants into battle and they dispensed justice and raised taxes at the local level. To activate this system of local government machinery, the king's chancery, which was staffed with educated clerics who developed the exchequer into a major instrument of strategic rule, issued commands through 'writs'. But competing with this system of royal administration and justice in the provinces were the manorial courts of the great barons. While this overlapping system of control provided the men and money to fight for territory in France, it also provided an economic basis for strategic struggle.

The unfolding conquest strategy, driven by elite warriors exploring profitable weaknesses in French defences, generated a demand for the above instruments of strategic direction and for institutions that embodied the strategic struggle. The most important of these was parliament. The struggle between the king and his nobles can be traced back to the earliest Anglo-Saxon times. A tribal chief, a regional warlord, or a king of all England could only command the support of his nobles for as long as he was successful in battle and could guarantee security for their newly acquired possessions. Strategic leadership was of paramount importance. The most famous of these strategic struggles occurred between the Angevin king, John, and his barons. It was an outcome of John's incompetent strategic leadership, which reduced rather than increased the wealth and income of his nobles. While he taxed his nobles very heavily, John failed utterly in his conquest ambitions. The outcome was Magna Carta – the Great Charter – imposed on John by his nobles, both lay and ecclesiastical, in 1215 in an effort to rescue a failing conquest strategy by reestablishing a proper balance between the rights and responsibilities of the king and his nobles.

The shadow of Magna Carta fell across the thirteenth century, a period of intense struggle between king and magnate that led to the baronial rebellion of 1258 against Henry III and the establishment of 'parliament' (meaning 'discussion') consisting of 27 men elected by the rebel barons. In the process of recovering his power, Henry III turned increasingly to the new men who had grown rich on the profitable wool trade. These included the knightly class who grew the wool and the merchants who traded with manufacturers in the Low Countries. It is one of history's fascinating ironies that the aristocratic warriors, in attempting to assert their power over the king, were responsible for driving him into the arms of the new men of commerce who, for the first time, were able to express their opinions about the nation's dynamic strategy.

In the mid-thirteenth century the new men of commerce were admitted to parliament. In 1258 and 1264 two knights from each shire, and in 1265 an additional two burgesses from each important borough, were summoned to meet with the king's council to approve the taxes raised on the profits of commerce. While this initially occurred under the rebel 'commune', the practice proved to be of value to Henry III in his battle against the barons once he regained his authority. By the 1330s, when Edward III was raising funds to embark on what became the Hundred Years War, parliament, although still an *ad hoc* institution that met only when the king wanted money, had achieved the institutional form that was to survive into the seventeenth century – the Commons consisting of knights and burgesses, and the Lords composed of the great magnates both lay and ecclesiastical. And by the mid-fourteenth century the king had accepted the concept that customs duties would not be imposed upon merchants without the agreement of a 'full parliament'. With this achievement the new men of commerce began to influence England's dynamic strategy.

The commerce strategy, 1450–1750

The nation-state, the major vehicle of the conquest strategy in Western Europe, was able to adapt to the requirements of the commerce strategy. But to do so it needed to be transformed. As shown elsewhere (Snooks 1997a), the commerce strategy leads to the development of either the city-state as in ancient Greece and medieval Venice, or to the large metropolis within the nation-state as in England and the Dutch Republic. And as the commerce strategy unfolds, the metropolis emerges as the centre of an overseas trading empire. In ancient Greece the city-state survived intact because the overseas colonies were self-governing replicas of the mother city-state, and in the Venetian Republic the overseas possessions were never regarded as more than maritime bases and trading posts. By contrast, the commerce empire of Britain had, by the early eighteenth century, begun to challenge the integrity of the nation-state. London became the great commercial and financial metropolis of a global empire. Between 1500 and 1800, London's population increased by a factor of nineteen from 50 000 to 950 000, to reach a total almost double that of Paris, its nearest rival.

Within this societal vehicle of change, a great struggle raged from 1450 to 1750 between the supporters of the competing dynamic strategies of conquest and commerce. With the exhaustion of the conquest strategy in the mid-fifteenth century, there emerged a pragmatic royal dynasty – the Tudors, from 1485 to 1603 – who realized that political survival depended on being able to gain financial support from the new men of commerce. Yet while the Tudors needed the support of commerce against the old warrior elite, they failed to provide particularly positive leadership for the new commerce strategy. Only in comparison with the uncomprehending Stuarts (1603 to 1649 and 1660 to 1688), who continually frustrated the commercial aspirations of parliament, do the Tudors appear to gain leadership credibility.

The fundamental problem in the transition period was that absolute monarchy, which emerged to lead the conquest strategy, was unable to provide appropriate leadership for the new commerce strategy. It was a problem that provoked the civil wars of the seventeenth century and which persisted until the establishment of limited monarchy between 1689 (Bill of Rights) and 1701 (Act of Settlement) and the acceptance in practice of constitutional monarchy by Victoria and Albert in the 1840s. What is of interest is that absolute monarchy in England was able to survive the exhaustion of the conquest strategy and the collapse of the old warrior elite by cleverly persuading the new men of commerce that its leadership was essential to their cause. Yet it was a compromise that lasted only two centuries, because it was discovered the hard way that leaders of conquest do not make effective leaders of commerce.

The first English monarch to make the transition from leadership of a conquest to a commerce society was Henry VII (1485–1509). As a rank outsider, Henry Tudor found it necessary to gain support from the gentry in his attack on those aristocratic interests aligned against him. Not only did Henry govern with the assistance of the gentry as members of parliament in Westminster and as justices of the peace in the counties, he also negotiated commercial treaties on their behalf. In his turn, Henry VIII (1509–1547) began dismantling the old aristocracy; turning against the wealth and power of the ecclesiastical lords by dissolving the monasteries and breaking the economic power of the Catholic Church. To do so he needed the support of the Commons. This led to the summoning of the Reformation Parliament (1529–1536), which enthusiastically supported a king determined to break the wealth and power of the church not only because they stood to gain from a division of the spoils but also because it gave them the opportunity to promote the cause of commerce. Not surprisingly, parliament provided Henry with the funds he required. Elizabeth I (1558–1603) continued the new tradition of governing through the gentry rather than the aristocracy in the counties as well as in Westminster. Accordingly, the size of the Commons doubled during the sixteenth century to 600 members, while the size of the Lords shrank by one-third to only 40 members. Increasingly parliament came to represent the views of the emerging middle class.

During the Elizabethan era the Commons became, for the first time in English history, the stage for the strategic struggle. In the past that stage had been either the king's council or the battlefield. The stage of conflict shifted because the dynamic strategy had changed. The conflict was about the nature of economic policy. While Elizabeth received financial support from the Commons for her leadership of the commerce strategy – which involved fighting to defend commercial interests (the Netherlands) against conquest societies (France and Spain) – she came into conflict with them, particularly from 1597, over the indiscriminate sale of monopolies to favoured individuals and groups. The Commons, which objected because the royal policy favoured antistrategic rather than strategic organizations (lobby groups), had some successes.

But this victory was short-lived. The Stuarts had no intention of working through the gentry as the Tudors had done. This Scottish/French dynasty failed to understand that England had been forever changed by the very rapid commercial expansion of the sixteenth century and that they were expected by the middle classes to act as leaders of the commerce strategy. They stubbornly refused. By seeking out alternative sources of finance, both James I (1603–25) and Charles I (1625–49) were able to rule for long periods without calling parliament, which refused to vote any 'subsidies' because the Stuarts failed to actively support the commerce strategy. Charles even refused to provide English merchants with naval protection against pirates in the seas around England or against their rivals overseas. When petitioned by the merchants for naval support in the Mediterranean, Charles merely told them not to sail in those waters! As Charles said, he refused to become 'a Doge of Venice' – a merchant prince elected by other merchants to represent their interests in the world. The Stuarts were more interested in dynastic wars in Europe and Scotland.

This struggle, which led to a collapse of strategic confidence and to civil war (1642–8), was a struggle between the commerce strategists and a monarchy – set adrift from its conquest origins – that refused to lead this new dynamic strategy. While the objectives of the Commons were completely materialistic, they rationalized their unprecedented action against their monarch in terms of their protection of the rights and liberties of the 'people'. But by 'people' they meant the small proportion of property owners – or new strategists – rather than the great majority of the population that had no property. As one member of parliament said at the time: 'when we mention the people, we do not mean the confused promiscuous body of the people'. A similar distinction had been made in 1624 between 'free men' and 'men who are not free': 'He that hath no property in his goods is not free'. This is a clear distinction between the strategist and the nonstrategist of the early to mid-seventeenth century. The civil wars of the 1640s, therefore, were all about strategic leadership.

With the death of Oliver Cromwell – the military dictator thrown up by the civil wars – in 1658, and the resignation of his son Richard soon after, parliament was summoned once more to Westminster. Reeling from military dictatorship, the Commons invited Charles Stuart, as the lesser of two evils, to become King Charles II (1660–85) of England. But the Stuarts still had not learned the real lesson of the civil wars – the need for the monarchy to lead and defend the dynamic strategy of commerce. In the end, a Whig-led parliament decided in 1688 to invite William of Orange, the effective ruler of the Dutch Republic and defender of the commerce strategy in Europe, to force James II (1685–8) from the throne. With William at its head, England thereafter became the leading nation in aggressively defending and extending the interests of commerce.

Parliament had, from the late seventeenth century, finally taken control of its own destiny. Like the Republic of Venice, it passed a series of acts (between 1689 and 1701) to establish a political leadership with powers limited by law. Never again would an English monarch misunderstand what was expected of him or her. The Commons had created a monarch in its own image. At the same time local government was in the hands of the gentry who had originally made their fortunes, either directly or indirectly, from commerce. Such an integration of governmental functions, at both the Westminster and county levels, had not existed since the height of the conquest strategy in the thirteenth century. When the exhausted commerce strategy was replaced with the technological strategy in the two generations after 1780, the monarchy meekly followed parliament's lead.

The technological strategy

The vehicle of England's dynamic strategy has changed considerably over the past millennium owing to the changing strategic demand generated by the conquest→commerce→technological strategic sequence. Conquest saw the rise of the nation-state; commerce the transformation of the nation-state into a global maritime empire with London as its metropolis; while the unfolding technological strategy has led to the recreation of the nation-state, the dismantling of empire, and the move to political union with its arch-rivals of the previous millennium. How do we account for the changes over the past two centuries?

With the adoption of the technological strategy, which led to the Industrial Revolution, Britain was able to generate extraordinary profits from new products and new processes within its own borders. Innovation has replaced monopoly access to resources and markets as the engine of growth. England, thereby gained a competitive advantage over its neighbours and created a wealthy and powerful nation-state that no longer depended heavily on its overseas possessions. While the post-industrial, or 'new', empire assisted in the penetration of overseas markets, it was not essential to England's new dynamic, as the successful dismantlement of the British Empire in the mid-twentieth century clearly demonstrates.

As the technological strategy unfolded in the West, other states – such as France, Germany, and the USA – adopted the latest production and organizational techniques and participated in the extraordinary profits that Britain had enjoyed as the first industrial nation. And, in the resulting competitive process, Britain's extraordinary profits were eroded. Britain responded at first (during the interwar years) by turning to its old empire to ward off international competition. But this failed owing to different interests in the Empire and to the emergence of the mega-states of the USA and USSR. Since the Second World War, the growing competition from the mega-states has forced old foes in Europe to abandon their empires, to bury their differences stretching back a thousand years, and to begin the process of building a European mega-state that could compete with those existing (USA and USSR) and those emerging (China). Over the past two centuries, therefore, the unfolding technological strategy, which will continue into the twenty-first century, has transported Britain from control of empire to active, if reluctant, participation in a new mega-state.

Within this transforming eco-political system a number of important institutional changes, driven by strategic demand, have taken place. They include the transition from a limited to a constitutional monarchy, the emergence of universal suffrage, and the development of a political system that is responsive to, and provides leadership for, the prevailing technological substrategies. Although these institutional changes were constructed on foundations laid down under the commerce strategy, they did not 'evolve' automatically from them. Had the underlying conditions been different, and had the commerce strategy been followed by conquest rather than technological change (as in ancient Greece and medieval Venice), these institutions would have turned back on themselves and would have been exploited by a new military elite.

The unprecedented economic transformation that occurred during the reigns of George III (1760–1820) and George IV (1820–30), led to a significant shift of authority from Crown to Commons as the new men of wealth asserted their determination to control the sources of their wealth. As we have seen, by the 1840s the supremacy of parliament was finally accepted by the monarchy. From this time it was taken for granted that state sovereignty resides in the prime minister and cabinet who are responsible not to the monarch but to parliament, which in turn is responsible to those – the 'people' or strategists – who elect them.

Of course, English parliaments, if not kings, have always held the view that they are responsible to the 'people'. But the composition, if not the definition, of the 'people' has changed as the dynamic strategies and substrategies have unfolded and been substituted one for the other. The 'people' are always those who actively participate in, and benefit from, the successful pursuit of the dominant dynamic strategy. They are, in other words, the strategists. In the conquest period the 'people' were the tiny proportion (about half of one per cent) of the population lucky enough to be the king's tenants-in-chief; in the commerce period they were the landowners, merchants, and financiers who invested in and profited from the wool and associated trades; and in the technological period they were those who invested, initially, in physical capital (the industrialists) and, later, in human capital (the workers), in the process of industrialization.

With the growing wealth of the new owners of industry and their purchase of land in imitation of the commerce gentry, came an increasing representation of their interests in parliament. And as their representation increased, they struggled increasingly against the old gentrified commercial interests for control of the new dynamic strategy. This struggle was not as disastrous for the old strategists as it had been during the earlier shift from conquest to commerce, because the technological strategy not only provided scope for the new industrial interests to earn extraordinary profits, but also made it possible for the more ambitious and entrepreneurial members of the old commerce faction to rebuild their fortunes. The explanation is that the technological strategy generated new products and processes that enable

British merchants to make rapid inroads into overseas markets and, thereby, to share in the profitability of the Industrial Revolution.

The conflict between old and new strategists, therefore, led to demonstrations (particularly concerning the Corn Laws) without, and struggles within, parliament rather than on the battlefield as had occurred in the seventeenth-century. The outcome of these strategic struggles was the abolition of the Corn Laws thereby reducing industrialists costs, and the passing of the 1832 Reform Act thereby increasing representation from the growing industrial towns. Yet at this time the ownership of physical property was still the accepted definition of the 'people'. Workers had to wait until the end of the First World War before they could directly influence the deliberations of parliament.

Working-class participation in the strategic and, hence, political process, only occurred gradually as various sections of the non-propertied classes gained skills that were essential to potential employers, as they responded to strategic demand. At first this involved the establishment of unions and, later, participation in parliament. The demand for 'skilled' factory and building workers – particularly engineering tradesmen, boilermakers, carpenters, and joiners – grew rapidly from the early nineteenth century, leading to employer recognition of skilled unions in the 1850s and 1860s and by parliament in 1871. In the 1870s 'semi-skilled' workers, and in the 1880s 'unskilled' workers (who were by this time investing in general education and on-the-job training), also formed unions as they began to actively participate in the technological strategy and desired to enjoy the resulting benefits. This was the organizational basis employed, through the Trade Union Congress (TUC), to lobby parliamentarians for the formulation of favourable policies.

By the end of the nineteenth century the unfolding technological strategy required the support of the non-propertied classes. It was, therefore, only a matter of time before they obtained the economic power to enter parliament and to influence, even formulate, policy. The vote had already been extended to all urban male householders in 1867 and all county male householders in 1884. Yet it was still difficult for the ruling elite to regard men, let alone women, without physical property as part of the 'people'. Universal male suffrage was finally granted in 1918, and was extended to females in 1928, when it was finally accepted that the 'people' really did include the entire adult population, both male and female. This was implicit recognition, for the first time in Britain's history, that all the people had a stake in the dynamic strategy of the nation. All the people had finally become strategists. Despite this long struggle to exercise control over the dynamic strategy of England, some new political economists (Brennan and Lomasky 1993) have argued with a remarkable lack of historical, or even empirical, understanding that the participation of citizens in the political process is motivated more by a sense of symbolic drama than by material advantage.[2]

By the early twentieth century, the political party structure we know today was emerging. The essential characteristic of the British political system is that, while each party represents fairly well-defined sectional interests, all parties support the dominant technological strategy/substrategy. A major reason Marx was wrong about 'capitalism' is that he took a 'mode-of-production' view rather than a strategic view of the modern world. Only unrepresentative organizations outside parliament, such as the TUC (in the 1970s and 1980s) or ecological extremists, have turned against the technological strategy. Such action is based on an erroneous view of the objectives of the 'people', and is ultimately self-defeating because the dominant dynamic strategy will always be defended by the state. That is the reason for its existence.

The economic policies of both major parties – the Conservatives and Labour – are very similar. In the past, but not the present nor probably the future, the main difference has been the extent of government ownership of major industries. This was a hangover from confused, Marxist-inspired views. These differences arose during the early years of the Labour Party, established in 1893, and were consolidated after 1918 owing to the influx of Labour members of parliament and after the Second World War when, in a flush of enthusiasm, Labour ruled for the first time in its own right.

The only real differences between the parties today, and even this is fairly marginal, concerns the pattern of income distribution. While market solutions to distribution are generally accepted, special-interest groups – such as farmers, other business concerns, unions, and ethnic groups – lobby the respective parties, just as they have always done, for laws and regulations (tariffs and subsidies) that limit competition and redistribute income in their favour. More generally, all groups look to government to provide the institutional framework in which the dynamic strategy can be pursued most effectively in order to achieve both rapid economic growth and the full employment of resources. In this respect, however, most recent Western governments seem to have lost their way.

CONCLUSIONS

Dynamic-strategy theory provides a new approach to both political change and policy formulation. It is the same theory that is employed in this book to analyse longrun economic growth and economic fluctuations. Because of this versatility, it is possible to integrate the analysis of political change with economic change. Also the theory is concerned with dynamic processes rather than the comparative – static outcomes of the new political economy.

Dynamic-strategy theory will form the basis of a different perspective on what needs to be done to improve the economic performance and the viability of the developed nations. This perspective is based on the new general principle of strategic policy developed in Chapter 17.

17 The General Principles of Strategic Policy

In this final chapter the general principles of strategic policy are explored. These principles have been derived from the dynamic-strategy model of economic and political change developed in this book. The policy implications of my model not only differ dramatically from those arising from neoclassical theory, which are applied throughout the developed world, but they are expected to counter the insidious tendency of contemporary policy to undermine the longrun viability of Western democracies.

While general principles and broad proposals are discussed, no attempt is made to formulate specific policies as these will vary according to the circumstances in which each developed society finds itself. The general principles, however, are relevant to all developed societies. The reason for highlighting these general principles is that in the process of policy formation they appear to be more important than the changing models to which they give rise (Snooks 1997a: 498–503). We will proceed by outlining the principles, policies, and outcomes of orthodox neoclassical economics, and by discussing the strategic policy principles and broad proposals.

ORTHODOX POLICY

The general principles

What are the general principles underlying orthodox economic policy? The central policy principles are the concepts of efficiency and market flexibility. I will deal with efficiency first. Ideally, the neoclassicist would like to view efficiency in terms of a social welfare function that can be maximized subject to the usual economic constraints. But this has not proved possible because, as is well known from Arrow's Impossibility Theorem, a unique social welfare function does not exist.[1] Our neoclassicist, therefore, is thrown back upon the concept of Pareto optimality, where any change can objectively be regarded as an improvement only if someone is better off while no one else is worse off. However that might be measured!

A number of subsidiary policy objectives can be derived from the central efficiency principle. These include economic stability, and internal and external balance. Economic stability involves full employment of resources consistent with a low and stable level of inflation. This has led to the adoption by many orthodox economists of the concept of the natural rate of unemployment, also known as the 'nonaccelerating inflation rate of unemployment' (NAIRU) – of estimating the rate of unemployment consistent with nonaccelerating inflation.[2] In addition, internal and external balance are thought to minimize the distorting effects of government intervention in the market sector. If these broad objectives can be achieved, then it may be possible to meet the central efficiency principle. Yet, although there is widespread agreement about the importance of these general policy principles, there is much disagreement about how they should be achieved. I will return to this shortly.

Needless to say, neoclassical efficiency is a static supply-side concept. Although it was developed for shortrun analysis, Pareto optimality is also applied to the longrun, mainly to support arguments for *laissez-faire* trade principles. I have argued earlier that Pareto optimality, by which all policy instruments and outcomes are to be judged, is an artificial construct made necessary by a supply-side theory with no role for dynamic demand. Instead of evaluating policy in terms of the degree to which it facilitates the exploitation of strategic opportunities, the neoclassicist judges it in terms of a static supply-side criterion. While I reject social welfare (or social choice) theory as an evaluative criterion in a dynamic framework, it no doubt has its uses in static economics, not the least of which is the provision of intellectual clarity. As Amartya Sen (1987: 389) has pointed out:

> As a methodological discipline, social choice theory has contributed a great deal to clarifying problems that had been obscure earlier... The vast literature surveyed in this article can be ultimately judged by what has been achieved in terms of clarifying the obscure and illuminating the unclear.

Yet, I will argue, the artificiality of Pareto optimality is the least of its problems. The universal use of this concept has led to a policy thrust, both for the shortrun and longrun, that emphasizes stability at the expense of dynamics. To the degree that governments have accepted expert neoclassical advice, this concept can be held responsible for undercutting the longrun viability of Western democracies.

The second general policy principle is market flexibility. Apart from the obvious connection with the related concept of efficiency, market flexibility is one of the props of the supply-side neoclassical paradigm. If supply is to create its own demand, the shape of the aggregate supply curve is critical. It must be vertical. And a vertical aggregate supply curve requires flexible markets. The same is true of the Phillips curve, on which the NAIRU rule of thumb is based.

Keynesian macroeconomics, as is well known, is based on the idea that markets are inflexible in the shortrun. In this case the shortrun aggregate supply curve slopes upwards to the right. But Keynesian economics has been on the defensive throughout the developed world since the mid-1970s. We hear much these days about the importance of labour market flexibility and microeconomic reform in restoring full employment and increasing the rate of economic growth. There is much wishful thinking here, because monetary and fiscal policy, which is currently directed to achieving low rates of inflation and minimal government intervention, has actually increased unemployment and restrained economic growth. Market flexibility is, in this paradigm, the only remaining hope for the unemployed. But, as I will argue in the following section, it is a vain hope.

The emphasis on market flexibility is reflected in the following typical extract from the influential *Economist* (5 April 1997: 17):

> Economists disagree about a lot of things but not about how to get people back to work. Labour markets, they say, need to clear and the best way to ensure they do is to keep them flexible... if Europeans want to create more jobs, they will have to change the laws and habits that make it expensive to employ people.

In other words, orthodox supply-side economics tells us that an increase in jobs, and an acceleration of economic growth, must come from a change in institutions designed to reduce costs, rather than from an expansion of dynamic demand. This is the outcome of a completely static view of the world.

The objective of neoclassical economists who are serious about their role in advising governments is to make the economy operate in a similar way to their macroeconomic model. This means 'creating' a static system in which prices and wages are downwardly (rarely upwardly) mobile. In such a world, they argue, we could virtually eliminate both inflation and unemployment. This dangerously simplistic view is further distorted by politicians who share this unfounded faith, which finds expression in rhetorical phrases such as: 'We can buy further employment by reducing wage rates'.[3] What is not said is that this could only be achieved in a static world where *all* prices are perfectly and instantaneously flexible. In the dynamic-strategy model, which embraces the dynamic nature of the real-world economy together with its imperfect but changing markets and institutions, rapid economic growth and low levels of unemployment – with moderate rates of inflation and nominal wage increases – are generated by an expansion of strategic demand. Policy inspired by neoclassical advisers will undermine strategic demand and help to create stagnant and depressed economies. These issues can be explored further with reference to the instruments and outcomes of orthodox policy.

Policy instruments

The issue of appropriate instruments of policy is highly controversial. There is considerable debate among contemporary economists about whether governments should pursue active or passive policies, whether they should be flexible in their policy response or abide by publicly announced rules, about what mix of monetary and fiscal policies should be employed, and what is the best way of applying the generally accepted policy principles. Much of this debate depends on whether the economists are monetarists, Keynesians, or neoclassicists, and to the extent that they believe in rational expectations. As neoclassical economics is concerned with shortrun static issues there is little debate about longrun policy measures. In the main it is assumed that if societies follow *laissez-faire* trade policies, attempt to keep internal markets free from intervention by governments and special-interest groups, and manage to eliminate inflation, then they will achieve optimum growth rates. But there is a problem that monopoly-busting state agencies and inflation-fighting central banks may destroy the incentives for profit-seeking strategists as well as rent-seeking antistrategists.

Yet these differences are more apparent than real. At least there is a major consensus throughout the developed world about a number of policy 'rules of thumb', based on the above general principles. These rules of thumb state that:

- inflation should be eliminated in order to achieve stability and sustained economic growth;
- the internal (budget) and external (current and capital) accounts should be balanced in order to minimize the distorting effect of government intervention;
- economic stability should be achieved through monetary rather than fiscal policy owing to the desire to balance budgets;
- any inflexibilities in the private sector should be removed through 'microeconomic reform' (ie breaking the power of special-interest, or rent-seeking, organizations, especially monopolies in the commodity, labour, and capital markets).

These rules of thumb, in effect, call for zero government deficits, zero government debt, zero inflation, and zero market imperfection. They are the policy rules of the four zeros.

Widespread agreement on these policy objectives marks the triumph of the precepts of neoclassical economics in policy circles. This viewpoint has become entrenched within policy-making bureaucracies throughout the developed world, which include the various national treasuries together with similar departments in super-national organizations such as the European Union and the OECD. The reason for this conformity is that the departments concerned are staffed by relatively young graduates from neoclassical schools of economics in North America and Europe. What is more difficult to understand is why this approach has been accepted by most national governments and even by the majority of the electorates in these developed countries. It is an instructive example of the working of the imitative mechanism. Rather than being intellectually evaluated, ideas with few competitors become the subject of fashion. Only once a set of ideas becomes associated in the public's mind with adverse material outcomes will they be rejected and other solutions sought. It is essential therefore to provide a viable alternative to existing orthodox policy. The people deserve a choice.

Contemporary economic performance

We need to evaluate the outcomes of contemporary economic policies. While it is always difficult to sort out the performance outcomes of deliberate policies from those of other causes, a few observations can be offered. By surveying data compiled by *The Economist* for fifteen developed nations during 1996 and early 1997 we can draw the following sketch for OECD countries:[4]

- the rate of inflation is very low, averaging 2.0 per cent per annum, and ranging from 0.1 per cent in Japan to 3.9 per cent in Italy;
- the prime bank rate of interest for the same group of countries currently averages 6.30 per cent, ranging from 1.63 per cent in Japan to 9.50 per cent in Italy;
- the unemployment rate, which is relatively high, currently averages 9.5 per cent, ranging from 3.4 per cent in Japan to 22.4 per cent in Spain;
- and the annual increase in real GDP, which is relatively low, currently is 2.0 per cent, ranging from −0.7 per cent in Switzerland to 3.8 per cent in Australia. In per capita terms it is just in excess of 1 per cent per annum.

Hence, the contemporary economic performance in the developed world, to which the prevailing orthodox policy contributed, can be characterized as involving low rates of inflation, moderate rates of interest, high rates of unemployment, and low rates of economic growth (particularly on a per capita basis). Certainly inflation has been brought under control, but the expected (by neoclassical economists at least) increase in economic growth and reduction in unemployment has not materialized. By contrast, this static outcome of deflationary policies aimed at stability is just what the dynamic-strategy model forecasts and the growth–inflation curve demonstrates. It is consistent with the strategic view that the longrun performances of developed societies are being undermined by policies formulated in the light of the static efficiency principle. To eliminate inflation is to eliminate sustained economic growth.

It is of the utmost importance to realize why supply-side economics, with its artificial equilibrium and Pareto optimality performance criteria, is eroding the long-term viability of developed nations. The unbalanced nature of the neo-classical model, which totally neglects dynamic demand, is distorting policy and economic performance. Each time the economy rises from its knees, its legs are kicked away again. An illuminating example of this approach is the advice given by the leader writer of *The Economist* (3 May 1997: 13) to the incoming Labour Prime Minister of Britain, Tony Blair. The new Prime Minister is advised to do two things: to appoint a 'resolute cabinet', and to 'reimpose an official grip on the economy... Either interest rates must be raised, or taxes increased, or some combination of the two, in order to moderate the economy's growth...' Economic growth is the enemy of the stability cult.

It is ironical that a supply-side discipline so concerned to eliminate the distorting presence of government is actually encouraging governments to pursue policies that are distorting the dynamic process. What is most disturbing in this respect is the mechanistic and binding ways in which anti-strategic policies are being applied. There is, for example, a growing tendency for the national governments of developed societies to hand over anti-inflationary policies to central banks staffed by supply-side economists, who are not directly responsible to their communities. Also in the EU a range of deflationary policies has been set as preconditions for countries wanting to join the European Monetary Union. These institutional arrangements are responsible for projecting antistrategic policies from the shortrun to the longrun. The crucial question now is: How long can this distorting process be endured before irreparable damage is done? There are signs in the 1997 French elections that the people have had enough. But in order to change economic policies as well as governments it is necessary to recognize an alternative to the orthodox policy model.

What are the mechanisms by which orthodox policies, based on static supply-side economics, lead to the undermining of the longrun viability of developed societies? First, the attempt by a government in any society to eliminate its budgetary deficit by large-scale expenditure cuts irrespective of the productivity of that expenditure, will inevitably lead to a downward growth spiral. Large expenditure cuts lead to deflationary pressures and a loss of strategic confidence that cause a decline in the rate of economic growth and an increase in unemployment, which in turn leads to a larger budgetary deficit through increased unemployment relief and reduced revenues, and a new round of expenditure cuts. If this policy is pursued to its logical conclusion, decelerating positive growth will lead to accelerating negative growth and high rates of unemployment. And this has perverse outcomes. In order to reduce the undesirable social impact of high rates of unemployment, governments dedicated to the principles of free markets and small government sometimes end up creating artificial 'dole jobs'. This is the height of absurdity.[5] The best way to reduce a budget deficit, if that is really desirable, is to promote rapid growth.

Secondly, by abandoning the essential role of strategic leadership – leadership of the dynamic strategy – the governments of Western democracies run the risk of frustrating the exploitation of strategic opportunities. As shown in Chapter 16, rejection of the role of strategic leadership by the ruling elite leads to the loss of political power, to the disruption of the prevailing dynamic strategy, and to a decline in real GDP per capita. The irony is that the impact of strategic leadership on government budgets and the current and capital accounts is not the problem claimed by neoclassical economists. A systematic study of history shows that the benefits are far greater than the costs (Snooks 1997a). This position is also supported by more perceptive economic theorists (Cornwall 1994; Pitchford 1995b).

Thirdly, the attempt to reduce inflation to zero is, as argued above, harmful for two major reasons. Not only is an attack on inflation in a viable society an attack on the strategic demand–response mechanism, but if it is to be successful it must inflict damage on the dynamic process. It is invalid to argue, as the orthodox concensus does, that any country pursuing economic growth rather than inflation elimination will just not be competitive in the world economy. The reason is that they have failed to employ a dynamic analysis. A country that promotes economic growth through the pursuit of a successful technological substrategy will be more efficient in a dynamic sense than other countries that have brought their dynamic strategies to a standstill through deflationary policies (in the mistaken belief that a downward shift in aggregate demand, owing to a vertical longrun aggregate supply curve, will reduce inflation but not growth). The evidence can be found in Figures 11.4 and 11.5, which show that those countries (Japan and Germany) aggressively pursuing economic growth in the period 1961 to 1994 actually experienced lower rates of inflation over a comparable growth-rate range (and of course they grew at rates twice those of the rest) than other countries attempting to reduce inflation to zero. It is the successful dynamic strategists, not the belt-tightening brigade, that are most competitive internationally.

Fourthly, the deliberate disruption of the dominant dynamic strategy by whatever means, and the emergence of negative economic growth, generates a loss of strategic confidence. And this loss of strategic confidence leads to a decline in expected yields and a further reduction in the rate of investment. Finally, if these antigrowth policies are pursued over the longer term, irreparable damage could be inflicted on strategic institutions, particularly education and the arts. While these institutions may be seen by some governments as dispensable in the shortrun, they are in fact essential for the continuing unfolding of the dynamic strategy. Not only do they contribute directly to the accumulation of human capital, but they carry forward the vital spirit of the prevailing dynamic strategy. As my systematic study of history (Snooks 1997a) shows, this community spirit is important in bringing disparate factions together for a common strategic purpose.

But why have governments throughout the developed world adopted these distorted policies? This is a particularly important question in view of the argument presented in Chapter 16: if governments are to survive they must serve the interests of the majority of strategists. They must provide competent strategic leadership. In fact, governments that fail to meet the expectations of their electorates for greater prosperity are swept away. The only problem is that the distorting policies responsible for this outcome remain. The same economic policies rise phoenix-like from the ashes of earlier governments. This dilemma can be explained in terms of the nature of the modern technological strategy.

The modern technological strategy has transformed virtually the entire adult populations of developed societies into strategists. While there are large numbers of minor differences between these strategists, they can no longer be divided into 'old' and 'new' strategists or, in more dated terminology, 'capital' and 'labour'. Consequently, as the major political parties are competing for the same middle ground, their objectives and policies are very similar. The more they compete for the attention of the same voters, the closer their policies become. It is very risky in this modern political environment to advocate radically different policies, because political parties run the risk of electoral defeat. Hence, while strategists can choose between different 'leadership teams', mainly on the basis of personality, they are rarely able to choose between radically different economic policies. Clearly this is a problem when both parties (in a two-party system) adopt the same distorting policies.

But why have most major political parties throughout the developed world embraced policies that are not only the same but are also distorting? The policy rules of the orthodox consensus – zero budget deficits, zero current account deficits, zero government borrowing, and zero inflation – appeal to managers rather than strategic leaders, because they are based on ideas of equilibrium and stasis rather than disequilibrium and dynamics. As it happens, today's politicians are largely cast in the managerial rather than the entrepreneurial mould, because democratic politics today provides few opportunities for individual rent-seeking. Potential strategic leaders are drawn away by the extraordinary profits to be made in the private sector. Accordingly, those who are attracted to politics feel more comfortable with the risk-averse policies of stability and order. They are easily frightened by stories about rapid growth leading to an awakening of the sleeping monster of inflation. They find reassuring the belt-tightening, hair-shirt policies currently being advocated by the orthodox consensus. They nervously embrace the policy rules of the four zeros.

While even the most educated electorates find it impossible to evaluate complex technical ideas about how economies work, they do know when they are worse off. It is important, therefore, to be able to provide them with a choice not only of political parties but also of economic policies. To do so it is essential to persuade the less risk-averse leadership teams that their political future will be more secure if they pursue economic policies that support dynamic rather than static interests, and if they provide positive strategic leadership. They would do well to take their lead from society's pioneering strategists, as the governments of successful civilizations have always done.

STRATEGIC POLICY

This section focuses on the role of economic policy within a changing institutional framework rather than the role of policy in changing that framework. As discussed above, institutions change in response to strategic demand in order to facilitate the exploitation of strategic opportunities. The need to alter 'constitutional' rules will be – as they have always been – obvious to the strategists and their representatives in special-interest groups and in parliament. And constitutional rules will be altered accordingly. Proponents of constitutional economics, such as James Buchanan, completely overlook the role of strategic demand in this process. Intellectuals wanting to 'reshape' the basic institutions of society will only be 'successful' if they work along with the requirements of strategic demand rather than against them.

The constitutional economics advocates also completely overlook the strategic leadership role of governments. They assert that the people believe that governments need to be constrained by formal rules, and that all special-interest organizations are dedicated to rent-seeking. What they do not realize is that the active strategists in society insist that governments carry out their strategic leadership role, which requires interventionist activity on the part of the state. Where they have been influential, constitutional economists have contributed to contemporary restrictions on the positive strategic activities of governments and, hence, to the undermining of the longrun prospects of developed societies.

General principles

Strategic demand provides a new central policy principle, namely maximizing the sustainable exploitation of strategic opportunities. But it should be emphasized that this is not equivalent to the optimum growth-path idea, because such a path can be identified neither in prospect nor retrospect.

This new general principle replaces, for the purposes of dynamic analysis, the artificial supply-side constructs of social welfare and the natural rate of unemployment. As argued above, Pareto optimality owes its existence to the absence of a theory of dynamic demand in neoclassical economics (or indeed of orthodox economics as a whole). In the dynamic-strategy model the **strategic test** replaces the Pareto efficiency test. Efficiency of production and distribution is, therefore, secondary to strategic development. The strategic test also displaces the 'Wicksell test' advocated by constitutional economists because it provides the ultimate and measurable basis for 'unanimity and consensus'. It is a test relevant to the longrun as well as the shortrun.

The strategic test also replaces the NAIRU rule of thumb. It does so by undermining the alleged causal relationship between unemployment and inflation. As argued above, in reality there is no causal relationship between these two outcomes of the dynamic process. While both are independent outcomes of the unfolding dynamic strategy, inflation is also part of the incentive process by which a society responds to strategic demand. To attack **strategic inflation** (including nominal wage rates) is to damage society's strategic response. Of course, if strategic demand is overwhelmed by a *temporary* exogenous shock (such as the OPEC oil crisis of the 1970s), which leads to an acceleration of **nonstrategic inflation**, then anti-inflation action is required. But policy-makers should target only nonstrategic inflation and make no attempt to reduce **nominal inflation** to zero. In other words, this policy can not be based upon the NAIRU rule of thumb, because the Phillips curve has no meaningful existence. Hence, we should think of a viable economy as one in successful pursuit of its dynamic strategy, experiencing relatively rapid growth with low levels of unemployment and moderate levels of strategic inflation.

The strategic test concerns the effectiveness of a policy in facilitating the exploitation of strategic opportunities. And the measure of this effectiveness is the rate of growth of real GDP per capita (or, better, of real Gross Community Income [market plus household] per household) rather than recently popular 'human development' or environmental indexes. If the rate of economic growth is significantly lower than that achieved by a particular society during a comparable period in the exploitation of an earlier substrategy, or is significantly less than that of other societies pursuing similar technological substrategies, then it is probably not maximizing the sustainable exploitation of its strategic opportunities. And if it is not maximizing the sustainable exploitation of its strategic opportunities, then it is running the risk of longrun crisis and poverty, which is a hopeless basis for improving either human development or the environment.

What subsidiary objectives arise from the central strategic principle? Basically, that other issues such as economic stability and external and internal balance should not conflict with the exploitation of strategic opportunities. More specifically this means that governments should provide strategic leadership and that moderate inflation (say, 4 to 6 per cent) and increases in nominal wage rates should be regarded as essential components and natural outcomes of the dynamic process. Stability will not be a problem for any society that is successfully pursuing a viable dynamic strategy.

The provision of strategic leadership is essential in any viable society. This is a role denied by neoclassical models. Strategic leadership involves investing in infrastructure (research, educational, transport, and communication facilities) where the social return is expected to exceed the private return; encouraging domestic innovations and providing assistance for their marketing; spearheading the penetration of new markets by negotiating external trade and technological deals on behalf of its strategists; protecting the dynamic strategy at home and abroad; and operating proactively to secure control over external strategic resources (such as oil) or strategic locations. It also involves going beyond the Keynesian policy prescription of augmenting aggregate demand. This can be done by detecting the strategic cause of downturn and assisting in the replacement of exhausted with new technological substrategies. This leadership may also justifiably involve the pursuit of a protectionist strategy. It is important here to distinguish between a protectionist strategy aimed at developing an innovative industrial base (as pursued by Germany against the economic hegemony of Britain in the early to mid nineteenth century, and by the USA against Western European hegemony in the late nineteenth and early twentieth centuries) and a rent-seeking tactic providing monopoly profits for antistrategists in a society with no innovative objectives (such as many Third World countries in the twentieth century). Also immigration and capital inflow policies should be closely related to the requirements of the unfolding dynamic strategy. They should, in other words, respond to strategic demand.

This means that policy rules aimed at restricting public debt to zero or very low levels of GDP are, strategically speaking, self-defeating. The real test of government borrowing is not solely the size but the effectiveness of these funds in promoting the dynamic strategy. As always, the measure of this effectiveness is the rate of economic growth achieved. The reason governments do not lurch out of control is that they are constrained by the process of strategic struggle discussed in Chapter 16. We do not need to bind governments with unnecessary intrusive constitutional rules; which is just as well as this would merely reduce the flexibility and the effectiveness of strategic leadership.

The stability issue is important but subsidiary to the sustainable exploitation of strategic opportunities. If we get the strategic issues right, then stability will follow. In this respect it is absolutely essential to realize that inflation is not a problem for societies that are successfully pursuing strategic opportunities. Throughout history, prices have risen and fallen with economic growth, only raging out of control during periods of crisis that are beyond the powers of modern advisers to resolve. It is sobering to remember that ancient societies were able to effectively exploit strategic opportunities without creating destabilizing inflation even in the absence of advisers trained in neoclassical (or any other kind of) economic theory! It was not a matter of chance, but of intuitively understanding the central role of strategic development – an understanding that has been dulled by the apparent sophistication of modern economic theory. As demonstrated empirically, as well as theoretically, in Chapter 11, inflation is a stable, nonaccelerating function of economic growth. Indeed, the typical modern growth–inflation curve approximates the horizontal. Rapid economic growth, in other words, can be pursued without 'overheating' the economy and unleashing the 'monster' of hyper-inflation. Hence, the pursuit of zero inflation in the name of stability and order will, if successful, actually derail the dynamic strategy of the Western world and unleash the very forces of chaos that orthodox policy-advisers so fear. In particular, to grant central banks – institutions not responsible to the community's strategists – the independence to suppress inflation is an invitation to disrupt the dynamic process.

A viable dynamic strategy will also generate low rates of unemployment. This should *not* be thought of as a trade-off with inflation – rather it is an independent outcome of the increase in strategic demand. But, when an unfolding dynamic strategy falters, it may be necessary to expand government expenditure in relation to revenue because of the impact on strategic confidence and, hence, on further private activity. In such circumstances the zero-deficit rule of thumb is completely inappropriate.

And how does microeconomic reform fit into the strategic-policy framework? In a dynamic world, market flexibility is important but secondary to the need to generate an expansion in strategic demand, which will generate the incentives for the required institutional change. The best way to reduce the importance of special-interest groups and to free up markets is by pursuing a successful dynamic strategy. As we have seen, the network of special-interest organizations grows and becomes more constricting during periods of strategic exhaustion or strategic disruption as a result of wrong-headed policies. Economic expansion leads to rates of return in strategic activities that are higher than those in rent-seeking activities. As this relationship will be reversed during periods of strategic exhaustion or disruption, the existence of special-interest organizations will increase and there is little that government regulations can do to alter the situation. But when a new dynamic strategy/substrategy emerges governments can display effective leadership by breaking up special-interest organizations that threaten to impede the recovery process. Even then it is essential to ensure that this does not artificially eliminate the extraordinary profits that provide the incentives for developing a new technological substrategy. It is vital to distinguish between the activities of profit-seeking strategists and rent-seeking antistrategists.

CONCLUSIONS

In this chapter the general principles of strategic policy have been outlined. As argued, they contrast with the policies advocated by neoclassical economists, both academic and bureaucratic, and adopted by governments throughout the developed world. Further, it is suggested that, unless orthodox anti-inflation policies are abandoned and the new strategic policies of dynamics and strategic leadership are adopted, developed societies throughout the world will continue to see their longrun prospects being undermined, will experience poor growth performance, and will stagnate and, even, collapse. While efficiency and market flexibility are important objectives, they will do more harm than good if they are pursued through anti-growth policies. In the longrun, dynamic efficiency arising from the pursuit of a successful dynamic strategy is more important than static efficiency.

This is not just another call for a change of policy. The general policy principles enunciated here were derived from a new dynamic theory of the developed economy. In other words, the policy programme advocated in this chapter is theoretically grounded. The radical core of these policies involves facilitating the expansion of strategic demand and strategic confidence by the provision of strategic leadership and the abandonment of zero inflation targets. Essentially the dynamic-strategy theory provides a dynamic model of demand and, in doing so, overcomes the unbalanced approach of supply-side neoclassical theory that is currently helping to distort the dynamic process of the developed world through the promotion of a fundamentally flawed policy programme.

Notes

1 Social Statics and Social Dynamics

1. Even for the Heilbroner 'school', history is the source of the ultimate questions about humanity, rather than the basis for systematic model-building; whereas, they claim, deductive economics – largely classical, Marxian, and post-Keynesian – rather than inductive economics is the way these questions must be answered.
2. It is significant that the orthodox attempt since the early 1970s to provide microeconomic foundations for Keynesian macroeconomics has focused on aggregate supply, which Keynes himself gave very little attention.

3 Growth Theory

1. The Keynesian growth model received further elaboration at the hands of Nicholas Kaldor (1996), who developed a multi-sector growth model to provide interacting demand based on increasing returns in the manufacturing sector and diminishing returns in the agricultural/mining sector, in order to analyse the Keynesian issue of stability. This focus on increasing returns, which precedes that of endogenous growth theory, also contradicts the claim by Barro and Sala-i-Martin (1995: 10) that there is little of interest in the Keynesian analysis of economic growth. Further, Geoff Harcourt (1997) makes the point that Kaldor's analysis of cumulative causation prefigures the contemporary interest in path-dependence. Also see John Cornwall (1977) and Edward Nell (1992) for an emphasis on the role of aggregate demand in the growth process. My strategic demand displaces Kaldor's interacting demand in the dynamic process.
2. The notation here follows that by Barro and Sala-i-Martin (1995). The derivation and proofs of these equations are given in that source.
3. See Barro and Sala-i-Martin (1995: 32–6).
4. See the pioneering article by Dowrick and Nguyen (1989).

5 Strategic Theory

1. As Gregory Mankiw (1990: 1648) has said: 'Heteroskedasticity has never been a good reason to throw out an otherwise good model'! So much for Popper's empirical falsification hypothesis. For a discussion of the irrational basis of deductive economics see Heilbroner (1990).

6 From the Invisible Hand to No Hand at All

1. Some sense of the invisible hand can also be found in the work of William Petty, John Locke, Bernard Mandeville, Adam Ferguson, and David Hume (Vaughn 1987: 997).

2. This account relies heavily on the persuasive interpretation of Fitzgibbons (1995) and also of Skinner (1987: 357–75) as well as on Smith (1759; 1776).
3. This feature of Smith's system did not occur to me until I read Fitzgibbons (1995) in November 1996, which was after I had completed *The Dynamic Society, The Ephemeral Civilization*, and *The Laws of History*.

9 The Dynamic Nature of 'Materialist Man'

1. The use of the term 'economic distance' in the concentric spheres model (Snooks 1994a) predated my knowledge of the kinship selection model which uses the term 'genetic distance'. It is an interesting parallel.
2. Further discussion of the concentric spheres model can be found in Snooks (1997a: ch. 2).
3. The way ideology is employed to raise strategic confidence is discussed more fully, and illustrated extensively, in Snooks (1997a).
4. Our modern epoch is not unique in this respect. All ages abound with information about successful individuals and the sources of their success, rather than about theoretical models and the data required to apply them to reality. Imitative information in conquest societies focuses on successful military and state leaders, in commerce societies on successful commercial leaders and practices, and in technological societies on successful money-making practices. See Snooks (1997a: 43–5) for a discussion of imitative information in pre-modern societies.

10 A Realistic Dynamic Form

1. Similar points have been made by Luigi Pasinetti and Robert Solow (1994: 359, 376).
2. This account is based on Snooks (1997a: ch. 12) which can be consulted for more detailed discussion of this issue.

11 Strategic Demand and the Growth–Inflation Curve

1. In Chapter 18 of *The General Theory* (1936), Keynes appears to be a little confused about the independent and dependent variables in his system. He includes the rate of interest as an independent variable.
2. It should be realized that the conquest aims of a technological society are irrational, because in the longrun the rate of strategic return is much higher on the technological strategy (Snooks 1996: 308–14).
3. It has only been possible to provide the briefest of outlines here of my model of technological paradigm shifts. Those who are interested can find a detailed discussion of this model and its application to the past and the future in *The Dynamic Society* (1996), especially chs 12 and 13.
4. The growth–inflation relationship was first suggested in Snooks (1993a: 256, 266), and was further developed in Snooks (1994b: 8–9, 16, 65, 66), Snooks (1996: 388–91), and, particularly, Snooks (1997a: 275–7).
5. The inclusion of all values, negative as well as positive, generates a very longrun growth–inflation curve possessing similar characteristics to that in Figure 11.2.

6. Negative values for the growth–inflation relationship are the outcome of exogenous shocks, such as unintended wars and epidemics. The growth–inflation curve for Britain 1370–1994 (positive values only), using the SHAZAM package, is:

$$y = 1.554 + 0.784\,x \qquad\qquad R^2 = 0.22 \quad \bar{R}^2 = 0.19$$
$$(3.869)\ (2.867) \qquad\qquad\qquad DW = 2.11$$

- It passes all seven chi-square tests for heteroskedasticity
- It passes all three Ramsey reset specification tests.

7. The growth–inflation curve for Britain 1870–1994 (positive values only) is:

$$y = 2.242 + 0.8674\,x \qquad\qquad R^2 = 0.111 \quad \bar{R}^2 = 0.094$$
$$(2.058)\ (2.595) \qquad\qquad\qquad DW = 1.51$$

- It passes the ARCH and HARVEY chi-square tests for heteroskedasticity
- One Ramsey reset test is satisfactory.

8. The similarity of the growth–inflation outcomes for the very longrun and the post-Second World War period provide even more reason to be confident about the historical estimates of real GDP per capita. The other reasons are to be found in Snooks (1993: ch. 7) and Snooks (1994b: ch. 3).

9. The shortrun growth–inflation curve for all OECD countries 1961 to 1993 (excluding the OPEC crisis years) is:

$$y = 2.444 + 0.779\,x \qquad\qquad R^2 = 0.259 \quad \bar{R}^2 = 0.219$$
$$(2.608)\ (2.573) \qquad\qquad\qquad DW = 1.55$$

- It passes the heteroskedasticity ARCH and HARVEY tests
- It passes the Ramsey reset specification test.

The data for this function were calculated as compound rates of change between end years for each subperiod 1961 to 1973 and 1983 to 1993, and weighted by the number of years. An alternative procedure, by which the annual rates of change are averaged, generates almost identical results. One method measures the average experience for the whole period, and the other measures the average experience for each and every year.

10. For reasons of economy of presentation in what is primarily a theoretical work, some empirical results have not been included here. They will be discussed fully in a forthcoming book.

13 The Orthodox Explanation of Fluctuations

1. This general framework for characterizing business-cycle theories was suggested by Haberler (1958).
2. There are a number of excellent surveys of the business-cycle literature, including Haberler (1958), Rostow (1990), Schumpeter (1939), and Schumpeter (1954).
3. In seeking support for his views about effective demand, Keynes overstated the insights provided by Mandeville, Malthus, and Hobson, but certainly there are elements of *The General Theory* in these writers (Blaug 1986).
4. These include Harrod (1948), Duesenberry (1949; 1958), Hicks (1950), Kaldor (1954), Matthews (1959), Smithies (1957), Goodwin *et al.* (1983), and Cornwall (1994).

14   The Strategic Explanation of Fluctuations

1. There is nothing novel in this suggestion – see Schumpeter (1954), Goodwin *et al.* (1983), and Rostow (1990) – but it is usually honoured in the breach.

2. The long-wave literature is far from orthodox. Apart from a few figures like Schumpeter and Rostow, it is dominated by Marxists of some description. This reflects the important role Marx granted to economic fluctuations in bringing capitalism to its knees. In *Capital*, economic fluctuations have an impact not only on living standards but also on the economic, political, and social structure. Many of those influenced by Marx have adopted the long-wave concept as if it were a *model* of the entire society, rather than just a dynamic pathway. It is for this reason that the Kondratieff long wave has survived the many doubts that empiricists have expressed. Like all theories, especially those tinged with faith, the Kondratieff 'cycle' is resistant to unaccommodating facts.

   The Kondratieff cycle is now attributed to the Russian Marxist A. Helphand (with the pseudonym Parvus), who in 1901 published a work on agricultural crises (Solomou 1987: 3), although some have suggested that he was pre-empted by W.S. Jevons, who in 1884 recognized a long wave between 1790 and 1849 in British prices (Tylecote 1992: 10). This early work on prices was followed in 1913 by the Dutch Marxist Van Genderen (pseudonym J. Fedde). It was not until 1922 that another Russian Marxist, Nikolai Kondratieff, after whom the 50-year cycle is now known, also examined – apparently independently – long waves reflected in prices. The reason Kondratieff is so closely associated with this concept is that he was popularized in the English-speaking world by Joseph Schumpeter (1939). It was Schumpeter who provided the first persuasive explanation – discussed in Chapter 3 – of the Kondratieff cycle.

   Most of the more recent literature on this subject has been contributed by the followers of either Marx or Schumpeter (or both). I will merely provide a few examples. Predictably Marxist writers, such as Mandel (1981), focus on the mystical role of capital accumulation (reinforced by technological change) which continues to accumulate even when the profit rate is in decline ('Accumulate, accumulate . . .'). In the end this overinvestment leads to a downturn and contraction and is succeeded by underinvestment which causes the whole process to begin again. This is a fairly standard Marxist approach.

   Schumpeter also has his followers. Mensch (1979) adopts the master's idea of 'clusters' of innovations that appear during the depression and lead to recovery as new leading sectors penetrate new consumer markets at home and overseas. The expansion comes to an end when these consumer markets are saturated, and the subsequent depression continues until a new cluster of innovations emerges to tap into a new source of consumer demand. This is an example of Say's Law – of supply (technological change) creating its own demand – and cannot be regarded as a demand-side model as some have suggested (Delbeke 1981). Further, Mensch's model fails to account for this clustering and, more problematically, his periodization of innovation clusters is not supported by the evidence (Solomou 1987: 100). Freeman *et al.* (1982: 67–8), in an attempt to rescue Schumpeter from the deficiencies of Mensch's model, substitute the concept of 'new technological systems' for the haphazard notion of innovation clusters, which they believe is more faithful to the original concept.

W.W. Rostow (1990: chs 18–20) also favours the original Schumpeterian idea of innovation clusters – with entrepreneurs responding to a growing supply of ideas (or 'backlog of relevant, increasingly sophisticated, hitherto unapplied technologies') once there has been a sufficient build-up of 'technological absorptive capacity' through the operation of 'non-economic' factors – which results in the emergence of leading sectors (ibid.: 432). Leading sectors, which are the mysterious driving force in Rostow's analysis, are claimed to possess 'optimum sectoral growth paths' that resemble S-shaped trajectories of rise and fall. Owing to investment lags these leading sectors are 'generally marked by rather massive undershooting and overshooting of optimum sectoral paths...[These oscillations reflect] my theory of the cycles which Kondratieff identified but for which he offered no systematic explanation' (ibid.: 431). This supply-side approach owes much not only to Schumpeter's idea of innovation but also to the orthodox deductive concept of convergence to an equilibrium growth path. Despite his historicist claims, Rostow has been unable to escape the artificial dynamic form (an optimum, or equilibrium, growth path) created by the deductivists. Rostow's optimum sectoral growth path is a non-operational concept because it cannot be identified in retrospect, let alone in advance. How is it possible, therefore, to determine whether an actual sectorial growth path has undershot or overshot the optimum? There is something of the teleological about this idea. In contrast, the neoclassical equilibrium growth path is merely an assumption, not a trajectory to which reality is expected to conform.

3. See the thorough but mechanistic empirical investigation of long waves since 1850 by Solomou (1987). He found evidence for 'major long-run variation throughout the period 1856–1973', but these surges were irregular and closer to 20 years than 60 years. This contrasts with evidence for Australasia, where long waves are about 40 years (Butlin 1964; Snooks 1994a; Hawke 1985).

4. The idea of a 'global cycle' within a 'world system' has been advanced recently by Gunder Frank (Frank and Gills 1993).

15 The New Political Economy

1. The dynamic issues for lesser developed societies is discussed in a forthcoming book.

2. Emmett Sullivan (1997), my former PhD student, introduced me to this trade policy literature. He went on to accept the challenge in Olson (1982: 135) to examine the reasons for the high level of tariffs in Australia in the early part of the century.

3. The so-called 'Dark Ages' are only dark in terms of Brennan and Buchanan's knowledge of them.

16 The Strategic Model of Politics and Policy

1. This, in highly summarized form, is only one of a number of case-studies, ranging from the ancient to the modern world, dealt with in *The Ephemeral Civilization*

(Snooks 1997a). Some of those include: Rome, Greece, Tenochtitlan, Venice, USA, Russia, Western Europe, and China.

2. While it is true that an individual voter on his or her own has little impact on political outcomes, concerned citizens make the effort to vote because they are aware that if they and others of like mind do not, then their strategic interests will not be represented in policy-making circles. Solidarity amongst strategists is important. Individuals consider their voting role not in isolation but as part of a wider strategic group. This is something overlooked by supporters of 'methodological individualism'. Those who fail to vote do so because they believe that there is no danger to their strategic interests. When such a danger arises, the proportion of the electorate that votes increases dramatically.

17 The General Principles of Strategic Policy

1. For a discussion of social choice and Arrow's Impossibility Theorem see Sen (1987) and Arrow (1987). For its application to policy see Pitchford (1996).
2. For a recent discussion of the NAIRU concept see the Symposium in the *Journal of Economic Perspectives*, vol. 11 (winter 1997), pp. 3–108.
3. This was stated by the Australian Prime Minister John Howard in July 1997 after his return from a trip to Britain and the USA where he sought the advice of neoclassical policy advisers.
4. The fifteen developed countries included in this survey are: Australia, Austria, Belgium, Britain, Canada, Denmark, France, Germany, Italy, Japan, Netherlands, Spain, Sweden, Switzerland, USA.
5. This was pursued by the Howard Liberal–National coalition government in Australia in 1997.

Glossary of New Terms and Concepts

As *longrun dynamics* is a new area of study it has been necessary to develop and employ a range of new terms and concepts. To assist the reader, these terms and concepts have been brought together and briefly defined in this Glossary. When a new term or concept is first mentioned in a chapter it has been printed in bold type. Italics in the Glossary have been used to indicate that additional concepts are also defined here. Unfamiliar terms not included here can be found in the Glossaries of *The Dynamic Society* (Snooks 1996) and *The Ephemeral Civilization* (Snooks 1997a). In this study 'longrun' is a single word because it refers to an important and integrated concept.

Antistrategists comprise those ruling elites who assume control of societies during times of strategic crisis and engineer repressive economic and political systems. These command systems are designed to eliminate existing *strategists*, to prevent the re-emergence of potential strategists, and to facilitate rent-seeking. Examples of societies dominated by antistrategists include Rome from the time of Claudius, Soviet Russia, Nazi Germany, and Maoist China. Control by antistrategists is the outcome of a military-backed takeover by a small band of professional revolutionaries who are able to exploit the chaos that emerges when the new strategists are unable to overwhelm the old strategists during the course of a difficult *strategic transfer*.

Commerce strategy   Commerce, like conquest, has been used by ancient societies to lift its populations and real GDP per capita above the optimum levels dictated by the neolithic technological paradigm. Through monopoly access to markets and commodities, commerce empires have been able to grow and prosper in the most remarkable way. But the cost of this rapid growth is eventual collapse because once the commerce strategy has been exhausted the empire superstructure cannot be financed from internal sources. This strategy is closely associated with colonization which develops in order to facilitate the commerce strategy. See also *dynamic strategies*.

Concentric spheres model of human behaviour   In this model the self is at the centre of a set of concentric spheres that define the varying strength of co-operative relationships between him or her and all other individuals and groups in society. The strength of the economic relationship between the self and any other individual or group – measured by the *economic distance*

251

between them – will depend on how essential they are to the maximization of his or her utility. Those aspects of his or her objective function – such as the generation of love, companionship, and children – will be located on spheres with the shortest distance from the centre, with other relatives, friends, neighbours, workmates, members of various religious and social clubs, city, state, nation, group of nations, and so on, occupying spheres that progressively radiate from the centre (see Figure 9.1). As the economic distance increases, the degree of co-operation diminishes. The force keeping the spheres apart is the incessant desire of the self to survive and prosper, and the force preventing the spheres flying into space (the model's economic gravity) is *strategic confidence* – the basis of trust and co-operation – generated by a successful dynamic strategy.

Conquest strategy   This is the main *dynamic strategy* employed by ancient societies to increase their size – in terms of population and material living standards – above the optimum determined by the neolithic technological paradigm. Conquest is a zero-sum game with the conqueror growing at the expense of the vanquished. The ultimate cost of this strategy, however, is collapse, because once it has been exhausted the former conquest society is thrown back upon its neolithic economic system which cannot support the structure of empire. See also *zero-sum dynamic change*.

Deduction, the problem of   It has become an article of faith in the social sciences that deduction is superior to induction, owing to the so-called 'problem of induction'. This problem arises from an absence of any 'rules of induction' and, hence, of a mechanical way to infer generalizations or laws from empirical data. It is claimed endlessly that the inductive method has no counterpart to the logical rules of induction. Some extreme deductivists, such as Karl Popper, claim that induction does not exist. In their enthusiasm to reject empiricism, the deductivists have overlooked a problem in their own methodology, in that deductive hypotheses are derived not from the systematic observation of the real world but from intuition. As fact is stranger than fiction, deductive assumptions or premises inevitably fail to embrace the totality of reality and, hence, provide a partial and distorted picture. This is 'the problem of deduction', which is well illustrated in the field of social dynamics. In the end, the problem of deduction is more debilitating than the problem of induction. Certainly the problem of induction can be reduced to manageable proportions through a procedure I have called the *quaternary system of induction*.

Dynamic form refers to the shape of the dynamic process. Dynamic models possess either an artificial or a realistic dynamic form. The neoclassical growth model has an artificial dynamic form – the steady state – because, by completely overlooking *strategic demand*, it has been necessary to transfer the concept of equilibrium from economic statics to economic dynamics. As the steady state is merely an extension of static equilibrium, the dynamic form of the neoclassical growth model is entirely arbitrary. A realistic dynamic form can only be modelled by observing the way societies grow over the longrun. See also *strategic pathways*.

Dynamic order is the process by which economic agents, all attempting to maximize the probability of their individual survival and prosperity, co-operate to achieve rapid and sustained economic growth. This is the outcome of an unfolding dynamic strategy that generates changes both in *strategic demand* for a wide range of inputs including institutions and organizations, and in *strategic confidence* concerning the future. While the strategic unfolding continues and society prospers, strategic confidence remains high, generating trust and co-operation between individuals at all levels of society and stability in its institutions. But when this unfolding falters, confidence will decline, causing a deterioration in former trust, co-operation, and institutional stability and, hence, in dynamic order.

Dynamic strategies are those wide-ranging programmes employed by decision-makers attempting to maximize the probability of survival and prosperity. In the Dynamic Society these strategies include family multiplication, conquest, commerce, and technological change. The adoption of any one of these strategies will depend upon factor endowments and, hence, relative factor prices, and will require investment in specialized infrastructure. This investment generates a stream of positive net returns. Economic growth, therefore, is strategy-led. A dominant dynamic strategy will be pursued until it has been economically exhausted, which will occur when the marginal cost of investment in this strategy equals its marginal revenue. This leads not to collapse but to stagnation. Over time any dominant strategy will consist of a sequence of substrategies by which the economic possibilities of the former are explored. For the modern era these substrategies have been called *technological styles*.

Economic distance is the measure of the strength of material relationships between the self and all other individuals and groups in society. Economic distance is inversely related to the importance of other individuals and groups in maximizing the material objectives of the self. Hence family and friends occupy the spheres closest to the self, and strangers are to be found on the most distant spheres (see Figure 9.1). It is an important component of the *concentric spheres model of human behaviour*.

Environmental dynamic change (EDC) is economic change achieved through the dynamic strategy of family multiplication. This involves an increase in the number of family units (households) for the purpose of gaining greater control over unused natural resources with a given state of technology (Snooks 1994a: 127). It leads to population increase and migration and is the basis of the 'primitive dynamic', which in palaeolithic times led to the occupation of all continents except Antarctica by modern man. This dynamic mechanism has involved economic expansion without economic growth. See also *zero-sum dynamic change*.

Existential schizophrenia   The actions we are forced to take in order to survive and prosper are often so repugnant to the intellectual image we have of ourselves that we are unable to face them openly, certainly not on a daily basis. The truth could, and sometimes does, lead to self-destruction. And this frustrates the biological desire to survive and prosper. Accordingly, over millions of years we have learnt to deceive ourselves with such facility that we are usually unaware that we are doing so. We compartmentalize our lives and build barriers between what we do and what we think we should do. This is a normal rather than a pathological condition because it is required in the struggle to survive and prosper. While it is essential for the continued survival of our species, it prevents us from understanding the nature of ourselves and our society. Human society is no more complex than the physical world around us. It is our reactions to it that are complex.

Gross Community Income (GCI) is a measure of total economic activity that takes place in both the household and market sectors on an annual basis. It is an extension of the concept of GDP to the Total Economy. It is a term coined in Snooks (1994a: 17). Both GDP and GCI are important measures of the effectiveness of a society in exploiting its strategic opportunities and, hence, of its ability to survive and prosper. They are measures of economic survival and not welfare or human development. They are also the medium through which *strategic confidence* is communicated to the people.

Imitative information, in contrast to the information required by *homo economicus* in the neoclassical model, is readily available and easily evaluated. It is gained from direct observation of those around us, from professional advice, from the media, and from books, magazines, and electronic sources. What we need to know is: who is successful and why, not how to perform miraculous rate of return calculations.

Intellectual economizing   This is the core of my theory about the imitation mechanism in human (and animal) decision-making. It is based on the historical observation that the world's scarcest resource is the intellect, and that decision-makers economize on this resource by making rules and by imitating the successful actions of others. This is the basis for the process of *strategic imitation* by which the *strategic pioneers* are followed by large numbers of *strategic followers*. See also *imitative information*.

Materialist man is a central concept in longrun dynamics. Materialist man is related, yet very different to the neoclassical concept of *homo economicus*. Rational economic man is not a dynamic force in society, but rather an abstract collection of preferences and rational choices concerning consumption and production. Economic theorists have divorced these behavioural outcomes from more fundamental human motivational impulses. Materialist man on the other hand is a real-world decision-maker who struggles to survive and, with survival, to maximize material advantage over his lifetime. This does not require perfect knowledge or sophisticated abilities to rapidly calculate the costs and benefits of a variety of possible decision-making alternatives, just an ability to recognize and imitate success. Materialist man includes the *strategic pioneers* who ruthlessly explore strategic opportunities, and the *strategic followers* who imitate their success and provide the energy for the *unfolding dynamic strategy*.

Nominal inflation This is total inflation which is composed of *strategic inflation* and *nonstrategic inflation*, a distinction that arises from the dynamic-strategy model.

Nonstrategic inflation is that part of *nominal inflation* not generated directly by the dynamic process. Instead, nonstrategic inflation is the outcome of exogenous shocks (such as wars, epidemics, and resource bonanzas/crises) and institutional problems (such as inappropriate action by central banks, trade unions, and arbitration commissions).

Nonstrategists are those groups in society that are unable to freely invest in, or profit from, the prevailing dynamic strategy. They are controlled and manipulated by the *strategists* or *antistrategists* who exercise a monopoly over society's resources and wealth. The nonstrategists are the dependent agricultural workers in medieval society, slaves in both the pre-modern and modern world, and the 'people' in modern command systems such as Stalin's USSR or Mao's China. It would be a mistake to think that the role of the nonstrategist has evolved over time. Quite the reverse. The last twelve thousand years have seen the nonstrategist follow a great circle. In the palaeolithic era, most adults were freely involved in the dominant strategy of family multiplication; in the neolithic era, very small ruling elites controlled either the conquest or commerce strategies; and only during the modern era have these elites given way to the democratic control of the technological strategy.

Problem of deduction   See *deduction, the problem of.*

Quaternary system of induction, the   Contrary to the claim of the extreme deductivists, it is possible to formulate an effective framework for the inductive process. Elsewhere I have proposed a four-step inductive procedure called the quaternary system of induction (Snooks 1998: ch. 7). The four steps are: the discovery of quantitative and qualitative patterns in reality called 'timescapes'; the construction of a general model to explain the whole class of timescapes; the application of the general model to particular historical episodes to derive specific dynamic models; and the derivation of a model of institutional change. This quaternary system goes a long way to resolving the 'problem of induction'. See also *deduction, the problem of.*

Strategic confidence, which is the outcome of a successful *dynamic strategy*, is the force that keeps human society together. A successful dynamic strategy leads to a workable network of competitive/co-operative relationships, together with all the necessary rules and organizations. In economic transactions, individuals relate directly to the successful strategy and only indirectly to each other. It is not a matter of mutual 'trust' as such – of having confidence in the nature of other individuals – but rather having confidence in the wider dynamic strategy in which they are all involved and on which they all depend. What we know as 'trust' is derived from strategic confidence. Once the dynamic strategy has been exhausted and cannot be replaced, strategic confidence declines and, in extreme cases, disappears. And as strategic confidence declines, so too does 'trust' and co-operation. Strategic confidence is communicated directly to individuals in a society by the rise and fall in material standards of living and indirectly and less effectively through religious and secular ideology.

Strategic costs rise as the *dynamic strategy* unfolds and society becomes increasingly complex. The reason is that increasing demands are made upon intellectual resources. Strategic costs have been viewed by institutionalists as transaction costs. These costs must be offset by rising benefits from the unfolding dynamic strategy.

Strategic-crisis hypothesis   A strategic crisis occurs when a civilization's dominant dynamic strategy is economically exhausted. This point is reached when the marginal costs of the dominant strategy equals its marginal revenue. Owing to the highly specialized nature of the dominant strategy, rapid switching to other strategies is not possible. Crisis is, therefore, inevitable. The approaching strategic crisis leads to a slowing down of the upswing and eventual downturn. Any future recovery must await the rejuvenation of the old strategy or the development of entirely new strategies. The strategic-crisis hypothesis encompasses the Malthusian hypothesis. In the Malthusian hypothesis, population is treated as an exogenously determined force which outstrips the productivity of agriculture and brings economic growth to an end. In the strategic-crisis hypothesis, population growth is endogenously determined as it is a response to man's dynamic strategies. Hence population expansion is not a determinant of the crisis but a response to it. The Malthusian crisis is a special case of the strategic crisis that emerges only when a society has been overwhelmed by the forces of chaos (see Snooks 1996: 397–8).

Strategic demand is the central concept in the dynamic-strategy model. It is an outcome of the *unfolding dynamic strategy*, and exerts a longrun influence over both the employment of resources and the institutional and organizational structure of society. Shifts in strategic demand occur as the dominant dynamic strategy unfolds and as one dynamic strategy replaces another. These shifts elicit changes in society's use of resources and its strategic institutions and organizations.

Strategic factions Although the changing political process is similar at both the strategic and substrategic levels – as it is the outcome of the *strategic struggle* – there is a major difference. At the strategic level the struggle is between supporters of entirely different strategies (such as conquest and commerce or commerce and technological change), whereas at the substrategic level it takes place between 'factions' within a single strategy. Hence, at the substrategic level, all participants accept and support the existing economic/social/political system, and the strategic struggle involves the pursuit of more advantageous positions within that system. Rather than pursue their struggle to the point where the existing system breaks down, the old and new strategic factions pursue their differences through existing democratic structures to achieve a marginal redistribution of income.

Strategic followers travel in the wake of the *strategic pioneers*. They seek information not about the costs and benefits of various investment alternatives, but about who and what is successful and why. When the pioneers earn extraordinary profits, they are emulated by large numbers of followers. This is the process of *strategic imitation*.

Strategic imitation is the process by which *strategic followers* emulate the activities of the successful *strategic pioneers*. The followers attempt to imitate not the intellectual mechanism of digital computers but the *dynamic strategies* of successful pioneers. And as the followers successfully imitate the successful pioneers, a new dynamic strategy emerges to challenge the old. This concept is based on the demonstrable fact that the human species is driven not by ideas but by desires. We develop rules not to economize on information and 'trust' but on the world's scarcest resource, intelligence. See also *intellectual economizing*.

Strategic inflation　In the dynamic-strategy model, the role of prices is central to the interaction between *strategic demand* and *strategic response*. The unfolding dynamic strategy generates an increase in strategic demand that places pressure on existing resources, technologies, and institutions, thereby leading to an increase in prices and extraordinary profits. This provides the incentives for the strategic response. It is the systematic increase in prices, which arises from the dynamic process, that constitutes strategic inflation. The more erratic impact of exogenous forces (war, epidemics, and natural resource bonanzas/crises) and of institutional difficulties, is called *nonstrategic inflation*. Total inflation is called *nominal inflation*.

Strategic leadership is a fundamentally important concept in this study. It is essential in facilitating the pursuit of the society's dominant *dynamic strategy*. This role exceeds the minimum laid down by neo-liberal advocates of all kinds, including neoclassical economists and constitutional economists such as James Buchanan. The test of strategic leadership is not that of static efficiency (Pareto optimality) but of effective and sustained development of the dominant dynamic strategy (strategic progress). Strategic leadership is also important in generating and maintaining *strategic confidence*, which binds society together through a network of co-operative relationships. It is strategic leadership rather than 'moral leadership' (Casson 1991: 3) that is essential for the wellbeing of society. Like 'trust', the moral integrity of society is an outcome of a successful dynamic strategy.

Strategic pathways are the trajectories traced out by the dynamic processes of societies pursuing one of the four *dynamic strategies* (or one of the more numerous substrategies). They are the outcome of the *strategic demand–strategic response* mechanism. For technological societies these pathways are best measured by real GDP and real GDP per capita, while for commerce and conquest societies they are best measured by territorial size as these strategies involve imperial expansion. See also *unfolding dynamic strategy*.

Strategic pioneers are those innovators who successfully invest in aspects of a new and emerging dynamic strategy. They operate not on detailed information about benefits and costs, but on intuition about outcomes and faith in their own abilities. They embody the various available investment alternatives. They are but a small proportion of other equally optimistic risk-takers – the ones who got it right at the right time. The rest are weeded out by competitive forces. Their reward is to reap the extraordinary profits of which they dreamed. They confound the supporters of rational expectations.

Strategic response This response is called forth by changes in *strategic demand* for natural and human resources, capital, and for technological and institutional ideas. This interaction, which is mediated by increasing prices, gives rise to the *strategic pathway*. In neoclassical economics the supply side is treated as the active force in society – supply creates its own demand – and in Keynesian economics the supply-side variables are treated as given. But in the dynamic-strategy model, Say's Law is reversed as supply responds to the *unfolding dynamic strategy*. See also *strategic inflation*.

Strategic reversals These occur when a traditional *dynamic strategy* exhausts itself and the only viable replacement strategy is one used in the past. An example is the conquest→commerce→conquest strategic sequence in ancient Greece or medieval Venice, or the family-multiplication→conquest→family-multiplication sequence in China after the year 500. This leads to the reversal of the earlier victory of one group of strategists over another, such as merchants over warriors followed by warriors over merchants – as in Greece and Venice. It leads to a corresponding reversal in institutional development, which confounds the idea of social evolution.

Strategic struggle The strategic struggle is a contest between various groups in society for control of the sources of society's resources and wealth. Although it employs political instruments it is fundamentally an economic struggle – a struggle for survival and prosperity in the face of scarce resources. This struggle involves a contest between either the new and old *strategists*, or between the strategists and the *antistrategists*. If the transfer of control between the old and new strategists does not occur smoothly, the strategic struggle will lead to civil wars or revolutions. And if the new strategists are not sufficiently powerful economically to overwhelm the old strategists quickly, the *antistrategists* may exploit the situation by hijacking the revolution through manipulation of the *nonstrategists*, and by creating a command system.

Strategic test The dynamic-strategy model introduces a new central policy principle, namely maximizing the sustainable exploitation of strategic opportunities, which is measured in terms of GDP per capita. But it should be emphasized that this is not equivalent to the optimum growth path idea, because such a path can be identified neither in prospect nor retrospect. In the dynamic-strategy model the 'strategic test' replaces the 'Pareto efficiency test' (as efficiency of production and distribution is secondary to strategic development), and the 'Wicksell test' advocated by constitutional economists (because it provides the ultimate and measurable basis for 'unanimity and consensus'). It is a test relevant to the longrun as well as the shortrun.

Strategic transfer   This is the process by which strategic control passes from the old *strategists* to the new strategists. This transfer may take place relatively smoothly if the new strategists are absorbed into existing institutions of power; it may take place violently through civil war and revolution if the old strategists are able to make a determined stand; and it may break down altogether and be hijacked by the *antistrategists* if the new strategists are not able to take control quickly. In the last two cases the strategic transfer turns ultimately into a *strategic crisis*. Strategic transfer is a critical phase in the history of any society, for it can lead to the continued development of more democratic institutions or to a return to more autocratic institutions.

Strategists comprise the dynamic group in society that invests time and resources in pursuing and profiting from one of the four *dynamic strategies*. The strategists are a diverse group. We must distinguish between the *strategic pioneers* (the more ambitious and less risk-averse) and the *strategic followers*; and between the old strategists (supporters of the traditional strategy) and the new strategists (supporters of the emerging strategy). While there is synergy between the pioneers and the followers, the old and new strategists are generally involved in a struggle for control of society's dominant dynamic strategy. This *strategic struggle* is at the core of institutional change and has been responsible for civil wars and revolutions. See also *nonstrategists* and *antistrategists*.

Technological dynamic change (TDC)   In societies where all natural resources are 'fully' utilized with the existing state of technology (in its broadest sense), economic growth and economic expansion can be regarded as component parts of a wider dynamic process of economic change called here technological dynamic change. The balance between growth and expansion will depend on the nature of the aggregate production function in a particular society at a particular time, which in turn will be influenced by the internal dynamics (family fertility and consumption) of the household (Snooks, 1994a: 127–34). TDC is the outcome of employing the technological dynamic strategy. It is contrasted with environmental dynamic change. This is the basis of the 'modern dynamic' which has generated the great linear waves of economic change.

Technological paradigm shifts   The progress of human society takes place within a dynamic structure defined by the great technological paradigm shifts in which growing resource scarcity is transcended by mankind breaking through into an entirely new technological era, thereby opening up extended possibilities for further economic growth. This involves the introduction of an entirely new set of techniques, skills, institutions, and outcomes. There have been three great technological paradigm shifts in human history: the palaeolithic paradigm shift when hunting displaced scavenging; the neolithic paradigm shift when agriculture displaced hunting; and the industrial paradigm shift when urban centres displaced rural areas as the major source of growth (see Figure 11.1).

Technological strategy This strategy is the dominant dynamic impulse of modern society and, in the past, has been employed by economic decision-makers to transcend exhausted technological paradigms. It was at the very centre of the palaeolithic (hunting), neolithic (agricultural), and modern (industrial) revolutions or *technological paradigm shifts*; and it will be the dominant dynamic strategy of the future. Unlike the conquest and commerce strategies it leads to an increase in material living standards not only for its host civilization, but for human society as a whole. See also *technological styles*.

Technological styles Within the modern technological paradigm, the dynamic *strategists* of competing nation-states attempt to secure a comparative advantage in their pursuit of extraordinary profits by developing new technological substrategies or technological styles. These technological styles – which historically have included: steam-powered iron machinery using coke (1780s–1830s); steel, synthetic chemicals, and complex machinery (1840s–1890s); electricity and the internal combustion engine (1900s–1950s); automated processes, microelectronics, lasers, new construction materials, and biotechnology (since 1950s) – emerge within the existing industrial paradigm as it unfolds at the global level. In turn they comprise a large number of 'strategic projects' that are co-ordinated through *strategic imitation*. See also *technological strategy*.

Unfolding dynamic strategy, the It is important to realize that when I refer to the 'unfolding' of a dynamic strategy I do *not* mean that the strategy is tracing out some preordained pattern of change like the emergence of a plant from a seed or the opening of a flower. A dynamic strategy 'unfolds' because economic decision-makers, operating in a competitive environment and responding to changing relative prices, attempt to achieve their objectives of maximizing the probability of survival and prosperity by exploring all the possibilities provided by a particular dynamic strategy at a given time or place. There is nothing inevitable or unilinear about this process. See also *dynamic strategy*.

Zero-sum dynamic change (ZDC) While *technological dynamic change* (TDC) involves an increase in material living standards for both the society employing the technological strategy and for human society as a whole, zero-sum dynamic change benefits the dynamic society at the expense of the rest of human society. ZDC results from a dominant society employing either the conquest or the commerce (in contrast to trade) strategies. This was the basis of the 'ancient dynamic' which generated the recurring cycle of war and conquest. In fact even ZDC may generate some increase in global material living standards owing to the concentration of resources in the hands of those who are able to employ them more efficiently because of economies of scale and more sophisticated organizational and human capital skills, but only if it is greater than the material losses inflicted by war. See also *environmental dynamic change* (EDC).

Bibliography

Aghion, P. and P. Howitt, (1992) 'A model of growth through creative destruction', *Econometrica*, **60**(2): 323–51.

Arndt, H.W. (1994) 'Full employment in historical perspective', *Australian Quarterly*, **66**(2): 1–12.

Arrow, K.J. (1962) 'The economic implications of learning by doing', *Review of Economic Studies*, **29**: 155–73.

Arrow, K.J. (1969) *Collected Papers of Kenneth Arrow* (Cambridge, Mass.: Belknap).

Arrow, K.J. (1986) 'History: the view from economics', in W.N. Parker (ed.), *Economic History and the Modern Economist* (Oxford: Blackwell) pp. 13–20.

Arrow, K.J. (1987) 'Arrow's theorem', in J. Eatwell, M. Milgate and P. Newman (eds) *The New Palgrave: A Dictionary of Economics*, vol. 1 (London: Macmillan) pp. 124–6.

Ashley, W.J. (1913) *An Introduction to English Economic History and Theory*, vol. 1: *The Middle Ages* (4th edn) (London: Longman).

Barro, R.J. and X. Sala-i-Martin (1995) *Economic Growth* (New York: McGraw-Hill).

Becker, G.S. (1976) 'Altruism, egoism, and genetic fitness: economics and sociobiology', *Journal of Economic History*, **14**(3): 817–26.

Bergstrom, T.C. (1995) 'On the evolution of altruistic ethical rules for siblings', *American Economic Review*, **85**(1): 58–81.

Blanchard, O. and L.F. Katz (1997) 'What we know and do not know about the natural rate of unemployment', *Journal of Economic Perspectives*, **11**(1): 51–72.

Blaug, M. (1986) *Great Economists Before Keynes: An Introduction to the Lives and Works of One Hundred Economists of the Past* (Atlantic Highlands, NJ: Humanities Press International).

Brennan, G. and J.M. Buchanan (1980) *The Power to Tax: Analytical Foundations of a Fiscal Constitution* (Cambridge University Press).

Brennan, G. and L. Lomasky (1993) *Democracy and Decision: The Pure Theory of Electoral Preference* (New York: Cambridge University Press).

Buchanan, J.A. (1980) 'Rent seeking and profit seeking', in J.A. Buchanan, R. Tollison and G. Tullock (eds) *Toward a Theory of the Rent-Seeking Society* (College Station: Texas A&M University Press) pp. 3–15.

Buchanan, J.A. (1987) 'Constitutional economics', in J. Eatwell, M. Milgate and P. Newman (eds) *The New Palgrave: A Dictionary of Economics*, vol. 1 (London: Macmillan) pp. 585–8.

Buchanan, J.A., R. Tollison, and G. Tullock (eds) (1980) *Toward a Theory of the Rent-Seeking Society* (College Station: Texas A&M University Press).

Butlin, N.G. (1964) *Investment in Australian Economic Development, 1861–1900* (Cambridge University Press).

Cassel, G. (1932) *Theory of Social Economy* (rev. edn) (London: Ernest Benn).

Casson, M. (1991) *The Economics of Business Culture: Game Theory, Transaction Costs and Economics* (Oxford: Clarendon; New York: Oxford University Press).

Colander, D.C. (ed.) (1984) *Neoclassical Political Economy: The Analysis of Rent-Seeking and DUR Activities* (Cambridge, Mass.: Ballinger).

Commons, J.R. (1934) *Institutional Economics: Its Place in Political Economy* (New York: Macmillan).

Comte, A. (1896) *The Positive Philosophy, Freely Translated and Condensed by Farriet Martineau, with an Introduction by Frederic Harrison*, 3 vols (London: Bell).

Cornwall, J. (1977) *Modern Capitalism: Its Growth and Transformation* (London: Martin Robertson).

Cornwall, J. (1994) *Economic Breakdown and Recovery: Theory and Policy* (New York: Sharpe).

Cyert, R.M. and J.G. March (1963) *A Behavioral Theory of the Firm* (Englewood Cliffs, NJ: Prentice-Hall).

Dawkins, R. (1989) *The Selfish Gene* (new edn) (Oxford and New York: Oxford University Press).

Delbeke, J. (1981) 'Recent long-waves theories: a critical survey', *Futures*, **13**(4): 246–57.

Denison, E.F. (1974) *Accounting for United States Economic Growth, 1927–1969* (Washington, DC: The Brookings Institution).

Domar, E.D. (1946) 'Capital expansion rate of growth and employment', *Econometrica*, **14**: 137–47.

Domar, E.D. (1957) *Essays in the Theory of Economic Growth* (New York: Oxford University Press).

Downie, J. (1958) *The Competitive Process* (London: Duckworth).

Dowrick, S. (1995) 'The determinants of long-run growth', in P. Anderson, J. Dwyer, D. Gruen (eds) *Productivity and Growth* (Sydney: Reserve Bank of Australia).

Dowrick, S. and D.T. Nguyen (1989) 'OECD comparative economic growth 1950–85: catch-up and convergence', *American Economic Review*, **79**(5): 1010–30.

Duesenberry, J.B. (1949) *Income, Saving and the Theory of Consumer Behavior* (Cambridge, Mass.: Harvard University Press).

Duesenberry, J.B. (1958) *Business Cycles and Economic Growth* (New York: McGraw-Hill).

Eldredge, N. and S.J. Gould (1972) 'Punctuated equilibria: an alternative to phyletic gradualism', in T.J.M. Schopt (ed.) *Models of Paleobiology* (San Francisco: Freeman, Cooper) pp. 82–115.

Eltis, D. (1987) 'Roy Forbes Harrod', in J. Eatwell, M. Milgate and P. Newman (eds) *The New Palgrave: A Dictionary of Economics*, vol. 2 (London: Macmillan) pp. 595–602.

Field, A.J. (1991) Review of D.C. North, *Institutions, Institutional Change, and Economic Performance, Journal of Economic History*, **51**(4): 999–1001.

Field, A.J. (1994) 'North, Douglass C.', in G.N. Hodgson, W.J. Samuels, and M.R. Tool (eds), *The Elgar Companion to Institutional and Evolutionary Economics: L–Z* (Aldershot: Elgar) pp. 134–8.

Fischer, S. (1977) 'Long-term contracts, rational expectations, and the optimal money supply rule', *Journal of Political Economy*, **85**(2): 191–205.

Fitzgibbons, A. (1988) *Keynes's Vision: A New Political Economy* (Oxford: Clarendon).

Fitzgibbons, A. (1995) *Adam Smith's System of Liberty, Wealth and Virtue* (Oxford: Clarendon).

Frank, A.G. and B.K. Gills (1993) *The World System: Five Hundred Years or Five Thousand?* (London and New York: Routledge).

Frech, H.E. (1978) 'Altruism, malice, and public goods', *Journal of Social and Biological Structures*, **1**(2): 181–5.

Freeman, C., J. Clark, and J. Soete (1982) *Unemployment and Technical Innovation: A Study of Long Waves and Economic Development* (London: Pinter).

Friedman, M. (1968) 'The role of monetary policy', *American Economic Review*, **68**(1): 1–17.

Friedman, M. and A.J. Schwartz (1963) *A Monetary History of the United States, 1867–1960* (Princeton University Press).

Friedman, M. and A.J. Schwartz (1982) *Monetary Trends in the United States and the United Kingdom: Their Relation to Income, Prices, and Interest Rates, 1867–1975* (Chicago: University of Chicago Press).

Galbraith, J.K. (1979) *The Nature of Mass Poverty* (Cambridge, Mass.: Harvard University Press).

Galbraith, J.K. (1983) *The Anatomy of Poverty* (Boston: Houghton Mifflin).

Galbraith, J.K. (1997) 'Time to ditch the NAIRU', *Journal of Economic Perspectives*, **11**(1): 93–108.

Gerschenkron, A. (1962) *Economic Backwardness in Historical Perspective* (Harvard: Harvard University Press).

Goodwin, R.M., M. Kruger and A. Vercelli (eds) (1983) *Nonlinear Models of Fluctuating Growth* (Berlin: Springer-Verlag).

Gordon, R.J. (1990) 'What is new-Keynesian economics?', *Journal of Economic Literature*, **28**: 1115–71.

Gossen, H.H. (1854) *Entwickelung der Gesetze des Menschlichen Verkehrs: Und der Daraus Fliessenden Regeln für Menschliches Handeln* (Braunschweig: F. Vieweg).

Gregory, R.G. and N.G. Butlin (1988) *Recovery from the Depression* (Cambridge University Press).

Grossman, G.M. and E. Helpman (1991) *Innovation and Growth in the Global Economy* (Cambridge, Mass.: MIT Press).

Grossman, G.M. and E. Helpman (1994) 'Protection for sale', *American Economic Review*, **84**(4): 833–50.

Haberler, G. (1958) *Prosperity and Depression: A Theoretical Analysis of Cyclical Movements* (London: George Allen & Unwin).

Hamilton, W.D. (1964) 'The genetical evolution of social behaviour', *Journal of Theoretical Biology*, **7**: 1–52.

Harcourt, G.C. (1972) *Some Cambridge Controversies in the Theory of Capital* (Cambridge University Press).

Harcourt, G.C. (1997) 'The Kaldor legacy: reviewing Nicholas Kaldor, *Causes of Growth and Stagnation in the World Economy*' (unpublished paper).

Harrod, R.F. (1936) *The Trade Cycle: An Essay* (Oxford: Clarendon).

Harrod, R.F. (1939) 'An essay in dynamic theory', *Economic Journal*, **49**: 14–33.

Harrod, R.F. (1948) *Towards a Dynamic Economics: Some Recent Developments of Economic Theory and Their Application to Policy* (London: Macmillan).

Hawke, G.R. (1985) *The Making of New Zealand* (Cambridge University Press).

Hawtrey, R.G. (1913) *Good and Bad Trade: An Inquiry into the Causes of Trade Fluctuations* (London: Constable).

Hayek, F.A. (1933) *Monetary Theory and the Trade Cycle* (London: Cape).

Hayek, F.A. (1952) *The Counter-revolution of Science: Studies on the Abuse of Reason* (Glencoe, Ill.: Free Press).

Hayek, F.A. (1988) *The Fatal Conceit: The Errors of Socialism* (W.W. Bartley, ed.) (London and New York: Routledge; New York: Routledge, Chapman & Hall).

Heilbroner, R.L. (1990) 'Analysis and vision in the history of modern economic thought', *Journal of Economic Literature* **28** (September): 1097–114.

Heilbroner, R.L. (1992) *The Worldly Philosophers* (7th edn) (New York: Simon and Schuster).

Henretta, J.A., W.E. Brownlee, D. Brody and S. Ware (1987) *America's History* (Chicago: Dorsey Press).

Hicks, J. (1937) 'Mr Keynes and the classics: a suggested interpretation', *Econometrica*, **5**: 147–59.

Hicks, J.R. (1939) *Value and Capital* (Oxford: Clarendon).

Hicks, J.R. (1950) *A Contribution to the Theory of the Trade Cycle* (Oxford: Clarendon).

Hicks, J.R. (1965) *Capital and Growth* (Oxford: Clarendon).

Higgins, B. (1959) *Economic Develoment: Problems, Principles and Policies* (London: Constable).

Hillman, A.L. (1982) 'Declining industries and political-support protectionist motives', *American Economic Review*, **72**(5): 1180–7.

Hillman, A.L. (1989) *The Political Economy of Protection* (Chur, Switzerland and New York: Harwood).

Hodgson, G.M. (1988) *Economics and Institutions: A Manifesto for a Modern Institutional Economics* (Cambridge: Polity Press).

Hodgson, G.M. (1993) *Economics and Evolution: Bringing Life Back into Economics* (Cambridge: Polity Press).

Hogarth, R.M. (1980) *Judgement and Choice: The Psychology of Decision* (New York: Wiley).

International Financial Statistics (IFS) Yearbook (Washington: International Monetary Fund).

Jevons, W.S. (1871) *The Theory of Political Economy* (London and New York: Macmillan).

Kaldor, N. (1954) 'The relation of economic growth and cyclical fluctuations', *Economic Journal*, **64**(253): 53–71.

Kaldor, N. (1957) 'A model of economic growth', *Economic Journal*, **67**(268): 591–624.

Kaldor, N. (1985) *Economics Without Equilibrium* (New York: Sharpe).

Kaldor, N. (1996) *Causes of Growth and Stagnation in the World Economy* (Cambridge University Press).

Keynes, J.M. (1936) *The General Theory of Employment, Interest, and Money* (London: Macmillan).

King, R.G. (1993) 'Will the new Keynesian macroeconomics resurrect the IS–LM model?', *Journal of Economic Perspectives*, **7**(1): 67–82.

Krueger, A. (1992) 'Government, trade, and economic integration', *American Economic Review*, **82**(2): 109–14.

Krugman, P. (1996) *Pop Internationalism* (Cambridge, Mass.: MIT Press).

Lavington, F. (1925) *The Trade Cycle: An Account of the Causes Producing Rhythmical Changes in the Activity of Business* (London: P.S. King).

Lenat, D.B. (1996) 'Artificial intelligence', *Key Technologies of the 21st Century – Scientific America: A Special Issue* (New York: Freeman) pp. 15–18.

Leslie, T.E. Cliffe (1888) *Essays in Political Economy* (2nd edn) (London: Longmans, Green & Co.; repr. New York: Augustus M. Kelley, 1969).

Lindert, P.H. (1994) 'Unequal living standards', in R. Floud and D. McCloskey (eds) *The Economic History of Britain Since 1700*, vol. I: *1700–1860* (2nd edn) (Cambridge University Press) pp. 357–86.

Lucas, R.E. (1976) 'Econometric policy evaluation: a critique', *Journal of Monetary Economics*, Supplementary Series, 1, pp. 19–46, 62.

Lucas, R.E., (1988) 'On the mechanics of economic development', *Journal of Monetary Economics*, **22**(1): 3–42.

Lucas, R.E. and L.A. Rapping (1969) 'Real wages, employment, and inflation', *Journal of Political Economy* **77**: 721–54.

Maddison, A. (1988) 'Ultimate and proximate growth causality: a critique of Mancur Olsen on the rise and decline of nations', *Scandinavian Economic History Review*, **36**(2): 25–9.

Maddison, A. (1995) *Monitoring the World Economy, 1820–1992* (Paris: Development Centre of the Organisation for Economic Co-operation and Development).

Magee, G.B. (1997) *Productivity and Performance in the Paper Industry: Labour, Capital, and Technology in Britain and America, 1860–1914* (Cambridge University Press).

Magee, S.P., W.A. Brock, and L. Young (1989) *Black Hole Tariffs and Endogenous Policy Theory* (Cambridge University Press).

Malthus, T.R. (1798) *An Essay on the Principle of Population* and *A Summary View of the Principle of Population* (republished Harmondsworth: Penguin, 1970).

Mandel, E. (1981) 'Explaining long waves of capitalist development', *Futures*, **13**(4): 332–8.

Mankiw, N.G. (1990) 'A quick refresher course in macroeconomics', *Journal of Economic Literature*, **28**: 1645–60.

Mankiw, N.G. and D. Romer (eds) (1991) *New Keynesian Economics* (Cambridge, Mass.: MIT Press).

Marshall, A. (1920) *Principles of Economics: An Introductory Volume* (8th edn) (London: Macmillan).

Marx, K. (1867–94) *Capital*, 3 vols (republished Moscow: Foreign Languages Publishing House, 1957–61).

Matthews, R.C.O. (1959) *The Trade Cycle* (Cambridge: Nisbet).

Menger, C. (1871) *Grundsätze der Volkswirtschaftslehre* (Wien: W. Braumuller).

Mensch, G. (1979) *Stalemate in Technology: Innovations Overcome the Depression* (Cambridge, Mass.: Ballinger).

Milgate, M. (1987) 'Equilibrium: development of the concept', in J. Eatwell, M. Milgate and P. Newman (eds) *The New Palgrave: A Dictionary of Economics*, vol. 2 (London: Macmillan) pp. 177–83.

Mill, J.S. (1843) *A System of Logic, Ratiocinative and Inductive: Being a Connected View of the Principles of Evidence and the Methods of Scientific Investigation* (9th edn, 2 vols; London: Longmans, Green, Reader, & Dyer, 1875).

Mill, J.S. (1848) *Principles of Political Economy* (London: Parker & Co.).

Mises, L.E. von (1958) *Theory and History* (London: Cape).

Mitchell, B.R. (1988) *British Historical Statistics* (Cambridge University Press).

Mokyr, J. (1990) *The Lever of Riches: Technological Creativity and Economic Progress* (New York: Oxford University Press).

Morgan, M. (1990) *The History of Econometric Ideas* (Cambridge University Press).

Muth, J.F. (1961) 'Rational expectations and the theory of price movements', *Econometrica*, **29**: 315–35.

Nell, E.J. (1992) *Transformational Growth and Effective Demand* (London: Macmillan).

Nelson, R.R. (1995) 'Recent evolutionary theorizing about economic change', *Journal of Economic Literature*, **33**(1): 48–90.

Nelson, R.R. and S.G. Winter (1982) *An Evolutionary Theory of Economic Change* (Cambridge, Mass.: Harvard University Press).

Newell, A. and H.A. Simon (1972) *Human Problem Solving* (Englewood Cliffs, NJ: Prentice-Hall).

Nightingale, J. (1996) 'Anticipating Nelson and Winter: Jack Downie's theory of evolutionary economic change', *Working Papers in Economics*, 13 (Griffith University, Brisbane, November).

North, D.C. (1981) *Structure and Change in Economic History* (New York: Norton).

North, D.C. (1984) 'Three approaches to the study of institutions', in D.C. Colander (ed.) *Neoclassical Political Economy: The Analysis of Rent-Seeking and DUR Activities* (Cambridge, Mass.: Ballinger) pp. 33–40.

North, D.C. (1990) *Institutions, Institutional Change, and Economic Performance* (Cambridge and New York: Cambridge University Press).

North, D.C. (1991) 'Institutions', *Journal of Economic Perspectives*, **5**(1): 97–112.

North, D.C. and R.P. Thomas (1973) *The Rise of the Western World* (Cambridge University Press).

Olson, M. (1965) *The Logic of Collective Action: Public Goods and the Theory of Groups* (Cambridge, Mass.: Harvard University Press).

Olson, M. (1982) *The Rise and Decline of Nations* (New Haven and London: Yale University Press).

Pagan, A. (1996) 'The rise and fall and rise...of the business cycle', *The Shann Lecture 1996* (Perth: University of Western Australia).

Pasinetti, L.L. (1981) *Structural Change and Economic Growth: A Theoretical Essay on the Dynamics of the Wealth of Nations* (Cambridge University Press).

Pasinetti, L.L. and R.M. Solow (eds) (1994) *Economic Growth and the Structure of Long-term Development* (London: Macmillan; New York: St Martin's Press).

Phelps, E.S. (1968) 'Money-wage dynamics and labour market equilibrium', *Journal of Political Economy* **76** (July/August): 678–711.

Phelps, E.S. (1994) *Structural Slumps: The Modern Equilibrium Theory of Unemployment, Interest, and Assets* (Cambridge, Mass.: Harvard University Press).

Phillips, A.W. (1958) 'The relationship between unemployment and rate of change of money wage rates in the United Kingdom 1861–1957', *Economica* **25**: 283–99.

Pigou, A. (1929) *Industrial Fluctuations* (2nd edn) (London: Macmillan).

Pitchford, J.D. (1960) 'Growth and the elasticity of factor substitution, *Economic Record*, **36**(76): 491–504.

Pitchford, J.D. (1974) *The Economics of Population* (Canberra: ANU Press).

Pitchford, J.D. (1995a) 'Variable returns to scale, resources and population' (International Conference in Honour of Professor K.J. Arrow, Monash University, 7–8 September).

Pitchford, J.D. (1995b) *The Current Account and Foreign Debt* (London and New York: Routledge).

Pitchford, J.D. (1996) 'Appraising fiscal deficits' (Conference of Economists, Canberra, 24 September).

Plato (1892) 'Republic', in *The Dialogies of Plato, translated into English with Analyses and Introductions by B. Jowett*, vol. III (Oxford: Clarendon) pp. 1–338.

Popper, K.R. (1965) *Conjectures and Refutations: The Growth of Scientific Knowledge* (New York: Basic Books).

Popper, K.R. (1972) *Objective Knowledge: An Evolutionary Approach* (Oxford: Clarendon).

Popper, K.R. (1992) *Unended Quest: An Intellectual Autobiography* (revised edn) (London: Routledge).

Ramsay, F. (1928) 'A mathematical theory of saving', *Economic Journal*, **38**: 543–59.

Rebelo, S. (1991) 'Long-run policy analysis and long-run growth', *Journal of Political Economy*, **99**(3): 500–21.

Robbins, L. (1934) *The Great Depression* (London: Macmillan).

Robertson, D.H. (1915) *A Study of Industrial Fluctuation: An Enquiry into the Character and Causes of the So-Called Cyclical Movements of Trade* (London: P.S. King).

Robinson, J. (1953–4) 'The production function and the theory of capital', *Review of Economic Studies*, **21**: 81–106.

Robinson, J. (1956) *The Accumulation of Capital* (London: Macmillan).

Rogerson, R. (1997) 'Theory ahead of language in the economics of unemployment', *Journal of Economic Perspectives*, **11**(1): 73–92.

Romer, P.M. (1986) 'Increasing returns and long-run growth', *Journal of Political Economy*, **94**: 1002–37.

Romer, P.M. (1987) 'Growth based on increasing returns due to specialization', *American Economic Review*, **77**(2): 56–62.

Romer, P.M. (1990) 'Endogenous technological change', *Journal of Political Economy*, **98**(5) part ii: S71–S102.

Rostow, W.W. (1971) *The Stages of Economic Growth: A Non-Communist Manifesto* (2nd edn) (Cambridge University Press).

Rostow, W.W. (1990) *Theorists of Economic Growth from David Hume to the Present: With a Perspective on the Next Century* (New York and Oxford: Oxford University Press).

Samuelson, P.A. (1983) 'Complete genetic models for altruism, kin selection and like-gene selection', *Journal of Social and Biological Structures*, **6**(1): 3–15.

Sandmo, A. (1990) 'Buchanan on political economy', *Journal of Economic Literature*, **28**(1): 50–65.

Sargent, T. and N. Wallace (1975) ' "Rational expectations", the optimal monetary instrument and the optimal money supply rule', *Journal of Political Economy*, **83**(2): 241–54.

Schedvin, C.B. (1970) *Australia and the Great Depression* (Sydney University Press).

Schumpeter, J.A. (1939) *Business Cycles: A Theoretical, Historical and Statistical Analysis of the Capitalist Process* (New York: McGraw-Hill).

Schumpeter, J.A. (1942) *Capitalism, Socialism, and Democracy* (New York and London: Harper).

Schumpeter, J.A. (1949) *The Theory of Economic Development: An Inquiry into Profits, Capital, Credit, Interest and the Business Cycle* (Cambridge, Mass.: Harvard University Press; first published in German, 1912).

Schumpeter, J.A. (1954) *Economic Doctrine and Method: An Historical Sketch* (London: Allen & Unwin).

Seaman, L.C.B. (1981) *A New History of England* (London: Macmillan).

Sen, A. (1987) 'Social choice', in J. Eatwell, M. Milgate and P. Newman (eds), *The New Palgrave: A Dictionary of Economics*, vol. 4 (London: Macmillan) pp. 382–93.

Sheshinski, E. (1967) 'Optimal accumulation with learning by doing', in K. Shell (ed.) *Essays on the Theory of Optimal Economic Growth* (Cambridge, Mass.: MIT Press) pp. 31–52.

Simon, H.A. (1947) *Administrative Behavior: A Study of Decision-Making Processes in Administrative Organization* (New York: Macmillan).

Simon, H.A. (1956) 'Rational choice and the structure of the environment', *Psychological Review*, **63**: 129–38.

Simon, H.A. (1982) *Models of Bounded Rationality*, 2 vols (Cambridge, Mass.: MIT Press).

Simon, H.A. (1987) 'Satisficing', in J. Eatwell, M. Milgate and P. Newman (eds), *The New Palgrave: A Dictionary of Economics*, vol. 4 (London: Macmillan) pp. 243–5.

Skinner, A.S. (1987) 'Adam Smith', in J. Eatwell, M. Milgate and P. Newman (eds) *The New Palgrave: A Dictionary of Economics*, vol. 4 (London: Macmillan) pp. 357–75.

Smith, A. (1759) *The Theory of Moral Sentiments* (republished, edited by D.D. Raphael and A.L. Macfie; Oxford: Clarendon, 1976).

Smith, A. (1776) *An Inquiry into the Nature and Causes of the Wealth of Nations* (republished, edited by E. Cannan in 2 vols; London: Methuen, 1961).

Smithies, A. (1957) 'Economic fluctuations and growth', *Econometrica*, **25**: 1–52.

Snooks, G.D. (1974) *Depression and Recovery in Western Australia, 1928/29–1938/39: A Study in Cyclical and Structural Change* (Perth: University of Western Australia Press).

Snooks, G. D. (1988), 'Government unemployment relief in the 1930s: aid or hindrance to recovery?', in R. G. Gregory and N. G. Butlin (eds), *Recovery from the Depression* (Cambridge: Cambridge University Press) pp. 311–34.

Snooks, G.D. (1993) *Economics Without Time. A Science Blind to the Forces of Historical Change* (London: Macmillan; Ann Arbor: University of Michigan Press).

Snooks, G.D. (1994a) *Portrait of the Family Within the Total Economy. A Study in Longrun Dynamics, Australia 1788–1990* (Cambridge University Press).

Snooks, G.D. (ed.) (1994b) *Was the Industrial Revolution Necessary?* (London and New York: Routledge).

Snooks, G.D. (1996) *The Dynamic Society. Exploring the Sources of Global Change* (London and New York: Routledge).

Snooks, G.D. (1997a) *The Ephemeral Civilization. Exploding the Myth of Social Evolution* (London and New York: Routledge).

Snooks, G. D. (1997b) Strategic demand and the growth–inflation curve. New theoritical and empirical concepts', *Working Papers in Economic History*, ANU, **195** (Canberra, July).

Snooks, G.D. (1998) *The Laws of History* (London and New York: Routledge).

Solomou, S. (1987) *Phases of Economic Growth, 1850–1973: Kondratieff Waves and Kuznets Swings* (Cambridge University Press).

Solow, R.M. (1956) 'A contribution to the theory of economic growth', *Quarterly Journal of Economics*, **70**: 65–94.

Solow, R.M. (1986) 'Economics: is something missing', in W.N. Parker (ed.), *Economic History and the Modern Economist* (Oxford: Blackwell) pp. 21–9.

Stadler, G.W. (1994) 'Real business cycles', *Journal of Economc Literature*, **32** (December): 1750–83.

Staiger, D., J.H. Stocks and M.W. Watson (1997) 'The NAIRU, unemployment and monetary policy', *Journal of Economic Perspectives*, **11**(1): 33–50.

Stiglitz, J. (1997) 'Reflections on the natural rate hypothesis', *Journal of Economic Perspectives*, **11**(1): 3–10.

Sullivan, R.E. (1997) 'Trade, protection and taxation: the formation of Australian tariff policy, 1901–14' (unpublished PhD thesis, Australian National University, February).

Swan, T.W. (1956) 'Economic growth and capital accumulation', *Economic Record*, **32**: 334–61.

Taussig, F.W. (1911) *Principles of Economics*, 2 vols (New York: Macmillan).

Temin, P. (1976) *Did Monetary Forces Cause the Great Depression?* (New York: Norton).

Tobin, J. (1993) 'Price flexibility and output stability: an old Keynesian view', *Journal of Economic Perspectives*, **7**(1): 45–65.

Tullock, G. (1980) 'Rent-seeking as a negative sum game', in J.A. Buchanan, R. Tollison and G. Tullock (eds) *Toward a Theory of the Rent-Seeking Society* (College Station: Texas A&M University Press) pp. 16–36.

Tullock, G. (1987) 'Public choice', in J. Eatwell, M. Milgate and P. Newman (eds) *The New Palgrave: A Dictionary of Economics*, vol. 3 (London: Macmillan) pp. 1040–4.

Tunzelmann, N. von (1994) 'Technology in the early nineteenth century', in R. Floud and D. McCloskey (eds) *The Economic History of Britain Since 1700*, vol. 1: *1700–1860* (2nd edn) (Cambridge University Press) pp. 271–99.

Tylecote, A. (1992) *The Long Wave in the World Economy: The Current Crisis in Historical Perspective* (London and New York: Routledge).

United States, Bureau of the Census (1960) *Historical Statistics of the United States, Colonial Times to 1957* (Washington, DC: Bureau of the Census).

Vanberg, V.J. (1994) 'Hayek, Friedrich A.', in G.M. Hodgson, W.J. Samuels and M.R. Tool (eds) *The Elgar Companion to Institutional and Evolutionary Economics: A–K* (Aldershot: Elgar) pp. 314–20.

Vaughn, K.I. (1987) 'Invisible hand', in J. Eatwell, M. Milgate and P. Newman (eds) *The New Palgrave: A Dictionary of Economics*, vol. 2 (London: Macmillan) pp. 997–9.

Veblen, T.B. (1899) *The Theory of the Leisure Class: An Economic Study of Institutions* (New York: Macmillan).

Veblen, T.B. (1904) *The Theory of Business Enterprise* (New York: Scribner).

Veblen, T.B. (1919) *The Place of Science in Modern Civilization* (New York: Huebsch).

Veblen, T.B. (1934) *Essays in Our Changing Order and Other Essays* (ed. L. Ardzrooni) (New York: Viking Press).

Walras, L. (1874–7) *Eléments d'économie politique pure; Ou, théorie de la richesse sociale* (Lausanne: L. Corbaz & Cie).

Williamson, O.E. (1975) *Markets and Hierarchies, Analysis and Antitrust Implications: A Study in the Economics of Internal Organization* (New York: Free Press).

Wilson, E.O. (1975) *Sociobiology: The New Synthesis* (Cambridge, Mass.: Belknap Press of Harvard University Press).

Witt, U. (ed.) (1993) *Evolutionary Economics* (Aldershot, Hants and Brookfield, Vt: Elgar).

Wrigley, E.A. (1994) 'The classical economists, the stationary state, and the Industrial Revolution', in G.D. Snooks (ed.) *Was the Industrial Revolution Necessary?* (London and New York: Routledge) pp. 27–42.

Index

278   *Index*

Menger, Carl, and general equilibrium
theory, 88; and the
Methodenstreit, 70
Mensch, Gerhard, and innovation
clusters, 248–9
Methodenstreit, 70, 72, 73
methodological individualism, 87
microeconomic reform, and dynamic-
strategy theory, 243–4
Mill, John Stuart, and empiricism, 67;
and historical method, 4, 34; and
social dynamics, 4; and social
statics, 4; and the stationary
state, 4, 27
Mises, Ludwig von, and antihistoricist
campaign, 73
modern evolutionary institutional
economics, 53–61
modern evolutionary institutionalism,
see modern evolutionary
institutional economics; neo-
Veblenians; new institutional
economics
monarchy (English), and dynamic
strategies, 224–5, 226
moral basis of institutions, Adam
Smith on, 81, 82–3, 83–4
'moral man', 52
motivation, *see* law of human
motivation

NAIRU (non-accelerating inflation
rate of unemployment),
see natural rate of unemployment
nation-states, and commerce
strategy, 224; and conquest
strategy, 221; and mega-states,
138–9; and technological
strategy, 137
natural rate of unemployment, 105,
192–3, 233, 241; and Phillips
curve, 173–5, 192
Nell, E.J., 245
Nelson–Winter model, and new
evolutionary economics, 62–6,
107–8
neo-Darwinism, 52, 57, 58, 64–5, 85,
106–7

neo-Veblenians, and modern
evolutionary institutional
economics, 53–6
neoclassical economics, and decision-
making, 99–101, 113–14, 119; and
efficiency, 232–3; growth theory
of, 34–48; and dynamic-strategy
theory, 40–1; and social
dynamics, 4; and inflation and
unemployment, 234; and market
flexibility, 233; and policy
instruments, 235–6; and rent-
seeking and profit-seeking, 9; and
shortrun fluctuations, 182–5, 192;
see also 'endogenous' growth
model; Solow–Swan growth
model
neolithic paradigm shift, 149, 150; *see
also* Neolithic Revolution;
technological paradigm shifts
Neolithic Revolution, 136, 149, 150
neolithic technological paradigm,
exhaustion of, 135
Netherlands, the, and inflation and
economic growth, 156
new evolutionary economics, 50, 61–6
'new' growth model, *see* 'endogenous'
growth model
new institutional economics, 56–61;
and decision-making, 103–4,
113–14; and political change, 204,
208–9, 211–12; *see also* Friedrich
Hayek; Douglass North
new institutional theory, *see* new
institutional economics
new institutionalism, *see* new
institutional economics
new political economy, 203–12, 220–1;
and rent-seeking and profit-
seeking, 9; *see also* collective-
action theory; new institutional
economics; public choice theory
new strategists, 214; in England,
228–9; and strategic struggle, 18,
19, 216
New Zealand, and inflation and
economic growth, 156
nominal inflation, 151, 241;
defined, 255